JAMES DEAN
An American Icon

JAMES DEAN
An American Icon

by

THOMAS BRENNAN

REGENT PRESS
Berkeley, California
2024

[Paperback]
ISBN 13: 978-1-58790-688-6
ISBN 10: 1-58790-688-0

[E-book]
ISBN 13: 978-1-58790-689-3
ISBN 10: 1-58790-689-9

Library of Congress Control Number: *forthcoming*

First Edition

0 1 2 3 4 5 6 7 8 9 10

Photo Credits:
All images of James Dean are publicity photos accessed from multiple sources. They were gathered on the web and are in the public domain. Please address any issues as to their provenance to the publisher.

Manufactured in the United States of America

REGENT PRESS
www.regentpress.net
regentpress@mindspring.com

CONTENTS

Introduction . . . 1

CHAPTER 1
The Early Years . . . 7

CHAPTER 2
New York City . . . 41

CHAPTER 3
East of Eden . . . 83

CHAPTER 4
Rebel Without a Cause . . . 139

CHAPTER 5
Giant . . . 183

CHAPTER 6
Tragedy Strikes . . . 223

CHAPTER 7
Dean's Lasting Impact . . . 257

Bibliography . . . 287

Index . . . 291

INTRODUCTION

ince James Dean's tragic death in 1955, his popularity has grown greater with each new generation. His name continues to appear in the lyrics of rock, country, and pop music throughout the world. James Byron Dean came from humble beginnings, but he left behind a legacy still revered to this day. Countless books, magazines, documentaries and films have been generated in an effort to explain why his legend continues to grow.

This book is not so much about Dean's personal life as it is about his growth and accomplishments as an actor. He revolutionized the art of acting like nobody before or since. He took to acting as seriously as Elvis Presley and the Beatles took to rock and roll music. The intensity he exhibited in all of his roles amazed even the most cynical of critics. His performances were such that all eyes fell on him. It was almost as if he was separated from the story itself – that his presence was all that mattered.

James Dean embodied feelings of distress and discord in his films and in his life. Young people recognized and shared these same feelings and he immediately became their idol. Dean epitomized the resentful and discontented teenager well before he began starring in feature films. For many years he portrayed them on live television. He represented discontented young adults at a time when it was unfashionable to do so.

At the time of his death, James Dean had starred in only three films, *East of Eden*, *Rebel Without a Cause*, and *Giant*. Of those three films, only *Eden* had been released while Jimmy was alive. He would become the only actor to have been nominated posthumously for Best Actor twice. He also left behind an incredible output of outstanding dramatic performances for television. It is truly remarkable that a film star who appeared in only three films could be so admired and loved by so many. And almost single handedly he created a whole new life style that lives on even to this day.

Frequently referred to as "The First Teenager" in film, he was much more than that. The young star came to represent the consummate outsider, a loner not willing to accept society's norms. The characters he portrayed rebelled against the status quo. Although the common thread in Dean's work symbolized a rebellious nature, each of the three characters he portrayed on film were distinctly different. This was an essential part of Dean's genius.

Friends and associates of Jimmy have never been able to agree on what kind of a person he really was. Some have described him as affable and empathetic while others thought he was moody and occasionally offensive. Depending on who one spoke to, film and television directors described Dean as arrogant and difficult while many others thought he was inventive and goodhearted. He also lived life to the fullest because he believed he might not reach thirty.

One word that perhaps best describes Dean the person and Dean the actor is 'nonconformist.' For this reason, many of his peers in the acting community detested him not just as an actor but also on a personal level. They looked at him as one would an alien from a distant galaxy. He rarely recited the prepared script as directed. He experimented while others towed the line. On a personal level, Jimmy never seemed to care much about making money in the movie business. He focused almost entirely on his craft and he refused to stray from his bohemian lifestyle.

Although many people in the entertainment industry recognized Dean's incredible talent, others were very critical toward his ability as an actor. Many film critics initially thought he was just another cheap knock off of Marlon Brando, one of Jimmy's idols. Even Elia Kazan, the brilliant director of *East of Eden* and *On the Waterfront*, mocked Dean for not being as technically equipped as Brando or even Montgomery Clift, another outstanding "Method" inspired actor. Many of these same critics changed their opinion of Dean once they witnessed his performances in *Rebel Without a Cause* and *Giant*. They finally recognized the essence of Dean's talent as an outstanding actor.

Soon after Dean's tragic ending, fan mail literally poured into Warner Brothers' mailrooms the likes of which had never been seen before. This was particularly stunning for an actor who had only spent a year and a half in Hollywood. Amazingly, letters were even addressed to Jimmy himself, evidence that many fans refused to believe that Dean was dead. Some rumors claimed Jimmy had not died in the crash but was instead merely disfigured and had gone into hiding, embarrassed by his grotesque appearance.

Dean's death is made even more tragic by the fact that he had shown so much promise as an actor. By the time he completed *Giant*, his acting had matured substantially. He proved he could convincingly portray a disillusioned adolescent as well as an aging Texas oil tycoon. Had he survived, he may well have convinced even his staunchest critics that he deserves to be considered one of the finest actors in the history of film. And there are certainly those today who will argue that he belongs at the top of that long list of incredible film actors.

Dean's popularity was so great, that when frenzied fans visited the Observatory where *Rebel Without a Cause* had been filmed, they fought to sit in the same seat Dean sat in during the famous "Moo!" sequence. When Henry Ginsberg, the producer of *Giant*, was told by a reporter that the fans reaction to Dean's demise was as big as the 1920s film idol Rudolf Valentino's, Ginsberg replied, "It's bigger than Valentino's."

After *Giant* was released in 1956, a full year after Jimmy's fatal car accident, Dean's enormous popularity was keenly evident to everyone at Warner Brothers and beyond. Movie mogul Jack Warner claimed that although Dean had given director George Stevens a lot of grief, he was well worth it because the young star was twenty-five percent responsible for the success of *Giant*.

Someone once observed that it wasn't so much what Dean said that mattered but how he said it. His unique delivery, facial expressions and mannerisms helped set Dean apart from his peers. His overpowering intensity shocked audiences everywhere. He made you feel his pain in a very personal way. It is generally recognized that *East of Eden* may have turned Jimmy into a film star, but it was *Rebel Without a Cause* and *Giant* that made him a legend.

CHAPTER 1

THE EARLY YEARS

A young Jimmy poses with his parents Mildred and Winton Dean.

James Byron Dean was born on February 8, 1931, in Marion, Indiana. His parents were Winton Arlando Dean and Mildred Marie Wilson Dean. The birth took place at 404 East Fourth Street in Marion, Indiana. After about five hours of labor, James Dean came into the world at around 2:00 a.m. on a Sunday. He reportedly weighed eight pounds, ten ounces. The family doctor and a midwife were in attendance during the delivery. The procedure cost the Deans fifteen dollars. They had no more children after their son was born. It is unclear why the parents chose Byron for Jimmy's middle name. Some have speculated Winton chose it in honor of one of his co-workers. Others have suggested that Mildred chose it in honor of the English poet Lord Byron.

Winton Dean was born on January 17, 1907, in Fairmount, Indiana. He was the son of a Quaker farmer and a local auctioneer. It has been said that Winton's family line can be traced back to the *Mayflower*. He was very reserved and kept to himself most of the time. He was also a dexterous tinker who found farm work uninteresting and tedious. Mildred Wilson Dean was born on September 15, 1910, in Marion, Indiana. She was the daughter of a factory worker from Gas City, Indiana. She was raised Methodist. Like her husband, she was very quiet and reserved. She played the piano and enjoyed reading poetry.

Six months prior to Jimmy's birth, Winton married

Mildred on July 26, 1930, at the Grant County courthouse in Marion, Indiana. Reverend Zeno Doan, a Methodist minister, performed the marriage ceremony. Winton was twenty-two and Mildred was not quite twenty. After their wedding ceremony they had no place to go on their honeymoon. They were invited to stay with David and Hazel Payne for two weeks before moving into the Seven Gables apartment complex in Marion, Indiana.

The young couple were very different in many ways. Winton did not enjoy the arts and he read very little. Although they were both reserved to a certain degree, Mildred did have a sense of humor. She read novels to help pass the time and she enjoyed listening to music. She even dreamed of one day traveling abroad, whereas Winton felt perfectly fine staying close to home. Mildred enjoyed reading poetry and liked to recite passages from the works of James Whitcomb Riley, who also hailed from Indiana. Winton never showed much of an interest in listening to his wife's recitations.

Winton worked at the Veterans Administration Hospital as a dental technician while Mildred worked in a drugstore. After Jimmy was born, Winton continued to work at the hospital while Mildred stayed at home and cared for Jimmy. The Deans moved to Fairmount, Indiana when Jimmy turned three. His father tried raising bullfrogs for a living, but Winton's attempt at self-employment failed miserably and so they moved back to Marion. They moved around quite often, but stayed in and around the vicinity of Marion and Fairmount.

Fairmount, Indiana was a town with a population of around 2,600. In 1850 the small farm town received its name after a famous park in Philadelphia. The town was large enough to support its very own weekly newspaper, the *Fairmount News*, an elementary school, a fire department, over a dozen churches, and several Quaker meeting houses. Surrounding the small town were vast swathes of farmland. Reportedly, the only movie theater in Fairmount was closed because many of its citizens, particularly Quakers, refused to allow it to stay open.

Mildred doted on her baby while Winton remained somewhat standoffish toward the newest member of the family. She frequently read books and recited poetry to Jimmy. She also built a small theater out of cardboard so they could produce skits using dolls to represent characters in the plays. They both enjoyed putting on shows for family members and friends. Mildred hoped that one day Jimmy would become a great stage and film star.

When Jimmy turned five, Mildred enrolled him in some tap dancing classes at the Marion College of Dance and Theatrical Arts. The school was owned by Zina Gladys Pitsor, a former vaudeville entertainer. The two women became very close friends. Jimmy became such a talented tap dancer that the owner featured him in the school's recital program. According to Pitsor, the audience adored Jimmy's intricate tap dancing routine.

Jimmy frequently suffered from rashes, nosebleeds, vomiting, and lethargy. Doctors determined that he was anemic but they could not ascertain the root cause. Perhaps Mildred's frequent use of paints containing toxins may have contributed to Jimmy's dire condition.

In 1936 Winton accepted a position as a permanent staff member at the Sawtelle Veterans Administration

Hospital in Los Angeles, California. It first opened its doors for disabled Civil War veterans in 1888, taking the name, "Old Soldiers Home." The offer was too attractive to turn down and so Winton and Mildred decided to move to California. The family rented a small duplex on Twenty-sixth Street, which was near Wilshire Boulevard in Santa Monica. At that time, Santa Monica was a tranquil, middle class suburb of Los Angeles. Their home had a parlor and two small bedrooms, a backyard with a garden, and a front yard with a palm tree.

Mildred enrolled Jimmy in Brentwood Elementary School in West Los Angeles. He performed poorly as a student at this school. He was constantly getting into fights with several of his classmates. He had difficulty making and keeping friends. His schoolmates occasionally teased Jimmy about his middle name. His peculiar Indiana accent added more fuel to their taunts. Jimmy wasn't the only family member to suffer. According to a friend, Mildred felt uneasy living in California. She missed her folks terribly and wished her family would move back to Indiana where she felt more at home. Mildred corresponded quite frequently with the folks back home. She always made sure to include several photographs of Jimmy in her letters.

Realizing that Jimmy was having difficulty adjusting to his new environment, Mildred devoted as much time as she could toward her only son. She kept him occupied with many activities, including learning how to play the violin. According to Winton, Jimmy was fascinated with the toys they bought him, but he quickly grew bored of them. On February 8, 1938, Mildred enrolled Jimmy in the McKinley Elementary School on Santa Monica Boulevard. Perhaps she thought her son needed a fresh start at another school.

When Jimmy was eight years old, his mother began complaining of excruciating abdominal pains. Tests revealed she had been suffering from cervical cancer. Winton's mother Emma Dean received a letter from her son explaining his wife's dire condition. Jimmy was kept in the dark in terms of his mother's diagnosis. Winton's mother and sister decided to visit the Deans in order to do what they could to lessen the burden of caring for Mildred. In an effort to help alleviate some of her discomfort, Mildred asked that the Bible be read to her. Jimmy would sit next to his mother and read passages from the Bible. He was fond of reading the Twenty-third Psalm to his dying mother. *"The Lord is my shepherd; I shall not want. He maketh me to lie down in green pastures; he leadeth me beside the still waters..."*

A few weeks later, Mildred suffered a life-threatening hemorrhage. Doctors determined she had only a short time to live. Jimmy watched helplessly as his mother's health deteriorated over the next several months. Her bedridden body wasted away until she looked almost unrecognizable. Jimmy was finally told about his mother's condition just prior to her death. She succumbed to her illness and died on July 14, 1940. She was only twenty-nine years old. Mildred died in the hospital with her family by her side. Jimmy's mother's death would haunt him for the rest of his life.

Emma Dean sat down with her son and made him a proposition. She told Winton that Ortense and Marcus Winslow would be more than happy to raise Jimmy as their own or at least until Winton's financial situation improved. Amazingly, Winton agreed without hesitation. Apparently, Winton had no problem sending his only son back to Indiana to live with relatives. Not only did Jimmy have to deal with his mother's tragic death, he had to contend with the agony of being abandoned by his own father. It was finally determined by all concerned that young Jimmy would live with the Winslows on their little farm in Fairmount, Indiana, for an undetermined amount of time.

A funeral service was held in Santa Monica and shortly thereafter, Mildred's body was transported back to Indiana. Jimmy and his grandmother rode in the same railway carriage that carried Mildred's body. Winton had decided not to accompany his mother and son on the train to Fairmount. He claimed his wife's illness had saddled him with a debt so enormous, he couldn't possibly afford to travel to Indiana. According to Winton, he had to sell his automobile in order to pay Mildred's medical expenses.

Winton's decision not to accompany Emma and Jimmy on their trip to Indiana is difficult to understand to say the least. His refusal to attend his own wife's funeral makes practically no sense since it is fairly certain his relatives would have helped him financially. In any event, Mildred was given a proper burial and was laid to rest in Grant Memorial Park in Marion, Indiana.

Jimmy took his mother's death very hard. He somehow managed to painfully retreat within himself, rarely expressing grief over his mother's passing and his father's abandonment. Years later Winton claimed that his son "Never liked to talk about his hurts."

The Winslows were sensitive to the fact that Jimmy was, for all practical purposes, an orphan. The sudden death of his mother and the separation from his father plagued Jimmy for the rest of his life. To help alleviate

Jimmy's anguish, they kept him busy with farm work. The Winslows raised a variety of farm animals, including sheep, chickens, and pigs. They also grew oats and corn. Jimmy milked cows, gathered eggs, and fed the stock. By the time he was ten he could skillfully operate a tractor by himself.

Marcus and Ortense had been married eighteen years by the time Jimmy moved in with them. They had a daughter Joan who was fourteen at the time. They had always planned on having a son and so they accepted their nephew that much more. The Winslows were a blessing to Jimmy. He told them how much he admired their bedroom and so they let him have it. Ortense encouraged Jimmy to pursue any artistic activity he wished, such as painting and drawing and molding clay.

The farm offered a great deal of recreational opportunities for Jimmy. There was a large pond on the Winslow property for swimming in the summer and ice-skating and hockey in the winter. A large barn was frequently used for basketball and anywhere between ten to thirty neighbors regularly showed up to play. Jimmy typically played against boys quite a bit older and bigger than him. However, his competitive spirit more than made up for his much smaller physique.

Jimmy kept busy drawing and painting. He also enjoyed listening to programs on the radio, such as the Lux Radio Theatre or shows featuring Jack Benny, Bob Hope, and Red Skelton. He was already telling the Winslows how much he wanted to perform on stage and in movies. Nobody took him very seriously until later when he started performing in skits and plays sponsored by the school district.

In the fall Jimmy started fourth grade at West Ward Elementary. At one time it had been a religious school. His teachers noticed that Jimmy was very shy and reserved as compared to the rest of the students. One grade school teacher, India Nose, recalled that Jimmy "had the sweetest laugh as a little boy." She also remembered that he "was sometimes moody, and often unexplainably stubborn." He was also easily startled by sudden, unexpected noises. One time in class he broke out crying for no apparent reason. His only explanation was that he missed his mother. Jimmy may have also suffered tremendously from his dad's abandonment, particularly at a time when he needed his father the most. He may have begun to develop a deep-seated feeling of resentment toward his father.

Jimmy constantly dreamed of becoming an actor. He finally got his wish when he volunteered to participate in some plays offered by the Back Creek Friends Church. His aunt and uncle attended services there every Sunday. In his very first performance he portrayed a blind boy who miraculously regains his sight in a play called *To Them That Sleep in Darkness*.

Jimmy was fascinated with the outlaw Henry McCarty, alias William H. Bonney, better known to the world as Billy the Kid. He enjoyed reading about the exploits of the young outlaw and how he died at the hands of his old friend Pat Garrett. He had hoped that one day he might portray the Western legend in a film.

In the fall of 1943, Jimmy left West Ward and started seventh grade at Fairmount High School. On November 2, Ortense gave birth to a son and named him Marcus Jr. Jimmy always thought of Marcus not as a cousin but as a younger brother. In turn, young Marcus thought of Jimmy as his older brother.

Ortense encouraged Jimmy to perform on stage for the Women's Christian Temperance Union. He agreed wholeheartedly without any hesitation. He preferred to recite gory odes rather than read poetry. He won a prize for his very first reading and from then on he was hooked. Not satisfied with winning just any award, he wanted to compete for the most cherished award, the Pearl Medal. He was given a reading called simply "Bars." Adeline Brookshire (the teacher would later go by the name of Adeline Nall), advised Jimmy to use a chair as a prop. For days he rehearsed his lines while peering from between the chair's rungs.

Bars! Bars! Iron bars! No matter which way I look I see them always before me! Long, menacing, iron bars that mock and sneer at me, even in my sleep. At times I think I hear them shout: "You killed a man! You killed a man!" Then I shout back at them: "I didn't! I didn't! I tell you, I didn't!" But did I? My God above, did I - I who as a boy could not bear to inflict pain on anyone?

On the night of the contest, the committee ruled that Jimmy couldn't utilize any props whatsoever. Jimmy stood on the stage and froze in front of the entire audience. He was subsequently ushered off the stage much to his embarrassment. "You couldn't make Jimmy Dean do things he didn't want to do," Ortense later explained. Jimmy blamed Adeline for his downfall. Unable to accept responsibility for his actions, he held a grudge against her for weeks.

Jimmy was a daredevil even at a tender age. He tried to ride a Brahma bull at a county fair and was unceremoniously thrown from it. He studied Yoga and attempted many of its exercises, such as holding his breath until he passed out. One day while playing in a barn, Jimmy fell out of the loft and knocked his two front teeth out. For the rest of his life he had to wear a dental bridge to compensate for his missing teeth.

Dean considered himself to be outside the norm as far as local interests were concerned. He didn't like farmwork and he found it difficult to accept the community's values and moral precepts. He felt very uneasy in terms of fitting in just to please the multitudes. He enjoyed talking about his passion for the dramatic arts, even though many of his classmates and neighbors frowned upon acting as a legitimate career. Jimmy was considered to be an outsider by many in his community. Rather than deal with their judgmental attitude, he kept to himself a great deal of the time.

Jimmy was an exercise enthusiast who enjoyed running, lifting weights, and practicing dribbling and shooting the hoops. In his freshmen year at Fairmount High School, he joined the basketball and track teams. He made the baseball team by his sophomore year. Dean had a strong tendency to break his glasses while playing basketball. He couldn't see without them. It seemed like every other week his glasses either needed to be repaired by the local optometrist or Marcus purchased Jimmy a new pair.

According to Paul Weaver, the basketball coach of the Fairmount High School team, Jimmy was a good player, but he had to be dealt with very carefully. Weaver didn't think Dean was very coachable and he learned never to criticize him in the presence of other teammates. Weaver also learned that Jimmy had to do things his way. If the coach tried to change his style of play on the court, Dean simply ignored his suggestions. Jimmy was excruciatingly sensitive to any kind of lecture and resented feeling embarrassed in front of his peers.

Keeping busy seemed to agree with Jimmy. He explored other school activities, including the debating society. He joined the high school band and became proficient at playing the clarinet. He listened to Benny Goodman records and enjoyed imitating Goodman's unusual style of playing. Dean spent part of his free time learning to play the bongos. He liked sketching landscapes and frequently gave them as gifts to friends and relatives.

Winton stopped by the farm after his discharge from the service. He proudly showed off his new wife, the former Ethel Case, to everyone. Jimmy felt apprehensive around his father and his new wife and he avoided them as much as possible. The thought of being abandoned by his own father still weighed heavily on him.

In the fall of his sophomore year, Jimmy began working closely with a teacher who would change his life forever. Adeline Brookshire had been teaching speech and English at Fairmount High School for several years. In addition to those duties, Adeline sponsored the Thespian Society and she directed school plays. She coached Dean, her star pupil, in public speaking and drama. She recalled that Jimmy could be "moody and unpredictable." One day Dean offered her a cigarette during class. She claimed he'd go off on a rant if he didn't win a competition of some sort. "Frankly, he couldn't take criticism," she recalled.

Dean appeared in a play called *Mooncalf Mugford* during his sophomore year. The short romantic story was written by Brainerd Duffield and Helen and Nolan Leary.

Jimmy played a delusional old man who lures his hapless wife into a kind of fantasy world. His performance was so powerful and convincing, Adeline began to seriously consider her protégé as someone with a bright future in the acting profession.

In his junior year, Jimmy played the part of Otis Skinner in *Our Hearts Were Young and Gay*. The story was written by Corneila Otis Skinner and Emily Kimbrough. Jimmy played a character much older than himself. He devised his own makeup to the point where no one recognized him onstage. He had applied a liberal amount of pancake base, talcum-powdered hair, and eyeliner.

Also during his junior year, Jimmy played a character named Herbert White in the supernatural thriller, *The Monkey's Paw*. The story was written by W.W. Jacobs and Louis N. Parker. White is a London factory worker who lives with his parents. In the end, he is accidently ripped apart inside a machine.

In March of his senior year, Brookshire urged Jimmy to enter a contest sponsored by the National Forensic League. He chose Charles Dickens' "A Madman's Manuscript" from *Pickwick Papers*. The monologue is told by a lunatic who drives his wife insane and ultimately to her death. He attempts to murder his brother, but is captured and locked away in an insane asylum. It is here where the madman recounts his tale of lunacy and murder. Jimmy studied the monologue and when he was ready, he performed it in front of Brookshire's drama class.

"Yes – a madman!" Jimmy screamed. "How that word would have struck to my heart many years ago! How it would have roused the terror that used to come upon me sometimes, sending the blood hissing and tingling through my veins, till the cold dew of fear stood in large drops upon my skin and my knees knocked together with fright!"

Jimmy's appearance suddenly changed as he rambled on, his teeth tightly clenched, and his eyes glaring at his classmates, some of whom seemed legitimately frightened. He continued on with abandonment.

"It's a grand thing to be mad, to be peeped at like a wild lion through the iron bars, to gnash one's teeth and howl through the long, still night, to the merry ring of a heavy chain – and to roll and whine among the straw…"

Brookshire recalled that Jimmy's most outstanding trait was his uncanny ability to concentrate on the matter at hand. She remembered vividly how he would crouch in front of the class and scream, "Hurrah for the madhouse! Oh, it's a rare place." When Jimmy completed his speech, he took a bow and walked to his seat and sat down. Many of his peers remained frozen in their seats, not knowing how to respond to fourteen minutes of pure insanity.

A few days later, Jimmy performed the same monologue at a final open rehearsal. Unfortunately, a student named David Fox began heckling Jimmy's performance. Dean was noticeably irritated by the interruption to his monologue and he had a difficult time getting back into character. Jimmy reportedly chased Fox out into the hall and down a flight of stairs. The principal and several teachers broke up the altercation between the two boys. Jimmy was promptly suspended from school and barred from competing in an upcoming basketball game.

When Jimmy returned to school he had the monologue down to near perfection. However, Adeline advised him to shorten his performance to twelve minutes, the allotted time permitted. Dean balked at this suggestion, telling her that each second was essential in telling the story. Adeline gave in to his stubbornness and she never criticized him again. He also refused to wear the required coat, white shirt, and tie while performing the madman's monologue. "How the heck can I go crazy in a shirt and tie?" he asked her. Once again, she didn't press the issue. She knew he was going to do it his way or not at all. Everything worked out well for Jimmy because he won first place in the National Forensic League's Dramatic Declamation Contest in Peru, Indiana. One of the judges at the contest was deeply moved by the "eerie expression in his eyes." She remarked that Jimmy looked insane at times during his presentation.

On April 27, Adeline and Jimmy boarded a train bound for Chicago where they would catch another train for Longmont, Colorado, where the National Forensic League Tournament Finals were being held. Jimmy would be competing against one hundred contestants from twenty-four states. A judge warned Jimmy not to go over the allotted twelve minutes allowed for each presentation. He ignored the suggestion and performed the monologue the only way he knew how. His way. He placed sixth in the semifinal round and therefore was not allowed to advance to the finals.

According to Adeline, Jimmy blamed her for his failure to compete in the finals because she did not take his side. He explained to her that the additional two minutes of monologue were necessary in order to help support the integrity of the piece. His failure was all the more troublesome because many of the judges thought his performance was outstanding. Dean's habit of stubbornly testing the boundaries of rules and regulations would continue unabated for the rest of his life.

Jimmy's sports prowess was clearly recognized in and around Fairmount. In 1948, Dean appeared in an article of the *Fairmount News*. The paper referred to him as "An outstanding threat on the high school team." It also indicated that he had accumulated forty points in three basketball games, a truly remarkable achievement.

Dean proved to be very competitive in everything he attempted. Ortense Winslow recalled that "when Jimmy was set to do something, nobody could stop him. He was tough-minded when he thought he had to be. And when he laughed, the whole world laughed, when he cried, it cried. He was always able to get people into his moods. It was a wonderful gift."

Jimmy was fascinated with speed. When he turned fifteen, Marcus bought him his first motorcycle at a little shop called Carter Motors. It was a 1.5 horsepower Czech-made CZ. Shortly after that, Marcus permitted Jimmy to ride the motorbike to school. He had a nasty habit of offering classmates a ride on the back of his motorcycle and then he'd abruptly take off at high speed. Several neighbors noted that he enjoyed performing dangerous stunts on his motorcycle, like lying flat on his stomach on the bike's saddle as he roared through town. According to Marcus, Jimmy never got injured riding his motorcycle. Not surprisingly, this prompted Dean to attempt more death-defying stunts.

Jimmy's senior year began in the fall of 1948. Having achieved a letter in basketball and track, he tried his hand at pole vaulting. He was told many times that he was simply too small to successfully compete in the sport, but Jimmy ignored the warnings. Not only did Dean excel in pole vaulting, he set a record for Grant County that went unbroken for years.

Roland DuBois, Fairmount High School's new principal, asked students to write a short essay about themselves. Jimmy wrote about his mother's death and how it still preyed upon his mind. He wrote that he wanted to devote his life to art and the dramatics. "As one strives to make a goal in a game, there should be a goal in this crazy world for each of us," he added.

Once Jimmy turned 18, he was required to register for the draft. He did this on February 14, 1949. His registration card indicated he weighed one hundred and fifty pounds and he was five feet, eight inches in height.

After graduation Uncle Marcus wanted Jimmy to enroll at Earlham, a small Quaker college in nearby Richmond, Indiana. It was Marcus' old alma mater. He thought his nephew should study agriculture. Jimmy told the Winslows he wanted to be an actor. He had also considered becoming a minister or a painter or a lawyer over the years. Being Quakers, the Winslows resigned themselves to whatever Jimmy wanted to do with his life.

Winton reached out to Jimmy and asked if he would like to move in with him and his new wife. Dean was grateful for his father's unexpected kindness and he agreed to take him up on his offer. Jimmy would be near Hollywood, the film capital of the world. His heart was also set on attending UCLA as a Theater Arts major.

May 16, 1949 was a memorable day for Jimmy. It was graduation day and he was asked to read a prayer at the end of the graduation ceremony. The school presented him with a medal for best all-around athlete and he was also awarded a prize for outstanding student by the art department.

Jimmy's high school grades were not sufficient enough to get him into UCLA. Reportedly, he had received mostly Ds. His best bet was to enroll in Santa Monica City College and then transfer to UCLA. Marcus and Ortense held a farewell party for Jimmy at their home. The *Fairmount News* even mentioned the farewell party under the headline JAMES DEAN HONORED AT FAREWELL PARTY MONDAY NIGHT.

Reportedly, friends drove Jimmy to Chicago where he boarded a Greyhound bus headed for Los Angeles. When he arrived at his destination, he had no idea how challenging living with his father and stepmother would be. It didn't help that father and son had hardly seen or written to each other for the past nine years. Winton rarely visited his son and Jimmy wrote to his father only when Ortense tactfully suggested that he do so. Bill Bast, a future friend and roommate of Dean's, confirmed that Winton was extremely mild-mannered and kept to himself much of the time. "I knew him in California because he was working at Sawtelle Hospital. But if you're looking for the source of Jimmy's dynamism you can forget the father."

The Deans lived in a small apartment close to the Veterans Administration Hospital. Jimmy made it a point never to address his father as 'Dad.' Winton was concerned about how his son would get along with his wife Ethel. Jimmy was pragmatic enough to develop some sort of rapport with his father and stepmother. However, Ethel still felt very uncomfortable around her stepson.

Dean's relationship with his father was cordial at first, but in time the battle of wills reared its ugly head. Winton thought his son was wasting his time dreaming of becoming an actor. Jimmy grew tired of his father's remarks about how acting was such an unmanly profession. According to Winton, there was no way Jimmy would amount to much in the entertainment world. He suggested that his son study the law or become a physical education instructor. Clarence Darrow was a hero of Jimmy's and so he considered becoming an attorney. However, the idea of studying law did not last very long. Jimmy told his father he wanted to attend UCLA and major in the dramatic arts. Winton told Jimmy to forget about becoming an actor and to enroll in Santa Monica City College, which was less expensive than UCLA.

Winton emphasized that Santa Monica City College offered practical courses in business and teaching. Jimmy reminded his father that he wanted to study acting in college, but Winton tried to discourage his son from majoring in what he considered a thoroughly useless field. He thought his son was throwing his life away by foolishly dreaming of becoming a movie star. Winton saw only the practical side of a college education and that pursuing a degree based on a foolish dream was sheer folly.

To his great credit, Winton made an effort to spend time with his son. They went bowling and golfing together. Jimmy did not enjoy playing golf at all so he quit taking lessons from his father. Winton was thoughtful enough to buy his son a 1939 Chevy so Jimmy could drive himself to college.

Dean finally decided to compromise with his father and so he enrolled in the much more affordable Santa

Monica City College in June 1949. He signed up for a class in Theater Arts as an elective. The college was under new construction and so for the 1949-1950 academic year, classes were held in several available classrooms at the Santa Monica High School. Jimmy signed up for classes in physics, Spanish and geology. He also signed up for two other courses, namely History of the Theater and Beginning Acting. Gene Nielsen Owen, chairperson of the drama department, taught both classes. Owen immediately recognized natural acting talent in her new student, but she also noticed he lacked formal dramatic training.

Jimmy joined the Jazz Club and he became an announcer for the college's FM radio station. Moreover, he joined the school's Honor Society. He even found time to play as a substitute guard for the college basketball team. Sanger Crumpacker, the college's basketball coach, remembered Jimmy as a very motivated individual who desperately wanted to win. He was the shortest member on the team, but he more than held his own by playing aggressive basketball on the court. Plagued by bad eyesight, he often refused to wear his glasses during a game because he was concerned about his appearance.

Dean joined the Miller Playhouse Theater Guild. It was a traveling summer stock company in partnership with UCLA. He did not perform in any plays, but he did paint scenery and worked with props. He also decided to go by the name of Byron Dean.

Jimmy's accomplishments were faithfully printed in the *Fairmount News*.

JAMES DEAN JOINS THEATRE GROUP AT SANTA MONICA, CAL.

Mr. and Mrs. Charles Dean received a letter last week from their grandson, Jimmy Dean, who recently went to Santa Monica, Calif., to make his home with his father, Winton Dean. He stated in his letter that he was enjoying his vacation bowling and playing golf with his father, and he also wrote, "I have registered for summer and fall session at UCLA...I am now a full-fledged member of the Miller Playhouse Theatre Guild."

In a letter he wrote to the Winslows, Jimmy referred to his acting peers as "the most catty, criticizing, narcissistic bunch of people you ever saw, always at each other's throats." He was awarded a small part in a musical called *The Romance of Scarlet Gulch*. His name was listed once again as Byron Dean. Jimmy may have thought his new name sounded more intriguing.

Dean enjoyed listening to jazz and he frequently hung out at Ray Avery's Record Roundup located on La Cienega Boulevard. He particularly liked listening to Bessie Smith and Jelly Roll Morton. He purchased old 78s of old timers like Edward "Kid" Ory, a New Orleans trombonist, and Frank Trumbauer, a saxophonist who once played with Bix Beiderbecke. Clearly, Jimmy enjoyed music from a bygone era.

Gene Owen, one of Jimmy's drama teachers, remembered him as "always polite and thoughtful; his enthusiasm for everything that pertained to the theater was boundless." Dean attended a radio class offered by Owen. She was impressed with Jimmy's rendition of Edgar Allan Poe's "Telltale Heart." Spurred on by Jimmy's talent, Owen asked him to read some lines from *Hamlet*. Impressed once again by Dean's dramatic reading, Owen had to look no further for her Prince of Denmark.

Owen recalled that Jimmy's articulation was inadequate. "He mashed his words and he was difficult to understand. In an articulation class someone pointed this out and blamed it on his Hoosier accent. Later, when we were alone in my office, Jimmy protested and removed the upper plate he wore across his hard palate for a dental problem. Obviously, it made some tongue positions difficult for certain sounds."

In order to help remedy the situation, Owen had Jimmy recite Shakespearian passages from *Hamlet*. "I told him that if anything would clear up fuzzy speech it would be the demanding soliloquies of Shakespeare. And so we began, on a one-to-one basis, what was to be a fascinating and revealing study for both of us."

Jimmy was absolutely adamant about enrolling in UCLA. The university offered more opportunity in dramatic arts than Santa Monica City College. He asked Gene Owen what she thought about his idea of transferring to the university. She didn't feel he was sufficiently prepared to succeed at UCLA and so she advised Jimmy against enrolling there. Completely ignoring her advice, he enrolled anyway. He realized UCLA's theater departments were among the country's finest and it had the reputation of providing the movie industry with talented directors, writers, and actors.

Winton was beginning to see the writing on the wall in terms of Jimmy's passion for acting. Dean's grades in drama and gym were great, but he could only manage a C average. Winton finally gave in to his son's passion for acting and allowed him to enroll in UCLA as a Theater Arts major. Jimmy decided to sign up for some pre-law classes as well. It was perhaps an attempt to appease his father.

Jimmy applied to UCLA in 1950 for the fall semester. His academic achievement at Santa Monica City College was good enough for him to be accepted and so at the end of his first year, Jimmy transferred to UCLA. To help pay for his tuition he worked as an athletic instructor at a camp for boys. He majored in Theater Arts as he had planned and joined the Sigma Nu fraternity. He also signed up as an air cadet in the ROTC program. He became friends with James Bellah, a fellow pledge brother at the fraternity. The 1948 film *Fort Apache*, directed by John Ford and starring John Wayne and Henry Fonda, was based on a story Bellah's father had written.

Jimmy moved out of his father's home and took up residence at a house near the campus. He took the pledge at the Epsilon Pi chapter of Sigma Nu, a national fraternity. According to Manuel Gonzalez, the commander of the chapter, the new resident kept to himself most of the time. Rather than partake in chapter activities, Jimmy spent much of his time reading and drawing in his room. He was often ridiculed by the other fraternity members. Because he wore jeans and a white T-shirt, he was frequently referred to as a plowboy and a hick.

The theater department announced it would be holding auditions for the production of *Macbeth* and that the play would run from November 29 through December 2. Jimmy showed up at the tryouts and read his assigned lines onstage in front of several dramatic arts teachers. Gene Owen's Shakespearian sessions with Jimmy apparently had paid off because he was offered a major role in the play.

Ecstatic over his good fortune, Jimmy wrote to Marcus and Ortense Winslow. "The biggest thrill of my life came three weeks ago, after grueling auditions for UCLA's four major theatrical productions, the major one being *Macbeth* which will be presented in Royce Hall (seats 160). After auditioning of 1600 actors and actresses, I came up with a wonderful lead in *Macbeth*, the character being Malcolm (huge part)."

In October Dean was officially chosen to play the role of Prince Malcolm in the university's version of *Macbeth*. Malcolm was the elder son of King Duncan of Scotland in the play. Jimmy was chosen to play Malcolm in William Shakespeare's *Macbeth* after the director thought he detected something that impressed him during Jimmy's audition. He sensed a certain intensity that was uncommon among other actors.

Jimmy had difficulty reading his lines without his glasses. He hated wearing them and he frequently fumbled with them. William Bast, a fellow student at UCLA, claimed that Dean spoke with an annoying Midwestern twang and his acting was subpar. Whenever Jimmy was confronted with criticism, he either argued with his critics or he turned his back on them. According to several of Jimmy's acquaintances, he wanted to come out ahead of everybody, that winning was the only thing that mattered.

The reviews regarding Jimmy's performance were generally disappointing. Gene Owen noted that he "was overshadowed by and in awe of Frank Wolff, who played Macbeth, so he sort of stayed back." Fellow student John Holden remarked that, "He just hasn't got it! He's never going to be an actor." Another witness to Jimmy's performance was Larry Swindell, who cracked, "Jim was terrible in *Macbeth* – really terrible." A student reviewer for the Theater Arts Department's newspaper chimed in that Jimmy "failed to show any growth, and would have made a hallow king."

Two UCLA students befriended Jimmy almost immediately. Jeanetta Lewis, a crew member of the *Macbeth* production, and theater major William Bast found Jimmy to be reserved but cordial. According to Bast, Dean made no real impression on him based on that one performance. He found him to be "quiet, almost sullen."

After the play, Dean rushed out another letter to the Winslows. "The play was very much a success," he claimed. "I was very much rewarded and proved myself a capable actor in the eyes of several hundred culture-minded individuals. Man, if I can keep this up, and nothing interferes with my progress, one of these days I might be able to contribute something to the world (theatrically)."

Dean was not happy with his experience at the fraternity house. He felt he was being judged as someone who had difficulty getting along with fellow fraternity brothers. Many of the fraternity brothers were upset with Jimmy's nonconformist ways. He was reportedly late for many of the fraternity meals and he rarely attended pledge meetings. Manuel Gonzalez, the chapter president, told Jimmy that he was only interested in personal endeavors and he couldn't care less about fraternity activities. Jimmy finally reached the end of his rope when a frat member suggested that he must be a "fruit" because of his acute obsession with acting. Dean punched his accuser in the face and he was subsequently thrown out of the fraternity.

With nowhere to live in the immediate future, Dean asked Bill Bast if he wouldn't mind sharing an apartment with him in order to save money. Bast immediately agreed. They found a furnished three-room Mexican style penthouse practically touching the Pacific Ocean. According to Bast, Jimmy's mood swings came and went at the drop of a hat. Jimmy's moodiness grew increasingly worse. Audition after audition yielded nothing but anxiety and depression. One day he could be moody and irritable and the next day he could be congenial and friendly. Bast quickly realized that Jimmy's whole reason for living was to become a serious dramatic actor. He was convinced nothing could stop Jimmy from realizing his dream.

Dean was low on funds most of the time. It was not unusual for Jimmy to ask his roommate for money so he could eat. Bast was not financially well off himself and so they were occasionally forced to eat oatmeal for dinner. Bast typically went to bed early, whereas Jimmy had difficulty sleeping. He frequently ventured out late at night to places like Venice Pier and hung out with whatever crowd happened to be mulling around at the time.

Disappointed with what UCLA had to offer, Jimmy decided to quit the university and face the real world on his own. He thought time was running short and UCLA was not satisfying his particular needs. Dean refused to abide by the guidelines imposed on him by the university. It was a decision that weighed heavily on Jimmy's mind.

Bast had been dating Beverly Wills, the daughter of the very popular comedienne Joan Davis. Soon afterward, Jimmy and Beverly began seeing each other. Eventually, Beverly told Bast that she was in love with Jimmy and so they broke up. Beverly's relationship with Jimmy was doomed from the start due primarily to Jimmy's sullenness and bad manners. Unable to tolerate his roommate's toxic behavior any further, Bast moved out of the penthouse and left Jimmy to fend for himself.

Dean landed a job parking cars at Ted's Auto Park to help make ends meet. The parking facility happened to be adjacent to a major entertainment studio. It is here where Dean met Rogers Brackett, the director of a half-hour radio series called *Alias Jane Doe*. Brackett was impressed with Jimmy's looks and demeaner and decided to audition him for a part in *Alias Jane Doe*. According to scriptwriter, John Michael Hayes, Jimmy worked on four episodes beginning July 28.

Brackett introduced Dean to Isabel Draesemer, manager for a talent agency in the Los Angeles area. Draesemer told Jimmy that an advertising agency was searching for some young adults for a Pepsi-Cola commercial. As soon as he heard about an opportunity to be seen on television, Jimmy jumped at the chance. Jerry Fairbanks, the commercial's producer, was interested in hiring all-American type teenagers. Dean was hired on the spot because of his good looks and pleasant disposition. Jimmy immediately agreed to act in it and so on December 13, 1950, he performed professionally for the first time. His role was to hand out Pepsi-Colas to teenagers on a merry-go-round. Dean was chosen over other actors to dance a jitterbug on the second day of filming the Pepsi commercial. He was paid twenty-five dollars for just a few hours of work. Sharing acting duties on that cold, wintery day were Nick Adams and Beverly Long, two actors who would someday cross paths with Dean on the set of *Rebel Without a Cause*. The commercial's location, Griffith Park, would someday play a critical part in Jimmy's most iconic and enduring film.

Dean managed to land a part in a one-act play called *The Axe of God*. It had been written by Richard Eshleman, a UCLA student. The 'Axe' referred to Martin Luther. Jimmy played a young monk who meets Luther, but eventually becomes disillusioned. Gail Kobe played Luther's wife, Kathryn von Bora. According to Kobe, Jimmy was outstanding. He was constantly experimenting during rehearsals. "If you would go along with what he was doing," she recalled, "you could find wonderful things."

Producer Jerry Fairbanks was so impressed with Jimmy's performance in the Pepsi-Cola commercial, he called Draesemer and recommended that she have Jimmy do an audition for an episode of *Father Peyton's Family Theater*. The audition went well and he was hired to perform in an episode called "Hill Number One." The holiday special was to be broadcast on Easter Sunday, 1951. The production included several well-established actors such as Ruth Hussey who portrayed Mary, Roddy McDowell as one of the American soldiers, and Leif Erickson as Pontius Pilate. The story begins with American infantrymen trying to capture an enemy hill during the Korean War. "War is a crucifixion," the army chaplain tells the soldiers. "It shakes the earth, darkens the sun, and makes men look for a meaning in life.

Why don't we think a moment about the first hill – hill number one. It was taken by one man alone." The story then takes us back to the time of Pontius Pilate. Jesus Christ has just been crucified and Pilate is mulling over what to do with Christ's body. Dean assumed the role of John the Apostle. He is seen seated at a table with all the other disciples and they are discussing Pontius Pilate's scourges. The other disciples have gone into hiding because they fear retribution. They also seriously consider disbanding and returning home. John rebukes the others, asking them, "Was it for this we gave up our nets? Just to go back to our boats again?"

Jimmy suffered from a severe cold during the entire production. Because of his slender build and youthful appearance, he seemed to look out of place. He was clean shaven whereas the other actors playing disciples appeared much older, heavier, and donned beards.

Jimmy was an immediate sensation with girls at the Immaculate Heart High School. They created the Immaculate Heart James Dean Appreciation Society. They held a party in his honor and he thoroughly enjoyed the recognition and adulation of his adoring fans. Jimmy was paid $150 for his performance. *The Hollywood Reporter* claimed over forty million viewers watched the program, thereby giving Jimmy unbelievable exposure. The *Reporter* even praised the performances of some of the smaller roles. Jimmy had hoped that after "Hill Number One" aired, offers for more roles would come pouring in. They did not. An article about the show appeared in *Variety*, but Dean's name was never mentioned. Depression soon set in due to the lack of opportunity he was experiencing in the entertainment business. William Bast still stayed in touch with Jimmy as much as possible, even during Dean's darkest episodes.

Draesemer found a small role for Jimmy on a television anthology series called *Bigelow Theatre*. The name of the episode was "T.K.O." and it featured a very young Martin Milner. Milner would later appear on the very popular television series *Route 66* in the 1960s and on *Adam-12* several years later. Jimmy was paid forty-five dollars for his efforts. To help pay for expenses, Jimmy got a job as a movie usher. Although he enjoyed watching movies for free, he hated wearing what he referred to as a "monkey suit." He was fired after only one week. Bast felt betrayed because he had fought so hard to get Jimmy hired.

Dean's first role in a feature film was that of an American infantryman. He was hired to play a small part in a Korean War drama called *Fixed Bayonets!* He was paid $44 for his role as a sentry near the end of the film. His only lines are "I think I hear 'em comin.' It could be the rear guard, huh?"

Fixed Bayonets! was panned for being "the most realistic war tale to date." The sarcastic remark was in reference to the fact that as many as nineteen injuries occurred during the filming of the production. Bill Hickman, a man Jimmy would later befriend, broke an ankle when he fell down a mountainside. Other injuries included a shell explosion and a bayoneted foot.

Jimmy landed a role in a Paramount production initially called *At Sea with the Navy*, starring Jerry Lewis and Dean Martin. The film was later renamed *Sailor Beware,* a presumably snappier title. He played one of the corner men for an amateur boxer scheduled to fight his opponent played by Lewis. Jimmy's only line in the entire film is "That guy's a professional!"

It was becoming painfully obvious to Jimmy that the movie studio system in Hollywood was not the answer to his dream of becoming a serious film star. New York City was the world's mecca for television productions. There were also Broadway and Off-Broadway productions to consider as well. Then too, New York City offered many opportunities in terms of legitimate acting schools. Chief among them were the Actors Studio, the American Academy of Dramatic Arts, and the Neighborhood Playhouse of the Theater. Jimmy met a man named Dick Clayton, an aspiring actor who decided acting was not his forte. Jimmy told Clayton about his plans to relocate to New York City. Clayton had some experience with agents and so he told Jimmy to look up Jane Deacy, an agent who might be able to help him find some badly needed roles.

Universal-International hired Dean to play an obnoxious college student in *Has Anybody Seen My Gal?* starring Charles Coburn, Piper Laurie, and newcomer Rock Hudson. In the only scene he is in, Dean's character orders a milk shake from an elderly server. "Hey, Gramps – I'll have a choc malt – heavy on the choc – plenty of milk – four spoons of malt - two scoops of vanilla ice cream - one mixed with the rest - and one floating." He then punctuates his order by slamming a hat over his head.

According to Bill Bast, veteran actor James Whitmore thought Hollywood was totally devoid of serious acting schools. He informed Bast that he would hold acting workshops on the following conditions: Bast would bring in eight or nine candidates from UCLA, Whitmore would not be considered a teacher, but rather a guide, and that he didn't want monetary compensation.

Bast told Jimmy about a proposed acting workshop to be headed by Whitmore. The veteran actor had been featured in several major movies, including the outstanding film noir crime caper *The Asphalt Jungle* directed by

John Huston. He had also been nominated for best supporting actor for *Battleground* in which he played a gruff, battle-weary infantryman. Whitmore had also won a Tony for his brilliant performance in the popular Broadway production of *Command Decision.*

Whitmore wanted to pass on all of his knowledge and experience concerning acting. He had attended the Yale University School of Drama as well as the Actors Studio in New York City. Initially, his teaching sessions were held at the Brentwood County Mart. Whitmore believed imagination, the senses, and the emotions were necessary functions of real acting. He taught, for example, the simple act of peeling an imaginary apple was an exercise in utilizing and developing one's imagination.

The veteran actor told his students that acting is a serious profession and not a hobby, unless you wanted to make it one. He also stressed that if they were looking for glory and wealth, they were probably barking up the wrong tree. He taught his students that serious acting required time, patience, and a lot of work. He said if a student in his class was looking for a sense of personal gratification, then acting was made to order. During one improvisational session, Jimmy played a thief and Bill Bast played the jeweler who traps the thief in his shop. At one point the two became so involved in the scene, they came to blows and had to be separated by fellow classmates.

Jimmy asked Whitmore for advice on the best way to develop as an actor. Whitmore told Dean to stop wasting his time looking for parts in Hollywood because he had reached a dead end. He urged him to go to New York City and learn serious acting. He suggested Jimmy try joining the Actors Studio.

"I owe a lot to Whitmore," Jimmy recounted years later. "I guess you can say he saved me when I got all mixed up. One thing he said helped me more than anything. He told me I didn't know the difference between acting as a soft job and acting as a difficult art. People ask me these ridiculous questions like, 'When did you first decide to become an actor?' I don't know that there was ever any such time. I realized I was an actor because of James Whitmore. There's always someone in your life who opens up your eyes. For me, that's Whitmore. He made me see myself. He opened me up, gave me the key."

Dean was at a crossroads and he knew it. He came to realize that a serious actor could spend years in Hollywood and get absolutely nowhere. He firmly believed he wasn't the leading man type or someone the bobby soxers could fall in love with. He was tired of casting directors telling him that he wasn't photogenic enough or that he was too short or that he wore glasses. "How can you measure acting in inches?" Dean was quoted as saying. It was a tremendous step to take, but Jimmy clearly saw there was no other viable option, and so he decided to move to New York City. It would turn out to be the best decision he could have made at this point in his career.

CHAPTER 2

NEW YORK CITY

Newcomer James Dean strolling through the streets of New York City.

immy left California and headed for New York City in search of a brighter future. He had given Hollywood a try, but the results were far from what he had expected. When he left California in the fall of 1951, he was essentially broke. On his way to the big city, he visited the Winslows and borrowed some money from them. They gave Dean what they could spare, but it would not be nearly enough to hold him over for very long. Not in New York City.

As soon as Jimmy arrived in New York, he rented a room at the Hotel Iroquois on West 44th Street. The city had an immediate and profound effect on Dean. He found it overwhelming and frightening. He spent the first few days walking the streets, acclimating himself to his new and very strange surroundings. He took long walks up and down Broadway late at night. He began doubting his chances of ever making it as a serious actor.

Dean spent a great deal of time and money going to the movies. He thought it might help ease his sense of loneliness and anxiety. Jimmy told a friend that he had watched the film *The Men* starring Marlon Brando four times in just a couple of days. A huge fan of Montgomery Clift, he watched George Stevens' *A Place in the Sun* three times. He regarded Clift and Brando to be the best actors in Hollywood – bar none. To Jimmy, most of the current crop of actors were wooden. In his view, they lacked a certain naturalness he thought was essential for an actor.

Dean wrote a heartfelt letter to eight-year-old Marcus Jr. on Hotel Iroquois stationary. He was responding to some pictures his cousin had recently drawn.

Dear Marcus Jr.

First I want to thank you for the fine pictures. I feel the urgent need to warn you about something. Anyone at all can draw soldiers, guns, and barred gates with locks on them. Why? Because there are a lot of those things to see. That shouldn't mean that they are good things to draw. We live in a world where these things become very important. And that is bad...It would be much better if you would spread your talents toward the greater arts. Everyone can't draw trees, clouds, sheep, dogs, all kinds of animals, the earth, hills, mountains...I beg of you – please do not draw buildings of confinement, jails, castles, or zoos. Rather, draw pictures of shelter...Do not draw things of destruction...Have your Daddy help you read this.

Love, Jim.

When Dean could no longer afford his room at the Hotel Iroquois, he took a small room at the YMCA on West 63rd Street near Central Park. He also got a job as a dishwasher in a tavern on West 45th Street. Jimmy listened to a lot of classical music in his room at the YMCA. He particularly enjoyed Bach and Bartok. He read quite a bit, including extensive passages of major philosophical works. He rarely read a book to its completion and only absorbed as much as he thought was necessary in order to understand the basic principles of an author's ideas.

Jimmy landed a job as a stunt tester for a popular television game show called *Beat the Clock*. Bud Collyer was its affable and quick-talking host. Before each broadcast, testers like Dean and future film star Warren Oates performed zany stunts to determine if they could be done successfully. Contestants were required to perform various stunts before the clock ran out. Frank Wayne, a writer for the show, remembered Jimmy was fiercely competitive during these lab sessions. "If Jimmy couldn't do a stunt in the lab session, he would stay on his own time doing it over and over again until he finally got it, and then he'd come over with this big grin on his face and say, 'Frank, I've got it.' And then he'd kind of giggle."

Wayne discovered that Dean had gone days without eating. One of the sponsors advertised tapioca pudding on the show. Because the program was live, gallons of the pudding had to be thrown out at the end of the day. Jimmy asked if he could eat some. "You sure you want to eat a lot of tapioca?" Wayne asked him. "Man," Jimmy replied, "anything would taste good now. I haven't had anything to eat in two days." Wayne graciously gave Jimmy the pudding and paid for his dinner that same evening. Dean was eventually fired from the show because none of the contestants could duplicate his ability to perform difficult stunts.

Dean frequented low-priced eating facilities in order to stretch what little savings he had. After dining at cheap eateries like Horn & Hardart, where some meals cost less than a dollar, Dean stumbled across Jerry's Bar and Restaurant on Sixth Avenue and 54th Street. The owner, Jerry Lucci, sometimes allowed Jimmy to eat for free. Jerry's Bar quickly became Dean's favorite go to place for sustenance.

Bill Bast introduced Jimmy to Ralph Levy, a television director friend. Levy wrote a letter of introduction for Dean to James Sheldon who was working on commercials for several television shows. Jimmy read a scene for Sheldon and the director was so impressed, he sent him to audition for a television series called *Mama*. The TV show was based on a Broadway play written by John Van Druten called *I Remember Mama*. The play premiered on Broadway in 1944 and ran for 713 performances. *I Remember Mama* was derived from Kathryn Forbes' novel, *Mama's Bank Account*.

Immediately after Dean's reading he was hired to play Nels, the son of a Norwegian immigrant family in early twentieth-century San Francisco. The part had recently been vacated by Dick Van Patten due to a pending military obligation. Coincidently, Marlon Brando had played Nels in the Broadway version.

According to Rosemary Rice, one of the actors in the series, Jimmy was terrible as Nels. She claimed Van Patten played the role with a sense of humor, whereas Dean played the role of Nels much too seriously. According to Rice, Dean made her feel anxious because of what she considered to be his dark nature.

Unfortunately for Jimmy, Van Patten received an exemption from the military and returned back to the show. Ralph Nelson, the director of the program, felt relieved when Van Patten resumed his old role. He thought Dean seemed uninterested in the role of Nels, almost as if the part was beneath him. He thought there was a strange side to Dean that unnerved him. Nelson was also struck by the fact that money didn't seem important to Jimmy.

Van Patten and Dean became close friends. Jimmy liked to talk extensively about his theories on acting. He told Van Patten that he thought it was vital for an actor not to know his or her lines verbatim. "You want to give the impression you're searching for the words," Jimmy explained. Van Patten frequently invited Jimmy over to the Forrest Hotel on Forty-ninth Street for a game of late-night poker. According to Van Patten, Dean never played poker, probably because he never had enough money to gamble. Instead, Jimmy quietly sat in the background for hours and watched the game. Referring to Dean as his "flunkie," Van Patten occasionally sent him out for some cigarettes and soda.

James Sheldon generally liked what he saw in Jimmy as an actor, but he thought Dean wasn't right for the projects he was currently working on. However, he referred Jimmy to a talent agent named Louis Shurr. The agent was well connected with several producers and directors. Unfortunately, Shurr wasn't impressed with what Jimmy had to offer. He thought he was too short, he wore glasses, and he looked much too young to play more mature roles.

Luckily for Dean, Shurr's assistant Jane Deacy sensed something special in the young actor. Jimmy's predicament was similar to what Elvis Presley initially experienced at Sun Records in 1954. The owner of Sun Records, Sam Phillips, disliked Elvis' music, but his secretary Marion Keisker thought the singer had great potential. Primarily because of Keisker's tenacity, Elvis was offered a record deal with Sun Records. Jane Deacy eventually left the agency to form her own company and in the process she brought Jimmy along as her first client. From that point on, Dean affectionately referred to Deacy as "Mom."

Jane Deacy had started her career as a switchboard operator at the Louis Shurr office. In time, she became one of Shurr's most successful talent agents. Deacy never faltered in her belief that Dean was destined to make his mark in the film industry. She may have also been influenced to a certain degree by Dean's lonely boy quality. In fact, it was a quality many women found irresistible once they got to know Jimmy.

Around this time, Jimmy met composer Leonard Rosenman. Rosenman would later go on to write the film scores for *East of Eden* and *Rebel Without a Cause*. Jimmy asked if he would teach him how to play the piano. Rosenman graciously accepted and attempted to teach Jimmy the basics. He noticed one of Dean's fingers was crooked. This affliction evidently kept him from making the necessary spread with his right hand. Rosenman's wife asked her husband how the sessions were going. He replied, "He doesn't have any talent for the piano and he's too lazy."

New York City was a vibrant metropolis in the entertainment world. Television was in full swing in the 1950s and dozens of dramatic shows were produced each week. This created a haven for veteran actors and newcomers alike. Mass auditions were very common in those days. They were referred to as 'cattle calls' because as many as several hundred actors showed up at these open auditions. Each actor was assigned a number. He or she would be called up on stage in groups of ten or more and they would file past casting directors. If a casting director liked what he or she saw, then that lucky actor would be asked to do a reading for a part in a project.

Rod Serling, one of the premier television writers,

explained that in live television "you had unexpected things happening all the time, like profanities, missed cues, left-over air time. But nobody at the stations let it bother them too much. Also, we were a close community in New York - the live writers. We compared notes, we socialized together. We used to practically hold hands with a story as it went through final rehearsal and onto the air."

Television in the 1950s attracted many up-and-coming young actors, including Paul Newman, Grace Kelly, Eva Marie Saint, Rod Steiger, and Anne Bancroft. Literally hundreds of live dramas filled the airwaves each year. It was nearly impossible for a serious actor not to find at least some work in television in New York City. The cost to produce a live television show in those days versus today was practically nil.

One night, Jimmy went to the Rehearsal Club, a hotel for aspiring actresses and dancers. He met a young and talented dancer named Elizabeth "Dizzy" Sheridan. Sheridan would later go on to play Jerry Seinfeld's mother on the enormously popular sitcom series, *Seinfeld*. They hit it off immediately. Jimmy and Dizzy began spending a lot of time together at Dean's favorite inexpensive eatery, Jerry's Bar and Restaurant.

The couple got along so well, they agreed to share a place together at the Hargrave Hotel. There was one habit of Jimmy's that Dizzy found most appalling. He liked to use an old, blood-soaked matador's bullfight cape as a blanket. Dean had a difficult time paying his share of the rent. He frequently borrowed money for food and traveling expenses. Eventually, the two lovers went their separate ways.

When Bill Bast arrived in the city, he agreed to share

a room with Dean at the Hotel Iroquois. For ninety dollars a month, the room came with two twin beds and a chest of drawers. After just a few months, Dean, Bast, and Sheridan agreed to share a place on West Eighty-ninth Street. Evidently, Sheridan and Dean remained good friends.

Jimmy met Martin Landau during one of many countless cattle calls. Landau would go on to star in the hugely popular dramatic television series, *Mission Impossible*. The two struggling actors hit it off immediately. They began hanging out together at Cromwell's Pharmacy, which was located in the lobby of the NBC Building at 30 Rockefeller Plaza. The meals were inexpensive and there was easy access to several phones so that actors could follow up on contacts with their agents.

Dean and Landau stayed in touch with each other during this period. Occasionally, they would lay out on a huge flat rock somewhere in Central Park and tan themselves as they discussed their acting goals. Both men were avid fans of Montgomery Clift and Marlon Brando. Landau remembered Jimmy was determined to become an actor before he turned 30. Sometimes they'd speak about dying young, but neither of them took this notion too seriously.

Dean frequently reminisced about his upbringing in Fairmount. He thought about how important conformity was to the folks back home. He questioned their overall ideology and religious fervor and their suspicions and fear of individualism. He wrote a poem called "My Town" in which he revealed his innermost thoughts about Fairmount.

My town likes industrial impotence
My town's small, loves its diffidence
My town thrives on dangerous bigotry
My town's big in the sense of idolatry
My town believes in God and his crew.
My town hates the Catholic and Jew
My town's innocent, selfistic caper
My town's diligent, reads the newspaper
My town's sweet, I was born there
My town is not what I am, I am here

Jane Deacy began finding work for her young client. *CBS Television Workshop* aired an episode on January 27, 1952 called, "Into the Valley." Jimmy played a G.I. His next television appearance occurred on February 20. On that date, CBS's *The Web* aired an episode called "Sleeping Dogs." The story takes place at a mountaintop resort. The plot deals with a young man played by Dean who attempts to solve the murder of his brother. *The Web* typically featured ordinary individuals caught up in unusual and dire circumstances. Anne Jackson and E.G. Marshall were the stars of the program. Marshall had starred on Broadway in *The Skin of Our Teeth* and *The Iceman Cometh*. At the time, Jackson was married to another fine actor, Eli Wallach. They married in 1948 and stayed married up until Wallach's death in 2014.

Eleanor Kilgallen, a casting agent at MCA, was instrumental in getting Jimmy that role. She thought he had an attention-getting quality. Franklin Heller, the producer, was looking for a young man who could play an eccentric. Kilgallen told Heller she was sending someone over who was 'strange,' but he would be a terrific fit for the role. When Heller first met Jimmy, he was not impressed at all with the actor. He found him unkempt and surly. The producer tried to work with Dean, but he didn't like Jimmy's attitude. He found Dean to be moody, unresponsive to suggestions, always late for rehearsal, and generally just a "pain in the ass." He told Kilgallen to send over another actor to replace Dean, but Kilgallen stood her ground and Jimmy stayed. Director Lela Swift and E.G. Marshall also helped persuade Heller not to fire Dean. Swift recalled the minute Jimmy started reading for the part, she knew "that boy had something special."

Heller recalled that Jimmy was a complete disaster to work with. He grew tired of Dean constantly asking the director what his character's motivation was. Heller finally told Jimmy that his motivation was to earn a paycheck. This response only made Dean more defiant. Heller was horrified by Jimmy's insistence on realism. If the teleplay called for him to be physically assaulted, he wanted to be physically assaulted. Naturally, Heller refused to allow Jimmy to get hurt, even though he pleaded with Heller to allow other actors to injure him. However, the director remembered that once the production went live, Jimmy put on a fantastic performance.

Anne Jackson recalled that Jimmy was difficult to work with. According to her, Dean took up too much of the director's time discussing his role. "I got to admire him when he wasn't competing," Jackson remarked. "I'd never seen such an appetite for being another Brando. Still, he could be disarming and sweet." Although Jimmy's attitude was horrible during rehearsals, Jackson admitted that his performance was marvelous once the show went live.

Actor William Redfield recalled working with Jimmy. The two actors were rehearsing a scene together for a television program. "Eventually in the show I had to hit him," Redfield recalled for a *New York* magazine interview. "Well, I had done a little boxing at the YMCA. So we staged the fight, and we got to the run-through. And I threw this so called knockout punch at him, and of course I missed him by about this much. And he stopped the run-through and he said, 'Billy, hit me.' And I said, 'No, I don't want to hit you. I'll hurt you.' And he said, 'But we gotta see blood or there's no scene.' I said, 'We're not supposed to put each other's eyes out! And Jimmy says, 'No. Hit me. Or at least promise me when we get on the air, you'll hit me.' Well, I did. I hit him. And he did bleed. It was a hell of a shot and he hit the ground, banged into the bar. So later on, I went to see him. He had a swollen jaw. I said, 'Jesus, you asked me.' But he says, 'Oh, it was good. Good, That was really good.'" Redfield would later star in the brilliant film adaption of *One Flew Over the Cuckoo's Nest* starring Jack Nicholson.

Dean continued to antagonize another director who was shooting an episode for a television drama series called *Martin Kane, Private Eye.* Unfortunately for Jimmy, television shows were 'shot tight' in those days. The idea was to produce a show as quickly and as cheaply as possible, almost like creating products on an assembly line. There was no room for creativeness or character development. Refusing to work with Dean any further, the director fired Jimmy after a couple days of rehearsals. Although he was let go, Dean received monetary compensation because he owned a union card. Jimmy explained to the Shurr office that he was trying to get into his character. He couldn't worry about positioning himself on a chalk mark.

On March 3 *Studio One* aired an episode called "Ten Thousand Horses Singing." It was directed by Paul Nickell and written by Robert Carson. John Forsythe and Catherine McLeod were the featured stars. Nickell would go on to direct several hit television series, including *77 Sunset Strip*, *Lassie*, and *Ben Casey*. Carson had distinguished himself by winning an Oscar for Best Writing for the 1938 film, *A Star is Born*. Jimmy played a hotel bellboy. Although his character had no lines, Dean took it upon himself to utter two very small lines of his own. He replies "Yes, sir" when told by the desk clerk where to take a guest's luggage. A moment later he tells the elevator operator what floor to stop at. Dean obviously tried to make the most out of a very inconsequential role.

Lux Video Theatre aired an episode called "The Foggy, Foggy Dew" on March 17. It was directed by Richard Goode and written by Albert Hirsch. It starred James Barton and Richard Bishop. Dean played a nineteen-year-old boy named Kyle McCallum. While on a hunting trip the boy crosses paths with his biological father. Jimmy played a relatively well-adjusted adolescent who never discovers who his real father is. According to Muriel Kirkland, the actress who played Kyle's adopted mother, Jimmy's performance was far too intense for what the part called for. She also claimed Dean stubbornly refused to appreciate James Barton's advice on how he should play the role of Kyle. Unfortunately, the soundtrack and picture negatives were destroyed in 1953 and all that remains are a few seconds of silent film.

Jimmy continued to snatch up roles for live television. His next appearance occurred on May 21 on the *Kraft Television Theatre* program. The episode was called "Prologue to Glory." Jimmy played a close friend of Abraham Lincoln. Patricia Breslin and Butch Clavell were the featured stars in the program. The story takes place in New Salem, Illinois at a time when Lincoln was just starting out in politics.

Jimmy sauntered into Deacy's office one day and noticed a young woman sitting at a desk typing. He tried to strike up a conversation with her, but she was too busy for small talk. She finally gave in to Dean's persistence and told him her name was Christine White and she was typing a scene for an upcoming audition. She explained to Jimmy that she was one of Jane Deacy's clients.

Later that day the two met at Cromwell's Pharmacy. White told Jimmy that she was an actress. She had been writing a scene for an upcoming audition at the Actors Studio. Jimmy asked Christine to include him in her story and she agreed. Dean created his own character and they collaborated together on a revised storyline and dialogue. The scene takes place on an isolated island prior to a hurricane. Two young people meet on the island at a crucial time in their lives. They rewrote the scene over and over again until it began to take shape. They rehearsed their lines on buses, subways, taxis, parks, coffee shops, and on crowded streets.

When it came time to audition, Jimmy was exceedingly nervous. He told White he couldn't do the scene, that he wasn't prepared to act in front of so many strangers. To make matters worse, the highly respected director Elia

Kazan was in the audience. To settle his nerves, Jimmy drank several cans of beer which were supposed to be used as props. Ignoring White's pleas to stay, Dean ran out and bought more beer for the scene. When it was their turn to audition, Jimmy and Christine ran up onto the stage and performed their skit. It lasted much longer than the allotted five minutes. After the scene had ended, the studio audience remained silent. Elia Kazan finally said to them, "Very nice." Lee Strasberg told them that the scene was well crafted and that he wished it had lasted longer. The pair were the only two contestants accepted by the Actors Studio out of one hundred fifty candidates.

During the 1950s, the Actors Studio was the most prominent and respected school for actors in New York City. The Studio had evolved from the Group Theater of the 1930s. Konstanton Stanislavsky was its founder. The Actors Studio was founded by Cheryl Crawford, Elia Kazan, and Robert Lewis in 1947. The sessions were conducted by the highly respected acting teacher, Lee Strasberg. Auditions were brutally rigorous but the sessions were free for life.

Jimmy finally got up enough nerve one day and performed a scene in which he played a matador preparing for his final bullfight. The scene was derived from a novel by Barnaby Conrad called *Matador*. After his performance, Lee Strasberg analyzed his acting. According to Jimmy, the teacher's criticism was so harsh, he refused to appear in front of the class again. Dean complained to his friend Bill Bast about how he loathed the Studio. "If I let them dissect me like a rabbit in a clinical research laboratory or something, I might not be able to produce again. For chrissake, they might sterilize me!"

Afterward, Strasberg and Kazan noticed when Jimmy did attend some of the meetings, he would just watch other actors participate in the exercises. Strasberg later admitted that he did notice some positive aspects in Jimmy's performance and recalled that "he was a natural-born actor with an unusual sense of naturalness and integrity." He also claimed he only dissected an actor's performance if he sensed unusual and distinct talent. Dean evidently didn't see it that way.

Over time, producers and directors came to realize that although Dean may have been untrained as a performer, his expressions and gestures were typically restrained, reflecting a naturalistic style of acting rarely practiced by his peers. Dean seemed to realize that he in fact possessed a special talent for delivering original and innovative performances rarely seen on television. This may have fueled his resentment toward anyone who dared to criticize his abilities as a serious, dramatic actor.

On May 26 *Studio One* aired an episode called "Abraham Lincoln." Jimmy delivered a deeply touching portrayal of William Scott, a Union soldier accused of sleeping while on guard duty. He is subsequently court-martialed, found guilty, and is sentenced to death by firing squad. During his visit with General Grant, Lincoln decides to talk with the young soldier. Unable to look directly into Lincoln's eyes, Scott tells the President that he had just come off a grueling twenty-three-mile march. He had also pulled double guard duty after volunteering to fill in for a friend who had fallen ill. Lincoln begins to sympathize with the young soldier. When asked where he's from, Scott tells Lincoln that he is from Vermont. "We got a place up there – a big farm," the soldier explains. He tells Lincoln the farm belongs to his mother and Lincoln is noticeably touched by this revelation. The soldier breaks down and cries. Lincoln is visibly moved by the soldier's remorsefulness and he pardons him. Dean's facial expressions throughout the sequence are subtle and heavily nuanced as he delivers a stunning and sensitive performance.

On June 22 *Hallmark Hall of Fame* aired an episode called "Forgotten Children." It was directed by William Corrigan and written by Agnes Nixon. The featured stars were Cloris Leachman and Elliott Sullivan. Leachman would go on to win an Oscar for Best Supporting Actress for her role in *The Last Picture Show.* She portrayed Martha Berry, an American philanthropist who devoted her life to teaching reading and writing to disenfranchised children in the Deep South after the Civil War. Jimmy played a well-dressed Georgian aristocrat who disapproves of women gaining employment outside the home. He does a fine job playing a character whose demeanor is both inappropriate and repulsive.

In October, Jimmy received a letter from his father indicating that he was driving to Fairmount for a visit. Winton wanted to give his son a brand-new partial dental bridge to replace Jimmy's old bridge. Bast and Dizzy agreed to accompany Jimmy, and so they set off on their journey the next day. They were given a lift by Clyde McCullough, a catcher for the Pittsburgh Pirates. McCullough was traveling to Des Moines, Iowa to play ball with a team that was barnstorming across the country. Noticing the hitchhikers appeared to be hungry, McCullough bought them food along the way. When they finally reached their destination, the Winslows greeted them with open arms. The trio ate enormous portions of food to make up for all the days they practically starved back home. Jimmy introduced his friends to several of his teachers, including Dean's drama teacher, Adeline Brookshire.

Bast and Sheridan discovered a sensitive and endearing side to Jimmy. They saw just how deeply affectionate he could be. He played games with his young cousin and he reminisced about growing up on the farm with Marcus and Ortense. Sheridan recalled that Dean rarely talked about American politics or world affairs. Winton gave Jimmy his new dental bridge as he had promised. Father and son got along as well as could be expected.

The Winslows enjoyed their company so much, they asked them to stay longer than they had intended. They probably would have stayed longer except for the fact that Jane Deacy called Jimmy to let him know that the producer for a new play called *See the Jaguar* wanted him to read for a part. Deacy informed Dean that more than eighty young actors had already auditioned for the role of Wally Wilkins. Jimmy and his companions thanked the Winslows for their hospitality and immediately thumbed their way back to New York City.

One of Jimmy's many competitors during the 1950s was none other than Paul Newman. In fact, the two actors were always in fierce competition for dramatic roles on television. Although Jimmy lost many a role to Newman and vice versa, they remained on friendly terms. Historical productions on television were very popular around this time. Newman had been featured in several historical dramas, including "The Assassination of Julius Caesar" and

"The Death of Socrates." In fact, Newman's very first starring role in a feature film required him to wear a toga. For the rest of Newman's life, he vehemently regretted making *The Silver Chalice*. He even wrote an open letter to the public apologizing for his appearance in the melodramatic biblical film.

Due to Dean's popularity with women, he was constantly inundated with fan letters from all over the country. Some of the letters were sent by ladies who belonged to a television club. Their ages ranged from fifty-five to seventy-five and according to Jimmy, "they'd sit there checking the cats out, then write these dirty letters. It's really hard to believe."

Dean prepared hard for his audition for *See the Jaguar*. Wearing clothing he had borrowed from a friend, he arrived at producer Lemuel Ayers' office on West 57th Street. The director handed him a script and indicated what he wanted read. Dean spent an hour reviewing the script. Director Michael Gordon recalled that "it was only a matter of minutes until I saw that he was what I'd been searching and hoping for. His impulses and criteria were right on the beam."

Jimmy read his part so well, he was asked to return for another reading by the play's author, N. Richard Nash. He read poorly the second go around and Nash asked him for an explanation. Jimmy replied that he had broken his glasses and couldn't see well. Nash gave Jimmy money to have his glasses repaired. Instead of using the money to fix his glasses, Dean bought a knife. When Jimmy returned a few days later, he told Nash that his glasses were never repaired, but that he had memorized the entire script.

Dean was finally hired to act in a Broadway play at the tender age of twenty-one.

N. Richard Nash recalled that Dean was "the only person in the play who caught the spirit of it from the beginning. He brought a great richness to the part. There are scenes of great puzzlement, and you have never seen such puzzlement as portrayed by Dean. He had it. It was deep down and quite beautiful."

The play centers around a young, backwoods boy named Wally Wilkins. In an attempt to shelter her son from the torments and cruelty of the real world, his demented mother imprisons Wally inside an icehouse. Wally's mother dies and he is taken in and cared for by a young couple. A ruthless racketeer tries to rob Wally of his inheritance, but seeing that Wally has no money, he imprisons the boy inside a cage meant for an elusive jaguar.

During a rehearsal for *See the Jaguar,* Jimmy and a prop man got into a heated altercation and Jimmy reportedly pulled out a knife. Arthur Kennedy, the star of the play, yanked the weapon out of Jimmy's hand and promptly broke the blade in half. He warned Jimmy not to pull any more stunts like that again. Miraculously, Jimmy was not fired and the show went on. Jimmy respected Kennedy, who at the time was an outstanding stage actor. Kennedy would later go on to star in such hugely successful films as *Peyton Place* and *Lawrence of Arabia.*

One day, Dean was sitting at a table in Cromwell's when he spotted his good friend Martin Landau. Sitting in a booth with Landau were three other individuals, including an actress named Barbara Glenn. Glenn immediately felt a strong attraction to Jimmy. She thought he was "physically gorgeous," but he also appeared somewhat lost and disconnected with the world. Shortly thereafter the two became lovers. Glenn later admitted that the "sexual attraction was so powerful."

Jimmy rode Glenn around New York City on his motorcycle. She did not enjoy her rides with Dean and feared that one day he might sustain a horrible injury or even die from an accident involving his motorcycle. Glenn discovered Jimmy had a dark side that she found disconcerting. He had a hard time communicating his true feelings to her and they began to argue a lot. She considered Jimmy to be insecure, uptight and unable to hold a normal conversation for very long. She recalled that they frequently argued off and on during their tumultuous relationship, which lasted about two years. Dean typically withdrew rather than discuss their grievances. Eventually, Dean stopped responding to Glenn's phone calls and letters and this deeply upset her. Remarkably, Jimmy and Barbara somehow remained friends to the end.

See the Jaguar opened on the evening of December 3, 1952, at the Cort Theatre and closed on December 6 after just five performances. *Jaguar* went over very poorly with the critics. Some reviewers described the play as "a mess," and "obscure." Jimmy's performance, on the other hand, received rave reviews. He was upset over the play's failure, but the praise he received from critics bolstered his confidence to push forward. Walter Kerr, a highly respected critic for the *New York Herald Tribune* wrote: "James Dean adds an extraordinary performance in an almost impossible role." Theater critic Richard Watts Jr. from the *New York Post* wrote: "James Dean achieves the feat of making the childish young fugitive believable and unembarrassing." "As the boy, James Dean is very good," wrote John Chapman of the *New York Daily News*.

After *See the Jaguar* closed, Jimmy went back to answering casting calls. New York City actor Bill Hickey remembered meeting Dean during one of those casting calls. Many years later, Hickey would be nominated for an Oscar for Best Supporting Actor in *Prizzi's Honor*. Hickey was working for the director who had been casting for the show. Jimmy laid on the floor and read the script while other actors read sitting up or standing. Hickey was asked to remove Jimmy from the premises because of his odd behavior. Hickey ignored their demands because Dean wasn't in anyone's way. When Jimmy was called on to read his lines, he sprawled out on the floor just as he had done earlier and read his part of the script. Hickey recognized Dean had made a physical adjustment for the part which he found very inventive and unique.

Dean's performance in *See the Jaguar* began to pay off. MGM offered to test him for a role in an upcoming film, *The Silver Chalice*. Jane Deacy carefully studied the script and concluded the project wasn't right for her client. The part would eventually go to one of Jimmy's arch rivals, Paul Newman.

Dean continued to wear the same shabby clothes he had brought with him from Los Angeles. He swallowed his pride and wrote a letter to Marcus explaining his dire circumstances. "The hard part is the maintaining of a respectable social standing. Meaning clothes. You must be fashionable even in the heat. Shirt, tie, and suit. Wow. You know how I love to dress up. I would greatly appreciate it if you could spare ten dollars or so. I need it rather desperately. I'm sorry that when I write I always need something. Sometimes I feel that I have lost the right to ask; but because I don't write isn't an indication that I have forgotten. I shall never forget what you and Mom have done for me. I want to repay you by being a success. It takes time and many disappointments. I'll try very hard not to take too long. If I had asked for help at the wrong time, please forgive me and I will understand." His folks sent Jimmy a check for twice what he had asked for and with the money he bought a suit.

Jimmy was given a copy of Antoine de Saint-Exupery's book *The Little Prince* as a gift. The novella follows a young prince as he travels to distant planets, including Earth. The prince searches for and discovers the nature of real and everlasting love and friendship. The story serves to differentiate between a child's world of imagination and an adult's world of needless cruelty. Jimmy identified with the little prince because he also saw himself as a lonely outsider who refused to adjust to a world of arbitrary rules set up by authoritative figures. He fell in love with the story and even quoted several passages from it to friends and acquaintances. Among his favorite quotes were, "It is only with the heart that we can see rightly, what is essential is invisible to the eye," and "Love does not consist in gazing at each other but in looking outward together in the same direction."

1953 proved to be a banner year for Dean. He was gaining confidence in his abilities as a promising young actor. Jane Deacy continued to believe strongly in her client's talent as well. She started finding more and more roles for him in several television productions, primarily due to the positive reviews Dean received for his earlier appearances on television and for his outstanding performance in *See the Jaguar.*

Dean had heard about a television drama featuring bullfighting. NBC had hired Ray Danton to star as a bullfighter and the producer was searching for someone to train Danton on matador moves. Jimmy told writer James Costigan that he knew all about the moves a matador makes and that he wanted to train Danton. Jimmy refused any compensation, but told Costigan to remember him in terms of future projects. Several months later, Costigan informed Dean he had written a teleplay with a part he thought was perfect for him, but the director refused to work with Jimmy due to his erratic behavior.

Jimmy played an angel for a twelve-minute drama called "The Hound of Heaven" on the *Kate Smith Hour* on NBC. It was written by Earl Hamner Jr., the future creator of *The Waltons* and *Falcon Crest*. The show aired on January 15. Recently drowned Hyder Simpson refuses to pass through the Pearly Gates if it means leaving behind his beloved hound dog Rip. An angel comes along and assures Hyder that had he entered through the Pearly Gates he would have mistakenly entered Hell. Dean's slaphappy, barefooted character wore a pair of large floppy wings and spoke with a thick Southern accent. Longtime character actor John Carradine played Hyder Simpson. Carradine had performed in many films, including the role of a down and out preacher in *The Grapes of Wrath.*

On January 29 Jimmy was featured in a popular NBC television drama called *Treasury Men in Action.* The name of the episode was "The Case of the Watchful Dog."

Director Daniel Petrie cast Jimmy as a gun-loving misfit who transports illegal moonshine to a secret distribution center. Jimmy's character Randy Meeker clashes with his father after he kills Randy's dog for fear the dog's barking might draw the law to the still. Petrie would go on to direct the 1961 film *A Raisin in the Sun* and *The Betsy* from 1978.

CBS's *You Are There* aired the episode "The Capture of Jesse James" on February 8. *You Are There* was a popular television series that focused on important historical events. The show was hosted by Walter Cronkite. He would go on to become an evening news icon for CBS. Jimmy played the role of Robert Ford, the man accused of assassinating the famous outlaw, Jesse James. Sidney Lumet directed the drama and John Kerr played Jesse James. Sidney Lumet would go on to direct serious dramas, including *12 Angry Men, Serpico* and *Network.* Dean considered the part of Bob Ford to be his most intriguing role. Sidney Lumet recalled that Jimmy "loved the part, loved handling guns, and used to practice 'quick draw' with all the pleasure of a child." After the episode aired on television, Jimmy told friends he dreamed of one day making a "great Western."

The television program *Danger* aired an episode called "No Room" on April 14. Sidney Lumet directed Jimmy in this drama about a brother who thwarts his kinsman's safe-cracking attempt. Two days later, Dean appeared in a television drama series called *Treasury Men in Action.* The episode, which also starred Ben Gazzara, was called "The Case of the Sawed-Off Shotgun." The episode was directed by David Pressman and written by Albert Aley. Jimmy played Arbie Ferris, a reform school graduate. Gazzara's character tries to persuade Ferris to attend Boys Club meetings instead of getting into trouble. Ferris discovers that Blackie, a notorious bootlegger, is in town. Ferris tries to hook up with Blackie, but the bootlegger tells him to get lost. Ferris steals Blackie's sawed-off shot gun and attempts to rob a gas station, but instead he bungles the job. Blackie tracks Ferris down and in the midst of assaulting him, he is arrested by federal agents.

Dean was hired to play a researcher's assistant for an episode of *Tales of Tomorrow*. The program was television's first ever science fiction series for ABC. The episode, "The Evil Within," aired on May 1. Director Don Medford cast Jimmy in a small supporting role. Rod Steiger played a scientist whose wife mistakenly swallows a serum meant for patients with mental disorders. Dean played a quiet, serious-minded, bespectacled lab assistant who attempts to find the formula for the serum that has gone missing. Making the most of a very small role, Dean occasionally slouches during moments of contemplation, rubs his eyes and nervously pushes his glasses up higher so he can see better.

Steiger's career would soar after his role as a mob boss's right-hand man in the film, *On the Waterfront*. Dean and Steiger became close friends during this period. Medford complained that Dean never performed the same way twice in all of his scenes. He thought Jimmy wasted too much time experimenting with his character. However, he admitted that Dean was indeed a very natural actor, that he was the antithesis of being mechanical in his approach to acting.

Frank Corsaro hired Jimmy to play a ghost in an Off-Broadway production of *The Scarecrow*. The play is based on a short story by Nathaniel Hawthorne. The show opened on June 16 at the Theater de Lys for a limited engagement. Also appearing in the play were Eli Wallach, Patricia Neal and Anne Jackson. Eli Wallach would go on to star in such hits as *The Misfits* and *The Good, the Bad, and the Ugly*. Years later Patricia Neal would win the Oscar for Best Actress in *Hud*, starring opposite Paul Newman.

Corsaro tried to convince Jimmy to bury the hatchet with Lee Strasberg and to return to the Actors Studio. Dean never really got over his repulsion toward the Actors Studio and Strasberg's rather harsh assessment of his qualities as an actor. Corsaro thought Dean definitely had talent, but he lacked formal training in the dramatics. According to the director, Dean's technique had much to be desired. Corsaro also thought Jimmy could benefit from therapy and he told him so, but Dean refused treatment.

Dean found what would become his last New York City home. It was a fifth-floor walk-up apartment at 19 West 68th Street. He called it a "wastebasket with walls." Though the studio apartment was somewhat dingy and quite small, there was room for a bed and a couch. The outer wall had a large porthole window and a small ledge. He stored his books and extensive record collection on several shelves near his bed. Sometimes Jimmy would sit in the corner and play bongos for hours at a time. Bill Gunn was amazed at his friend's concentration while indiscriminately changing beats and rhythmic patterns.

On July 17, NBC's *Campbell Summer Soundstage* aired an episode called "Something for an Empty Briefcase." The teleplay was directed by Don Medford and written by S. Lee Pogostin. Pogostin would go on to write the screenplay for *Papillon*, which was released in 1973 and starred Steve McQueen. The teleplay featured veteran actor Robert

Middleton, who would go on to play opposite Humphrey Bogart in *The Desperate Hours* and opposite Elvis Presley in *Love Me Tender*.

In the episode, Jimmy played a 22-year-old character named Joe Adams. He had recently been released from prison on a charge of petty larceny. Don Medford recalled that Jimmy was "absolutely brilliant during an early rehearsal." Dean reportedly tried to convince the director to change the title of the teleplay to "Rage and Passion" because he thought the proposed title was silly and confusing. Though Medford felt Jimmy's performances during some early rehearsals were brilliant, he discovered Dean had difficulty remembering his lines for the next set of rehearsals. Some critics came down hard on Dean's performance. "His mugging and repetitive hand gesturing were on the ludicrous side," wrote one reviewer.

On August 17, *Studio One Summer Theatre* aired an episode called "Sentence of Death." The director was Matt Harlib and the teleplay featured Betsy Palmer and Gene Lyons. Harlib had been told that Jimmy was a hard case, but apparently the warning did not phase the tough New Yorker. The story begins when the owner of a drugstore is murdered. The owner's widow picks out the wrong suspect from a police lineup. Jimmy played a character named Joe Palica, the man falsely accused of murder. He is tried, convicted and sentenced to die in the electric chair. Another woman comes forward and claims she saw the real killer but no one believes her except a couple of cops who eventually nab the real killer. It turns out the killer and the widow were having an affair and they wanted the husband out of the picture. In the end Joe Palica is set free.

Harlib thought Dean's portrayal of someone preparing to die, but who still feels the loss of his family and his love for his girlfriend, was intense. He was particularly impressed with Dean's ability to facially express both grief and fear simultaneously. Martin Landau recalled that Dean told him he wanted to vomit on camera during a death row scene. When that idea was turned down, he suggested dry retching, but that suggestion was also vetoed. At least Jimmy was thinking in terms of a more realistic reaction from a prisoner facing impending doom.

Palmer claimed Dean and her were romantically involved for several months. She further recounted that they got along reasonably well, even though she sensed that Jimmy was generally unhappy and very apprehensive. She recalled that Dean usually cut his own hair, the 'Jim Trim' as he liked to call it. She also claimed he would occasionally dart in front of a car for no apparent reason other than to shock people.

Dean was hired to perform on CBS's television series, *Danger*. The episode, "Death is My Neighbor," aired on August 25. The script was written by Frank Gregory and John Peyser was the director. Peyser would go on to direct such noteworthy television series as *The Untouchables*, *Bonanza*, *Perry Mason*, and *Hawaii Five-0*.

In *Danger*, Jimmy played the part of a psychotic janitor who is eventually arrested for attempted murder. The star of the show was 75-year-old Walter Hampden, the distinguished and popular stage actor. Hampden had portrayed Shakespearean characters such as Macbeth, Shylock, and Richard III. In 1939 he played the Archbishop of Paris in *The Hunchback of Notre Dame* opposite Charles

Laughton. At one point during rehearsals, Jimmy tossed his copy of the script across the floor and yelled, "This is shit!" Producer Franklin Heller took Jimmy aside and warned him not to act up, particularly in front of Hampden. Dean ignored Heller's warning and threw the script across the floor again. Heller threatened to fire him after this latest incident. Surprisingly, the veteran stage actor took Heller aside and advised him against firing Jimmy. Hampden thought Dean was a little rough, but he saw talent in him nonetheless. Hampden remarked that Jimmy "put me on my toes as I'll wager he'll have the same effect on any other actor he works with…" Heller kept Jimmy on and there were no more serious incidents.

Heller held the highest regard for Hampden and always addressed him as "Mr. Hampden." Heller recalled that when he introduced Jimmy to the distinguished actor, Jimmy addressed him as "Walter." Once again Heller pulled Jimmy aside and scolded him for his apparent lack of manners. Dean responded by complaining why everybody made such a stink over "some old cat."

Jimmy's attitude abruptly changed after Hampden put on a brilliant performance during a rehearsal. Dean sat stunned as he watched tears well up in the older actor's eyes during an important scene. This moment had an overpowering and profound effect on Dean. Peyser recalled that Jimmy's attitude toward the veteran actor changed dramatically. "From that moment on," Peyser recalled, "Mr. Hampden could not open a door, a chair, need a pencil, but that Jimmy was right by his side. When Mr. Hampden wanted to go over a scene, there was Jimmy, ready to do his every bidding."

A reviewer for *Variety* enthusiastically applauded Dean's performance in a September 2, 1953 article. He wrote that Jimmy's "magnetic performance brought a routine meller (melodrama) alive. Dean's performance was in many ways reminiscent of Marlon Brando's in *Streetcar*, but he gave his role the individuality and nuances of its own which it required. He's got quite a future ahead of him."

Omnibus aired an episode called "Glory in the Flower" on October 4. Broadcast through CBS, *Omnibus* became the longest running cultural series in commercial television history. Many of the shows were based on the writings of John Steinbeck, T.S. Elliott, James Thurber, Ernest Hemingway, William Faulkner, and Carson McCullers. The episode's writer was William Inge, a Midwesterner. He had written the hugely popular Broadway hit, *Picnic*.

The teleplay was set in a rundown roadhouse somewhere in the Midwest. It was a favorite hangout for teenagers looking for some excitement. The featured stars of the play were Jessica Tandy and her husband, Hume Cronyn. Tandy had recently performed on Broadway as Blanche DuBois in *A Streetcar Named Desire*, acting opposite the incomparable Marlon Brando.

Inge had enjoyed Jimmy's performance in *See the Jaguar*. He asked director Andrew McCullough to hire Dean for an important role, that of a marijuana smoking juvenile delinquent named Bronco. McCullough agreed to call in Jimmy for a reading even though he had the reputation of being difficult. In an attempt to impress the director, Jimmy sat down with the script and as he read it, he pulled a knife out of his boot and jabbed it into the table. Annoyed by Dean's antics, McCullough grabbed the knife and told Jimmy to read the script. After Dean had read just a few lines, McCullough hired him right on the spot.

Hume Cronyn wrote this in his memoir about his first encounter with Jimmy on the set of "Glory in the Flower." "He was blond, thin, handsome, and had a very definite presence. He was also infinitely laid back. Not rude, not quite arrogant but with a manner that said 'I'm here-pay attention-and I don't give a damn what you think.'"

In one scene, the bar owner tries to confiscate a bottle of liquor brought in by Bronco, a gang member. During a rehearsal, Cronyn looked everywhere for the bottle, but he couldn't locate it. After several failed attempts, he gave up and asked Jimmy where the bottle was. "Why don't you just find it?" Jimmy asked him. McCullough stepped onto the set and asked Dean to hand over the bottle. It was supposed to have been hidden in Jimmy's hip pocket, but instead Dean had tucked it down the front of his jeans.

In another scene, the bar owner was supposed to wade into a group of rowdy teenagers and break up a fist fight. Jimmy happened to be one of the juveniles fighting. Cronyn looked for Dean, but he couldn't find him anywhere. Jimmy quietly positioned himself behind Cronyn and said, "I'm here!" Outraged, the director yelled, "Cut!" and approached the set. Cronyn yelled at Jimmy for not standing where he was supposed to be. Dean explained that he was trying something new. He wanted Cronyn to be totally confused for real instead of acting confused. Cronyn yelled, "I can act confused – keep that experimental shit for rehearsal or your dressing room! You're not alone out here!" Several weeks later, the two actors ran into each other on the street. Jimmy flung his arms around the veteran actor and said, "I forgive you - you were nervous."

McCullough recalled that Jimmy was constantly flocked by teenage girls who had small parts in the episode. At no time did Dean respond to their adoration, but instead remained focused throughout rehearsals. "I never saw any young actor with more magnetism," McCullough recalled, "and no matter how he turned, Jimmy was perhaps the most photogenic person I ever directed – he had no bad angle."

"Glory in the Flower" made television history in quite an unusual way. The episode's soundtrack featured the song, "Crazy Man, Crazy," the first recognized rock and roll recording to be played on a nationally televised program in America. The song is regarded as the very first recognized rock and roll recording to appear on the national American charts. It peaked at number 12 on the Billboard Juke Box chart for the week ending June 20, 1953. The song was written by the legendary rock and roller himself, Bill Haley, and performed by his band, then known as Bill Haley with Haley's Comets.

Director Fred Zinnemann spotted Jimmy on a television show and liked what he saw. In fact, he enjoyed Dean's performance so much, he brought him in to test for the part of Curly in the film version of *Oklahoma!* He thought Dean's screen test was sensational. In a letter he wrote to an associate, he stated that "Dean seems to me to be an extraordinarily brilliant talent. I am not sure if he has the necessary romantic quality. Just the same I shot his scenes with great detail because I felt that with an actor of his calibre, a standard of performance would be set up which would later on become very helpful as a reference and comparison."

NBC's *Kraft Television Theatre* aired an episode on October 14 called "Keep Our Honor Bright." An ex-actor named George Roy Hill wrote the teleplay. He would later go on to direct such highly successful films as *Butch Cassidy and the Sundance Kid* and *The Sting*. Maury Holland, a former vaudeville performer and Broadway actor, produced and directed the teleplay.

In the episode, Jimmy played a college student who masterminds a cheating scheme. He took the role of Jim Cooper, a student who is caught cheating on a senior final examination. Cooper tries to convince his college fraternity brothers not to have him expelled. He is expelled anyway and the distraught student overdoses on sleeping pills. Cooper recovers from the attempt on his own life and subsequently rats out several other alleged cheaters. After the show aired, Jimmy received letters from heart-stricken young girls begging him for a date. Also starring in the teleplay was a very young Bradford Dillman, a student from the Actors Studio. He would go on to star in several hit films, including *Compulsion*, which was inspired by the Loeb and Leopold murder case, better known at the time as the "Crime of the Century."

"Jimmy was not at all gregarious or forthcoming," recalled Dillman. "You could never describe him as friendly nor indeed as particularly likeable. He did have an impish sense of humor and enjoyed shocking people...Even then I was tremendously impressed by and envious of his singular talent." Dillman vividly remembered one occasion when the two actors met at Cromwell's. Dillman complained to Dean about how hard a day he was having. "Who asked you?" Dean blurted out. Shocked by Jimmy's cold response,

Dillman asked him what he meant. "You think I give a shit you want to be an actor?" Dean asked him. "You think that guy over there or that woman in the booth cares about you being an actor? Oh, maybe your mother does, I don't know, but get this straight. Absolutely nobody in the world gives a flying fuck."

On October 16, NBC's *Campbell Summer Soundstage* aired an episode called "Life Sentence." It was written by S. Lee Pogostin and directed by Garry Simpson. Jimmy played Hank Bradon, a psychotic convict. Jean Ryder, played by Georgann Johnson, is Bradon's object of affection. Johnson would go on to play a small but crucial role in *Midnight Cowboy*. She played the first woman Jon Voight's character Joe Buck attempts to seduce after the aspiring gigolo arrives in New York City. She is probably better known as the mother of the title character in *Dr. Quinn, Medicine Woman*, which ran from 1993 through 1998.

In "Life Sentence," Dean's character works in the prison garden where he watches Jean Ryder intently. He grows fond of her and plans to approach her once he is set free. When he does meet Ryder, he begs her to go away with him. Frightened, she threatens to call the police, but Bradon responds by telling her, "If you do, I'll bash your skull in." He tells her about his fantasies and then he grabs her. Fearing for her life, she shouts "You're hurting me!" Staring into her eyes, Bradon tells her, "That's the first time I've touched a woman in five years." Jimmy's role in "Life Sentence" was perhaps one of his darkest. He received high praise for his outstanding performance.

On November 11, *Kraft Television Theatre* aired an episode called "A Long Time Till Dawn." The writer was

Rod Serling, one of the most brilliant writers in television. Beginning in the late 1950s his television series, *The Twilight Zone*, would become a huge hit. The director Dick Dunlap held a dim view of Jimmy's attitude. He thought he was undisciplined, scruffy, and always late for rehearsals. But Dunlap could not escape the fact that Dean was an unusually talented actor. Rod Serling saw Jimmy's character as a sensitive young man who was also without remorse or conscience. He may have been extremely intelligent, but he lacks emotional growth. Jimmy played an ex-convict who accidently kills an old man. He tries to reconcile himself with his family, but he is met only with derision. The police locate his whereabouts and kill him.

"Jimmy Dean played the part in 'A Long Time Till Dawn' brilliantly," Serling recalled. "I can't imagine anyone playing that particular role better. I think this was his first big role in television and his behavior was very restrained and uncomfortable, but even then, there was an excitement and intensity about him that transmitted viscerally to the television audience." In one scene he is seen sitting, hunched over a table while nervously fiddling with a cigarette. Some critics panned Jimmy's performance as just another imitation of Brando.

NBC's *Armstrong Circle Theatre* aired an episode on November 17 called "The Bells of Cockaigne." The teleplay was written by George Lowther and directed by James Sheldon, one of Jimmy's friends. Veteran actor Gene Lockhart was the star of the show. He had worked with Jimmy during the religious drama, "Hill Number One." The veteran actor was famously known for his role in *Miracle on 34th Street*. Future *Rebel Without a Cause* star

Natalie Wood had also appeared as a young girl in that film.

Lockhart was very leery about working with Jimmy because of his reputation for arriving late on the set and needlessly improvising. Lockhart complained constantly to director James Sheldon about Dean. He claimed that during rehearsals, Dean never repeated his lines the same way and sometimes made up his own lines. He also claimed Jimmy was too wrapped up in his own character and didn't care about the other actors and their roles. Sheldon was well aware of Jimmy's apparent selfishness, but realized there wasn't much he could do about it. Sheldon advised Jimmy to be more cooperative with the other actors, otherwise he might get the reputation of being difficult to work with. Dean appeared surprised that any cast member would regard him as difficult – especially Gene Lockhart. In any event, Dean's attitude toward his work never wavered.

In "The Bells of Cockaigne," Jimmy played a stevedore who is married and has a son who suffers from asthma. The stevedore is upset because he can't afford medical treatment for his ailing child. He attempts to raise money by joining a gambling ring run by several of his co-workers. Unfortunately, he loses his entire paycheck in the process. Meanwhile, Lockhart's character wins a lottery worth $500. Instead of spending it on a trip to Ireland, his mother country, he gives his winnings to the young stevedore.

Dean's final television appearance in 1953 occurred on November 23. He played a naïve young man who falls head over heels for a 'street-smart' woman in an episode of *Robert Montgomery Presents* called "Harvest." Robert Montgomery had been a popular film star during his heyday. He had appeared in several major movies, including

They Were Expendable with John Wayne. He helped legitimize television productions and encouraged other established film stars such as James Cagney, Grace Kelly, Angela Lansbury and Jack Lemmon to appear in television dramas.

In "Harvest," the woman rejects the young man's advances. Distraught, he joins the navy. Jimmy's acting by this time had become more nuanced and subtle, particularly during close-up shots. He was becoming very adept at holding back his emotions because he had learned that the camera never misses anything. "Jimmy was wonderful to work with," director James Sheldon remarked, "malleable and cooperative, and everybody loved him."

Ed Begley starred as Jimmy's father in "Harvest." Begley would later perform in such critically acclaimed dramas as *12 Angry Men* and Tennessee Williams' *Sweet Bird of Youth*. Begley had no problem working with Jimmy and even thought he might become a successful actor. However, he regarded Jimmy as rather reckless.

According to many of Dean's peers he had an irritating habit of discovering nuances in terms of character development. He experimented with various facial expressions and manners of speech. Many cast members thought these experiments were not only unprofessional and time consuming, but totally unnecessary. Dean also made a point of not memorizing his lines because he realized most people in real life situations don't speak fluently. They typically mispronounce words as well as stutter and stammer. He wanted his characters to look and sound natural rather than appear well-rehearsed.

Dean began to develop a keen interest in photography. He met a professional photographer named Roy Schatt at a party one night. They hit it off immediately and Schatt even offered to teach Jimmy how to correctly utilize a camera. He explained all the intricacies involved in taking pictures, including how to frame a shot, the complexities of using proper lighting, and shutter speeds. It wasn't unusual to see Jimmy photographing Martin Landau in and around the stoop at Dean's apartment on West 68th Street. The only real downside to Dean's experience with photography had to do with his impatient nature. He absolutely hated the slow and tedious process of developing and printing photographs.

In December 1953, Jimmy auditioned for a small role in an adaption of Andre Gide's novel, *The Immoralist*. Jane Deacy thought this opportunity could significantly bolster her client's career. French actor Louis Jourdan played archaeologist Michel and Geraldine Page played Marcelline, his alcoholic wife. The guilt-ridden archeologist hopes that his recent marriage will help him become heterosexual. Jimmy was hired to play Bachir, a scheming, blackmailing Arab houseboy who attempts to lure Michel back to a gay lifestyle. Dean threw himself into the role of Bachir by studying Middle Eastern accents and listening to Arabian music.

The play's production was rampant with confusion and turmoil, and it appeared to be doomed from the start. Herman Shulman, the director, disliked how the actors read their lines, correcting them each time. When it was Jimmy's turn to read, no one could make out what he said because he mumbled. When Shulman tried to correct him, Jimmy spoke up in his defense. "Mr. Shulman," Jimmy reportedly said, "Why are you insulting my intelligence?" The other actors were appalled by what they had just heard. Jimmy explained that it was his first reading and he needed time to figure out how he should deliver his lines. Shulman allowed Dean to continue his reading.

Producer Billy Rose fired Shulman and drastically reduced Jimmy's onstage presence in the play. Daniel Mann, a highly respected theatrical director, replaced Shulman. Mann and Jimmy did not get along at all. One day, Dean was late for rehearsal and Mann called him on the carpet. He asked Jimmy how long had he been in the theater. Dean looked at his watch and replied, "About four minutes." Mann didn't appreciate Jimmy's humor, but the other actors did.

On opening night in Philadelphia there was a massive blizzard, but theater goers braved the elements and came out in droves anyway. The following morning a Philadelphia newspaper wrote that the play was "colorful as the thieving, blackmailing Arab boy." Jimmy hated the whole experience and wrote to Barbara Glenn about it. He claimed he had never worked with such a boring play and cast.

During a matinee in Philadelphia, Jimmy did something rather unusual on stage that nearly cost him his job. While Louis Jourdan was speaking, Dean reached for an imaginary piece of candy, held it in his hand, and then pretended to taste it. It was not in the script. Afterward, Mann told an Actors Equity representative that he wanted Jimmy fired immediately and replaced with Bill Gunn, Dean's understudy. Nothing came of it.

The play officially opened on February 8, 1954 at the Royale Theatre on West Forty-fifth Street in New York City. Dean had just turned twenty-three. Jimmy turned some heads when he announced that he was quitting the show in two weeks. It may have been his way of retaliating against Rose and Mann.

Marcus and Ortense had flown in from Fairmount to attend the premiere. Barbara Glenn, Dean's former girlfriend, was also in attendance. Judging by the audience's reaction at the end of the play, it appeared to be a major hit. Unfortunately, reviews for *The Immoralist* were mixed. On the other hand, Dean received very good reviews. He even won the highly respected Daniel Blum Award for the year's most promising personality.

Jimmy had spent a relatively short period of time in New York City learning his craft. His determination to succeed was about to pay off in a way no one could have foreseen. Fate stepped in one night while Dean played the poor seductive Arab boy, a role Jimmy later admitted he despised. Sitting in the audience was a man who would, unknowingly, introduce to the world one of the greatest actors to have ever graced the silver screen. That man, that genius, was none other than the incomparable director, Elia Kazan.

CHAPTER 3

EAST OF EDEN

**Dean alongside fellow actors Burl Ives and Raymond Massey
in Elia Kazan's powerful film adaption of
John Steinbeck's *East of Eden*.**

lia Kazan was born Elias Kazanjioglou in 1909 in what is now Istanbul, Turkey. His family relocated to America in 1913. He attended the Yale School of Drama and performed in films over the next several years. He co-founded the Actors Studio in 1947 and under the tutelage of Lee Strasberg, Method acting was introduced to members of the Actors Studio.

Kazan directed films that focused primarily on serious social issues that still resonate today. In 1945 Kazan directed his first movie, *A Tree Grows in Brooklyn*. Author Betty Smith had written a story about a family of second-generation immigrants who try desperately not to sink into despair and hopelessness. Kazan had read the novel several times and remained deeply moved by its story line.

On March 20, 1948, Elia Kazan was awarded an Oscar for Best Director for *Gentleman's Agreement*, starring Gregory Peck and John Garfield. It was perhaps Garfield's finest performance. The film dealt with antisemitism. Kazan followed that effort with *Pinky* in 1949. That story dealt with racism against African-Americans.

By 1955 Kazan had won two Tony Awards for direction for *All My Sons* and *Death of a Salesman*. Regarding *Salesman*, Kazan felt that Willy Loman's "fatal error is that he built his life and his sense of worth on something false: the opinion of others. This is the error of our whole capitalist system. We build our sense of worth not with ourselves, but through our besting others."

Kazan went on to make three films featuring the latest acting sensation, Marlon Brando. The first was *A Streetcar Named Desire* which was released in 1951. Brando's performance was electrifying and groundbreaking. No other actor had captivated moviegoers the way Brando did in *Streetcar* with the possible exception of Montgomery Clift. The picture garnered several Oscars, including Best Actress, Best Supporting Actor and Best Supporting Actress. Humphrey Bogart, who starred in *The African Queen*, beat out Brando for Best Actor. Kazan lost out to George Stevens (*A Place in the Sun*) for Best Director.

In 1952 Kazan and Brando teamed up once again for the film *Viva Zapata!* Anthony Quinn would go on to win an Oscar for Best Supporting Actor for *Zapata!* Two years later Kazan and Brando teamed up again for *On the Waterfront.* The film would garner eight Academy Awards, including Best Picture, Best Actor, and Best Director. Regrettably, Kazan and Brando would never make another film together.

Kazan was a huge believer in getting to know his actors. He insisted on meeting an actor's significant other in order to observe how they interacted with one another. He once suggested that a director needs to know what an actor has so that a director can "reach in and arouse it." "Without knowing the mindset of an actor," he explained, "you don't know what he has, you don't know what the hell is going on."

John Steinbeck had not written a best-selling novel in over thirteen years. His last novel, *The Grapes of Wrath*, was considered his masterpiece. He had remained one of the world's most famous authors, but he had been out of the spotlight for what seemed like an eternity. Steinbeck decided to write a book about his experience growing up in California. It took him over a year to complete *East of Eden*, and it became a smash hit with many of the critics and the public alike. By November of 1952 the novel had become the number one bestseller.

Elia Kazan walked into producer Jack Warner's office and announced that he was interested in making a film based on the latest novel by John Steinbeck. According to Kazan, the first words out of Warner's mouth were: "What'll it cost?" Kazan explained that it would cost 1.6 million dollars. Warner agreed with the figure and that was that. Kazan told Warner he wanted to use newcomers for the young characters and Warner agreed. Apparently, Elia Kazan was gold to Jack Warner. Kazan explained his idea of adapting the novel to the screenplay. He understood the importance of taking an epic story and focusing on the most essential and intriguing elements.

Jack Warner had absolutely no intention of ever reading *East of Eden*. He was primarily interested in the fact that *Eden* was a best seller and that John Steinbeck had written it. Apparently, he didn't care that the novel received mixed reviews as long as the public at large loved it. Warner was not alone in his thinking. Studios were constantly searching for 'pre-sold properties' to base their movies on. Hit novels and plays were a great source of material for Hollywood, particularly if the writer had a successful track record.

Kazan reached out to Steinbeck and told him that he was interested in making a film based on the author's latest novel. A deal was struck and John Steinbeck was paid

$125,000 for the rights to his novel. He was also promised 25 percent of the film's profits. Kazan and Steinbeck were not strangers. The author had previously written the screenplay for Kazan's *Viva Zapata!*

Steinbeck wrote the original script for *Eden*, utilizing the entire saga. However, it was decided that the script was much too long and so it was discarded. Kazan came to the rescue and breathed new life into the project. He insisted that the film focus entirely on the last part of the novel. Kazan had determined that the most intriguing section of *Eden* involved the rivalry between brothers Cal and Aron and their father's alienation toward Cal. He believed the importance of a story's unity is derived from the ending. He thought every element of a story should lead up to the climax. In Kazan's mind, the last part of *East of Eden* brought all of the key elements to the forefront and therefore a good film could be derived from the novel's ending.

The director realized his idea of utilizing just the last few pages of the novel would probably irritate the novelist. But he also knew that Steinbeck was an extremely sensitive man. Kazan believed that Steinbeck was exceedingly vulnerable to harsh criticism. Kazan explained to Steinbeck in as tactful a manner as possible that he wanted to "fool around" with the novel. Kazan had to be careful because he wanted Paul Osborn to write the screenplay rather than Steinbeck. Osborn was a well-known playwright who frequently wrote stories featuring small town, pastoral settings. The novelist eventually agreed and so that gave Kazan the green light to work with Paul Osborn exclusively on the script without any interference from Steinbeck.

Basically, the script they collaborated on focused on

Caleb Trask, the main character. Kazan's primary idea for the story was an "attack on the puritanical point of view." He wanted to convince the film's audience that "a boy whom people thought was bad was really good, and a boy whom people thought was good was actually quite bad and destructive."

The story Kazan decided to tell is fairly straightforward. A tormented and rebellious young man named Cal Trask discovers that his mother is a madam who owns her own brothel not far from where the Trasks live. Cal lives with his father, Adam, and his twin brother, Aron. Adam had told his sons years ago that their mother had died when they were very young. Cal tells his father that he knows his mother is still alive and her manner of employment. Adam begs Cal not to tell Aron about their mother. When his father loses money on a business venture, Cal succeeds in borrowing $5,000 from his estranged mother in order to help pay for his father's loss. Adam rejects Cal's money based on moral grounds. Angered by his father's coldness, Cal introduces Aron to their mother, the town madam. Deeply traumatized, Aron runs off and joins the military. On witnessing his favorite son being shipped off to war on a troop train, Adam suffers a massive stroke. The film ends as Adam lays helpless in bed while Cal sits by his bedside.

East of Eden was Kazan's first film dealing with color and CinemaScope. He was initially unsure about how best to shoot each sequence using these novel features. Because CinemaScope utilized a wide screen, Kazan learned to block off a third of a frame in the foreground with someone's shoulder or a door or some other object in order to fill the screen. Kazan wanted to emphasize the color grey, thinking that it would help convey the tone of the story. He spoke with his camera man Ted McCord about the idea. They decided the color green should be emphasized throughout the film and indeed it was. In fact, the room where Adam lies helpless from his stroke was painted with a particular shade of green. Furthermore, *East of Eden* is loosely based on the story of Adam and Eve and their two sons, Cain and Abel, and the color green is supposed to symbolize the Garden of Eden.

While Kazan strategized the best way to tell the story of *East of Eden* on the big screen, he started interviewing and auditioning dozens of actors who had performed on stage or appeared in films or both. Kazan grew increasingly frustrated in his attempt to find an actor who could play Cal Trask convincingly. They all seemed to lack a sense of rebelliousness and vulnerability. Out of pure desperation, Kazan interviewed John Kerr, another up and coming young film actor. He decided to offer the part of Cal to Kerr, but the actor would not be available until June due to prior commitments. Kerr was now officially out of the running. Kazan seriously considered Marlon Brando for the part of Cal, but ultimately decided against it. For one thing, Brando was too old to play a young farm boy. Moreover, his demeanor was such that it may have been hard for Brando to convey a sense of loneliness and vulnerability. After all, many of his earlier roles were those depicting men of power and substance such as Marc Antony and the rebellious Mexican leader, Emiliano Zapata. Attempting to portray a sensitive farm boy might be too much of a stretch even for an actor of Brando's stature.

Paul Osborn told Kazan that he should check out a

newcomer on Broadway. His name was James Dean. He had been playing a bit part in *The Immoralist* and his acting was electrifying. Kazan took Osborn's advice and went to see the play at the Royale Theatre. Although Kazan was sadly disappointed with Dean's performance, he contacted Jimmy anyway, perhaps as a favor to Osborn. He scheduled a meeting with the young actor to discuss the part of Cal at Warner's New York offices.

Kazan recalled that when he walked into his office, Jimmy was "slouched at the end of a leather sofa in the waiting room, a heap of twisted legs and denim rags, looking resentful for no particular reason. I didn't like the expression on his face so I kept him waiting. I also wanted to see how he'd react to that." Kazan further claimed that Jimmy looked unruly and impatient. Kazan tried to hold a meaningful conversation with Dean, but any semblance of a discussion ended abruptly. After a few moments of complete silence, Jimmy asked Kazan if he'd like to ride on the back of his motorcycle. Kazan took him up on the offer and soon regretted it. According to Kazan, Jimmy rode like a lunatic, dangerously weaving in and out of traffic like somebody trying to prove something. He later claimed that Dean "was showing off – a country boy not impressed with big-city traffic."

While Kazan fumed about Jimmy's uncouth demeaner, there was also something about Dean's sullenness and aloofness that Kazan found fascinating. He thought long and hard about the young actor's disruptiveness during their initial meeting. He came to the conclusion that Jimmy was exactly who he was looking for. He fired off a memo to Jack Warner about the perfect actor for the part of Cal Trask. Kazan was also impressed by Jimmy's use of his entire body while acting. He confessed to an associate that he was attracted by Jimmy's "wonderous use of a very athletic body and that body-acting is a natural facility that can't be taught."

It was quite clear to anyone who truly knew Dean that he abhorred Hollywood's elitists. Director Nicholas Ray later revealed that Jimmy had absolutely no intention of ever befriending bigwigs for the sake of succeeding in the film industry. "He shied away from social convention, from manners, because they suggested disguise. He wanted his self to be naked."

In March 1954, Kazan sent a letter to John Steinbeck explaining his attempt to discover a suitable actor to play Caleb Trask in *East of Eden*. "I looked through a lot of kids before settling on this Jimmy Dean. He hasn't Brando's stature, but he's a good deal younger and is very interesting, has balls and eccentricity and a real problem somewhere in his guts. I don't know what or where. He's a little bit of a bum, but he's a real good actor and I think he's the best of a poor field. Most kids who become actors at nineteen or twenty or twenty-one are very callow and strictly from a N.Y. Professional school."

Kazan recalled that when Steinbeck finally met Jimmy, the author found him to be disruptive and rude. Kazan agreed wholeheartedly with the author, saying that Dean had "a real mean streak and a real sweet streak." He further described Jimmy as "twisted and sick – a very hurt person. He was suffused with self-pity and the anguish of rejection, and the main thing I sensed was hurt, which was also the main thing everybody else felt. You wanted to put your arm around him and protect him and look after him." Perhaps the director overlooked the possibility that Dean may have been acting ornery in order to convince Kazan that he need not look any further for a sullen, rebellious actor to play Caleb Trask.

Jimmy was certainly not the only actor to vigorously campaign for the role of Cal Trask. Many promising young actors were keenly interested in testing for *Eden*. Paul Newman tested for the role of Cal while Newman's close friend Joanne Woodward tested for Abra, a major character in the picture. During one screen test, Dean and Newman were told to stand close to each other and improvise. Newman wore a white dress shirt and bowtie while Jimmy donned a plain opened collared shirt. Dean occasionally tossed what appeared to be a switchblade in the air with the intent of perhaps creating an atmosphere of impending danger. Newman brought no such prop to play with.

Kazan pored over all the test footage he had shot and concluded that Jimmy was indeed perfect for the role of Cal Trask. A formal contract was soon drawn up. That contract stipulated Dean would be paid $1,000 per week for a term no fewer than ten weeks of production. An unknown actor earning that kind of money was very fortunate in those days. The 46-page document indicated that he would be paid $1,250 per week for a second picture. And if he was lucky enough to star in a tenth movie, he would be paid a weekly salary of $4,000. Looking back, it appears Jimmy's future compensation was much lower than what it should have been. Assuming he worked for ten weeks on a film at $4,000 a week, that only amounts to $40,000, a far cry from what an established star like Elizabeth Taylor would probably earn. Kazan told the studio he didn't want them to send out glowing press releases about Jimmy. He was afraid his new star might feel a sense of entitlement, thus making him more difficult to handle.

On March 30, 1954, Jimmy performed on CBS's popular *Danger* television series. Andrew McCullough had offered him the lead in an episode called "The Little Woman." Jimmy played opposite a child actress named Lydia Reed. She would later become famous as the daughter in the enormously popular hit television series, *The Real McCoys*, starring Walter Brennan as her grumpy grandfather. Jimmy played Joe Scully, a counterfeiter on the run. Scully hides out with a poverty-stricken girl who lives in an alley. Lee Bergere, who played a police officer, claimed Jimmy acted professionally throughout the entire production. He had heard that Dean was difficult to get along with, but he found him to be very polite and cordial. Bergere would later play the role of Joseph Anders in the hit television series *Dynasty*.

In early April, Kazan arranged for Jimmy to be picked up at his home. Kazan and Dean were then driven to the Idlewild Airport for a 9:00 a.m. flight to Los Angeles. The facility was originally called New York International Airport when it opened in 1948. It was renamed John F. Kennedy International Airport after Kennedy's assassination in 1963. Kazan thought Dean looked like a homeless person. He carried two packages covered in paper which were held together with string. Dean informed Kazan that he had initially planned to ride his motorcycle all the way to the coast. He decided not to because he had recently been injured in a motorcycle accident. Jimmy didn't talk much with Kazan the entire time, and that suited the director just fine. The limousine finally made it onto the tarmac leading to the American Airlines passenger plane headed for Los Angeles.

Kazan recalled in an interview what transpired during their trip to Hollywood. "I took Jimmy out to California. He hadn't been there since he was a kid. I picked him up in a car and he had his clothes in a paper bag. He'd never been in an airplane before. He kept looking down over the side of the fucking plane, just watching the ground. He was totally innocent. It was all new to him."

The flight was affectionately called the "noon saloon" because a tremendous amount of alcohol was served in mini-bottles. Approximately nine hours after their departure from New York, the plane touched down in Los Angeles. After they disembarked, Jimmy asked the director if they could stop somewhere on the way to the studio. Kazan agreed and so Jimmy directed the driver to the Veterans Administration Hospital where his father worked as a lab technician. When they arrived at the facility, Jimmy jumped out of the limousine and entered the hospital. Shortly thereafter, Jimmy introduced Winton Dean to Kazan. Kazan got the distinct impression that father and son did not get along all that well. He sensed a great deal of awkwardness and tension between the two men. Kazan remembered that Winton Dean resembled in many ways the domineering and judgmental father in *East of Eden*.

"Obviously there was a strong tension between the two and it was not friendly," Kazan related in an interview. "I sensed the father disliked the son. He didn't seem to think his son's future was promising. They stood side by side but talk soon collapsed and we drove on."

Kazan decided to take some photographic tests to see how Jimmy would behave in front of a camera. The film crew thought Dean was just a stand-in for the male lead in the picture. They were not in the least impressed with Dean's presence as a film actor. Kazan announced to the crew that standing before them was the star of *East of Eden*, James Dean. No one on the set had even heard of him. They were confused as to why Kazan would choose someone who was unknown, bespectacled, intense, and in their opinion, too short. They believed these were not the proper qualifications for a leading man.

Kazan recalled that shortly after they arrived in Hollywood, Jimmy became upset and it was affecting his work. Kazan grew more concerned about Dean's inability to conform to his new surroundings. Dean was flat broke when he arrived in Los Angeles. He was compelled to spend several nights at his father's new home near Santa Monica Boulevard. Evidently, Kazan thought Jimmy was in desperate need for somebody who could relate to him and so he set Jimmy up with a dressing room close to his own. "We lived in adjoining dressing rooms on the lot," Kazan recounted later. "The star dressing rooms were rather luxurious. We both had these two-room apartments with a toilet and a place to cook. I kept my eye on him day and night."

Leonard Rosenman first met Jimmy in 1954 in New York City. He had composed several pieces of music in the classical vein. He greatly admired composers such as Arnold Schonberg, Luigi Dallapiccola, and the incomparable American composer Aaron Copeland. Dean and Rosenman had met during rehearsals for *Women of Trachis*.

Jimmy had a very small role in the play. He enjoyed listening to Rosenman as he played classical pieces on the piano. He asked the composer if he would teach him to play the keyboard and the composer readily agreed. However, after several lessons, Dean lost interest in learning the piano. The two men still remained close friends.

Kazan had yet to select a composer for the film. Jimmy told Kazan about Rosenman's score for *Women of Trachis* and that he should listen to it. Kazan listened to Rosenman's work and liked what he heard. Kazan immediately offered Rosenman the job of writing the score for *Eden*. Rosenman did not accept the offer because he felt writing movie scores was beneath his stature as a serious composer. Leonard Bernstein intervened on Kazan's behalf and convinced Rosenman to take the job. Just a year earlier, Bernstein himself had written a brilliant and moving film score for Kazan's *On the Waterfront*.

The director thought Jimmy was much too skinny and frail looking to play a hard-working farm boy, so he put him on a special diet to beef up his physique. He also ordered Dean to hang out in sunny Palm Springs because he desperately needed a good tan. Bill Gunn, a close friend of Jimmy from his New York City days, humorously related the following: "Kazan sent Jimmy to the desert to get a suntan and made him drink a pint of cream every day. It was kind of ironic to fatten him up to make him look like a farm boy because he was a farm boy. He had that lean look from doing it. And suddenly he had this rubber tire. And this suntan. I'd never see him suntanned! But this was Kazan's conception of the farm boy. Healthy. Fat. Cornfed. I think he got the pigs mixed up with the farmers."

Kazan ordered his assistant director Horace Hough to send Jimmy to live on a ranch so that he could observe the local lifestyle of the people living and working there. Hough reportedly contacted Marvin Roberts and informed him that Kazan wanted Jimmy to learn about growing and harvesting vegetables. Roberts resisted the assignment at first, but quickly accepted the project when he was offered a substantial amount of money to supervise Jimmy. Roberts was a veteran of nearly one hundred films produced by Warner Brothers. He was an excellent horseman who had doubled for numerous stars, including Elizabeth Taylor and Roddy McDowell.

After Paul Newman lost the part of Cal to Dean, he campaigned hard for the part of Aron. Unfortunately for Newman, Richard Davalos won the role of Caleb's twin brother. Based on several screen tests, Kazan believed Dean and Davalos had better chemistry than Dean had with Newman.

Kazan arranged for Dean and Davalos to share an apartment together over the Olive Drug Store. It was on the opposite side of the street from the Warner Brothers Studio. Apparently, he wanted the two actors to see how they would interact with one another. Kazan realized that Dick Davalos would have a difficult time living with Jimmy in such close quarters. He may have been hoping that they would get on each other's nerves much the same way Cal and Aron acted toward each other in the story. He would get his wish in just a few days.

Kazan chose Julie Harris for the role of Abra, a major character in the film, in spite of how Jack Warner felt about her. Warner didn't think Harris was pretty enough for the female lead. Kazan felt otherwise. He thought she was beautiful and sensitive and a fantastic performer. "She also had the most affecting voice I've ever heard in an actress; it conveyed tenderness and humor simultaneously. She helped Jimmy more than I did with any direction I gave him."

Julie Harris had performed in Kazan's short-lived play *Sunset Beach* in 1948. She also performed in the 1952 film *The Member of the Wedding*. In 1955 she appeared as Sally Bowles in the film *I Am a Camera*. The Sally Bowles character would later appear in the hugely successful film version of *Cabaret*, featuring Liza Minelli as Bowles.

The director primarily chose actors who had performed on the stage. Jo Van Fleet, for example, had many years of experience on Broadway, but surprisingly had never been in a film. She was chosen to play Cal and Aron's mother Kate, another significant character in the film. Remarkably, Kazan did not cast the role of Adam, the father of the twin boys. Evidently, Raymond Massey had agreed to play a role in the film *Battle Cry* with the understanding that he would be chosen for the role of the patriarch in *Eden*. Massey's father, a Canadian, was a wealthy co-owner of the successful Massey-Harris tractor company. Beginning in the 1920s, Massey appeared in several plays and films. In 1938 the actor's big break occurred when he played Abraham Lincoln in the Broadway version of Robert Sherwood's Pulitzer Prize winning play, *Abe Lincoln in Illinois.*

Kazan hired Burl Ives, Timothy Carey, and Albert Dekker to play supporting roles in *Eden*. Dekker, whose film career started in 1937, had a small part in Kazan's *Gentleman's Agreement*. Like Dekker, Carey usually played a heavy in several B movies. In *Eden*, Carey plays what one film critic accurately referred to as "dumb muscle." Burl Ives would go on to play his biggest role, Big Daddy, in Tennessee Williams' smash hit, *Cat on a Hot Tin Roof*, starring opposite Elizabeth Taylor and Paul Newman. Kazan chose a very young Lois Smith to play Ann, a bar maid who works for the town madam. Smith would go on to perform in such films as *Five Easy Pieces*, *Minority Report*, and *Twister*.

The film crew for *Eden* flew to Mendocino to begin shooting. This location represented the vicinity in and around Monterey where much of the story takes place. This is the area where Cal stalks his mother, the town madam. After about a week of filming, the cast and crew traveled to Salinas for several days of exterior shots. One of the initial sequences filmed is the beautiful scene where Cal proudly examines his crop of beans. Julie Harris recalled that it was Jimmy's idea to run through the bean field like an excitable adolescent.

At one point Jimmy stayed at the Little River Inn which was three miles north of Mendocino. During his stay there he suffered from a horrific case of poison oak. The symptoms were so severe, he was confined to a bed for several days. Kazan was forced to suspend shooting until he recovered.

Jimmy grew apprehensive about his new, strange surroundings. He felt awkward most of the time and never acclimated himself to the people or the locations shot in and around Northern California. He wrote a letter to Barbara Glenn describing his predicament. In part it read:

I don't like it here. I don't like people here. I like it
home (N.Y.) and I like you and I want to see you. Must I
always be miserable? I try so hard to make people reject me.
Why? I don't want to write this letter. It would be better to
remain silent. "Wow! Am I fucked up"...I DON'T KNOW
WHERE I AM....Wow! Am I fucked up! I got no motorcycle. I got no girl. HONEY – shit, writing in capitals doesn't
seem to help either....Kazan sent me out here to get a tan.
Haven't seen the sun yet (fog & smog). [He] wanted me
healthy looking. I look like a prune...I'll be home soon.
Write me please. I'm sad most of the time. Awful lonely too
isn't it. (I hope you're dying.) BECAUSE I AM.

    Love,
    Jim (Brando Clift) Dean

    Jimmy enjoyed wandering around Hollywood
Boulevard in his spare time. He observed and took note
of the nightlife with all its strange and unusual characters.
He'd stop and talk to complete strangers, absorbing and
memorizing their speech patterns and mannerisms. He was
constantly analyzing the peculiar way many people carried
themselves. According to Kazan, Jimmy liked to stand in
front of a mirror in his room and snap close-ups of his face.
It was a very unusual pastime Jimmy had carried over from
his days in New York City.

    Jimmy's unorthodox way of preparing for a scene
proved to be very annoying to the cast and crew, particularly
Raymond Massey. He pleaded with Kazan to make Jimmy
"say the lines the way they're written." Kazan listened to
Massey's complaints but that was about all. Almost without exception he allowed Jimmy the freedom to perform

the way he thought best in terms of his character. Kazan
found out almost immediately that Dean had to be han-
dled very carefully as a performer. "Jimmy wasn't easy to
work with because it was all new to him. He was like an
animal might be. Fretful, uncertain. But Julie Harris was
very helpful because she was terribly patient and understanding. When Jimmy sensed affection and understanding and patience, he got awfully good."

"But Jimmy could be impossible," Kazan recalled.
"He was always cutting in on someone's lines or saying the
wrong lines. Raymond Massey had studied the script with
his wife, had gone over it and knew it exactly. And then
onto the set came this little son of a bitch with the wrong
lines!"

"So I let Jimmy say his lines the way he wanted – just
because it irritated Massey. Would I do anything to stop
that antagonism? No. I increased it, I let it go. It was the
central thing of the story. What I photographed was the
absolute hatred of Raymond Massey for James Dean, and
of James Dean for Raymond Massey. That was precious.
No director could get it in any other way."

Raymond Massey vehemently loathed Jimmy. Massey
was never a Method actor nor did he care to become one.
He was strictly old school and he didn't have the patience
required to deal with Method actors. Jimmy's long preparations for a scene were excruciating to the veteran actor.
He simply didn't see the point in achieving a certain mood
based on emotional states of mind brought on by personal
memories. He hated watching Dean get into his character
by shaking his wrists, jumping up and down and crawling
on the floor. He despised Jimmy's whole demeaner when he

wasn't acting as well. For a young actor not to acknowledge the elder actor's presence was unacceptable to Massey. He complained to Kazan countless times and each time Kazan dutifully listened to his heartfelt complaints. However, Kazan elected not to alleviate the situation between the two actors. He enjoyed the fact that Dean and Massey despised each other. It fed into exactly what Kazan was sorely looking for in the film – the incompatibility between an authoritarian father and his rebellious son.

The beginning of the film introduces us to Caleb Trask. He is seen stalking an elderly woman dressed entirely in black. He manages to keep his distance from her, but she soon realizes someone is following her. As soon as the lady arrives home she sends a man out to confront the stranger. Cal is certain the woman is his mother, Kate, the town madam. Cal tells the man he hates her. In the next sequence there is a closeup of Cal shivering on top of a train as he returns home. Kazan wanted to empathize Cal's loneliness and his mother's abandonment. Cal is angry with himself as he utters the lines, "I should have gone right on in there. I should have gone right on in there and talked to her."

In the next scene, Adam tells a friend that he wants to do something for mankind before he passes on. He thinks he might be able to freeze lettuce as a way of preserving it for future consumption. At one point he suddenly glances over at Cal and asks if he has anything to say for himself. Adam angrily blurts out to his son, "Don't you have anything to say to me Cal?" Happy to oblige, Cal replies that Adam should plant beans instead of growing lettuce and going through all the bother of freezing it. Cal explains to Adam that you don't have to freeze beans because they're easy to keep. Not only that, the price of beans is expected to increase dramatically once America joins the war effort in Europe. Adam coldly tells Cal that he's not particularly interested in making a profit. Cal stares at his father, obviously hurt by his rebuke, but he doesn't say a word. One gets the sense that Cal is seething inside, injured by his father's insensitive response, but he decides to hide his frustration and disappointment from his father.

The next sequence calls for Cal to angerly push huge blocks of ice down a long chute attached to an ice house. He feels resentful toward his father and his brother, who is plainly Adam's favorite son. But when it came time for Jimmy to push the ice down the chute, nothing happened. According to Massey, all Jimmy did was pace up and down as he glared at the ice. Massey asked another actor, "What the hell goes on?" To which the other actor replied, "Jimmy's got to get to hate the ice. It takes time."

In the next scene Adam orders Cal to read a passage from the Bible as a way of atoning for his earlier transgression. Sensing his brother doesn't want to read scripture, Aron volunteers to read the verses instead. Undeterred by Cal's reluctance to read, Adam once again orders Cal to read from the Bible. Cal slumps forward in his chair as he begins to read scripture. Kazan used this scene as a device to show how different in temperament Cal was to his father and his brother. Kazan wanted to emphasize how pressurized the atmosphere was in the Trask household, even during mealtime. Kazan also shot the sequence at odd angles to further convey awkwardness and incongruity between Cal and Adam. Some critics complained that Kazan over emphasized the father and son conflict by shooting the scene this way. Cal reluctantly reads one verse and Adam chides him on his manner of reading from the Bible. "And I suggest a little slower, Cal – and you don't have to read the verse numbers." Adam insists that Cal should read the verses properly. When Cal stubbornly refuses to read the passages exactly the way his father wants him to, Adam loses his temper and yells at Cal for being disrespectful and rebellious. "You have no repentance!" Adam shouts. "You're bad! Through and through! Bad!"

Unfortunately for Massey, he had to be cajoled into raising his voice in anger. In order to accomplish this, Kazan realized the veteran actor had to step out of his comfort zone. He desperately wanted Dean and Massey to despise each other in order to pull this off. After all, the storyline called for a puritanical father to relentlessly upbraid and scold his inquisitive and rebellious son. What better way to elicit tension and deep apprehension between father and son than to pit the two actors against the other. The scene called for Adam to raise his voice in anger at Cal over his son's perceived transgressions. Massey simply could not bring himself to yell at Jimmy and so Kazan devised a plan. According to Leonard Rosenman, Kazan whispered something into Jimmy's ear and then stepped aside. Kazan called for action and Jimmy stared down at the Bible and said, "The Lord is my shepherd, I shall not suck cock, up your ass, fuck you, shit, piss…" Massey jumped to his feet and screamed at Kazan, "Gadge – I will not play with such a person – You'd better call my lawyers." Kazan immediately yelled "Cut!" He told Massey that he had ordered Dean to say those words in order to get a rise out of the veteran actor.

In Massey's 1979 autobiography, *A Hundred Different Lives,* he wrote about how Kazan tolerated Jimmy's idiosyncrasies. "Gadge did nothing to dissuade Dean from these antics. Most directors would not have tolerated such conduct, myself included, but Gadge knew his boy and he must have figured that his only course was to pamper him. After all, he had drawn great performances from Marlon Brando, and Dean was of the same breed. So Gadge endured the slouchings, the eye-poppings, the mutterings and all the willful eccentricities. He said to me one morning as I waited near my camera marks for that damn whistle to blow (Jimmy's), 'Bear with me, Ray, I'm getting solid gold!'"

Jimmy was given $300 a week from the studio to spend as he wished. He had some time to kill in between takes so he rented a car and headed down to Santa Monica City College to drop in on some old acquaintances. He located Gene Owen and Richard Shannon. The pair did not appreciate Jimmy's bohemian lifestyle or his crude manners. Perhaps in an attempt to make up for his lack of civility, he invited them to dinner in Santa Monica. His behavior shocked his dinner guests and he stormed out of the café.

Dean always wanted to own a horse and so he drove to Pickwick Stables to see what they had available. He examined several horses before purchasing a two-year-old buckskin for $250. He told Kazan how happy he was with his new horse and the director allowed him to keep it at the studio corral.

Kazan later claimed that if not for Julie Harris' presence, "Jimmy would never have got through *East of Eden* except for an angel on our set." Kazan recalled that the young actress was very patient and sympathetic with Dean. She would adjust her performance based on Jimmy's improvisations. Julie Harris appeared to be a positive force on the set of *Eden*. Harris recalled that she never felt offended by Jimmy. "I think he loved to be a naughty boy, and he was always looking to irritate others. But I never let it get through to me. He reminded me of Tom Sawyer, always looking for adventure, always looking to mix it up, not wanting to go smoothly – and no manners, to hell with manners and good feelings. He was desperately lonely and had many problems, so it was hard to get close to him. He was a strange and sensitive young man, and he had a tremendous imagination. I liked him very much, but he was not easy to know."

There is a pivotal moment in the film when Cal and Abra spend some time together. The scene takes place in a field of bright yellow mustard flowers. Cal opens up to Abra because she is kind to him. She in turn tells him how her father upset her so much, she threw his $3,000 ring into a river. Abra continues to prod Cal into opening up about himself. He suddenly grows anxious and tells Abra he doesn't have to answer to anyone. Kazan succeeded in showing Cal's distrust in expressing his true feelings to another person and how easily it is for him to resort back to feeling resentful toward the world.

In early June the cast and crew traveled to a new location to shoot Adam's horrific lettuce fiasco. His plan to ship fresh lettuce by freight rail to New York fails miserably. Jimmy had recently purchased a used Triumph T-110 motorcycle. Kazan ordered Dean not to take any unnecessary chances. He was determined to ensure that if Jimmy did take a bad spill, it wasn't going to happen during the filming of *Eden*. Dean promptly replaced his bike with a red MG TA convertible sports car. Against her better judgment, Julie Harris agreed to ride with Dean as he tore through the winding country roads at terrifying speeds.

Dean wandered over to the set of *The Silver Chalice* during some down time to chat with Paul Newman. He was introduced to another cast member, Anna Maria Pierangeli, better known as Pier Angeli. She had been an art student in Rome and was discovered by director Vittorio De Sica. She lived with her mother and two sisters in Brentwood, California. Shortly after Jimmy and Pier met, they became very close. They were frequently seen holding hands and spending their lunch breaks together. On June 29, 1954, Sidney Skolsky wrote in his entertainment column, "James Dean has the lead in *East of Eden* and you'll be hearing of him soon. Pier Angeli, who isn't in the movie, has discovered him already."

Jimmy and Pier took long walks along the beach, holding hands and talking about topics that mattered most to them. They were careful not to be seen by too many people for fear that Pier's mother might find out about their relationship. Sometimes they invited Pier's friends to accompany them so Pier could tell her mother that she had been out with some friends. Pier was careful never to divulge the whole story to her mother about her relationship with Jimmy.

The couple enjoyed exchanging gifts with one another. Dean charmingly referred to her as "Miss Pizza" to his friends and she called him by her favorite name, "Baby." Jimmy shot countless pictures of Pier and kept many of them on top of his bureau in his apartment.

Their relationship was doing fine until one evening when Jimmy and Pier arrived at her home, supposedly after her curfew. Pier's mother reproached Jimmy, whereupon he told the mother she was too strict with her daughter. The mother tried to end their relationship right then and there, but she quickly relented when Pier threatened to leave home for good.

Pier seemed to have a positive impact on Jimmy as far as social graces were concerned. He combed his hair more frequently and he dressed neater. The biggest shocker occurred when he stopped speeding, particularly when Pier was in the car with him. Allegedly, Jimmy told a close friend that he was considering becoming a Catholic so that the two lovers could get married in a Catholic church. However, he had supposedly confessed to someone else that he may not be ready for marriage. When Pier heard about his indecision to marry her, the couple started arguing for the first time.

Pier introduced Jimmy to the Villa Capri. Frank Sinatra was a frequent patron as well as some of his pals. The famous gangster Mickey Cohen frequented the restaurant as well. Johnny Weissmuller, perhaps the most famous Tarzan of them all, liked to emit an earth-shattering Tarzan yell as he entered the establishment. When the mood hit him, Weissmuller pounded his chest for good measure.

According to Joe Hyams, an acquaintance of Dean's, Jimmy had every intention of marrying Pier. He was willing to raise their children Catholic as a way of satisfying Mrs. Pierangeli, Pier's mother. Jimmy and Pier agreed to be married at St. Timothy's and they even discussed names for their children. There is no credible evidence to suggest that Jimmy formally proposed to Pier. He reportedly told a friend that, "We've got to grow up a little first," when asked if the couple would ever get engaged.

There were many moments when the young couple argued over Pier's overbearing mother. Jimmy frequently got drunk after his altercations with Pier. Then one day, Jimmy heard a rumor that Pier had announced her engagement to crooner, Vic Damone. He tried to call Pier, but she refused to respond to any of his phone calls.

In mid-June the cast and crew relocated to the Warner Brothers lot in Burbank for the amusement park sequences. An entire amusement park was built exclusively for the film. The scene where Abra and Cal share a seat together on the Ferris wheel was critical to the story. It is here where Abra reveals her attraction to Cal. Dennis Hopper recalled that Jimmy wanted to appear anxious and so he worked on a method to suit the situation. "So to get himself really uncomfortable," Hopper recalled, "he told me he didn't pee all day. Until they did the shot."

Jimmy was having a particularly difficult time with one scene. "One time we spent all afternoon on a scene and he couldn't do it," Kazan recalled. "So I got him loaded on red wine that night. He couldn't drink a lot because he was unstable and liquor would affect him, but I gave him two glasses of wine and he did the scene great."

The sequence where Cal presents a birthday present to his father is a key element in the film. The original script reflected a lot less emotion in terms of Cal's disappointment with his father. Adam refuses the $5,000 gift that Cal presents to him. Cal stares at his father and then walks to where the money is, picks it up and lets out an emotionally charged scream and storms out of the room, feeling deeply humiliated and horrified. Jimmy improvised a totally different reaction. Cal clings to his father and cries hysterically as Adam looks on, terrified of Cal's reaction. Not knowing what else to do, Massey, amazed and stupefied by Dean's improvisation, simply yelled out, "Cal! – Cal!" while Dean cries hysterically in Massey's arms. Kazan decided to keep this version of the scene in the film.

Richard Davalos recalled that Jimmy frequently cried during the filming of *Eden*. "He loved to do that. And he could do it very well most of the time. Kazan would just let him go through with it and then carry on with the scene. But in the birthday scene, Kazan left it in, and it really worked there. The worst scene for me to do in the entire movie was when we have an argument and Cal hits me, but it was so real…and I believed he hated me, I believed he hit me, because it was real for him too. I went off the set after the take and cried for about four hours, I was so upset. Julie Harris had to come over and try to calm me down."

Film critics began to accuse Dean of aping Brando's style of acting. Jimmy had this to say about comparisons between him and Brando. "People were telling me I behave like Brando before I knew who Brando was. I am not disturbed by the comparison, or am I flattered. I have my own personal rebellions and I don't have to rely on Brando's. However, it's true I am constantly reminding people of him. People discover resemblances: We are both from farms, dress as we please, ride motorcycles and work for Elia Kazan. As an actor I have no desire to behave like Brando – And I don't attempt to. Nevertheless, it is very difficult not to be impressed, not to carry the image of a highly successful actor. But that's as far as it goes. I feel within myself there are expressions just as valid and I'll have a few years to develop my own style."

Lee Strasberg was adamant about his feelings in terms of comparisons between Brando and Dean. "Never! They're two totally different kinds of personalities. What was common at that time was the *characters* they played. I don't care what the authors may have intended, they brought onto the stage what we call today the anti-hero, the person who cannot express himself, the person who is not a hero in the ordinary sense of the word."

During the filming of *Eden*, Kazan invited Marlon Brando to stop by the set to meet the cast members. The actor was in the midst of filming *Desiree* at another studio. The director noticed that Jimmy spoke "in a cathedral hush" while in the presence of his idol. Brando acted like a big brother to Jimmy, giving him much needed advice. He warned Dean to lay off the motorcycling, to bring it down a notch. He told him that he was in danger of destroying the greatest gift an actor can have – his face. He also encouraged Jimmy to seek psychiatric help. It is unclear if Dean ever took Brando's advice.

When asked to explain the essence of Cal, Kazan offered the following thoughts. "Hatred/love. Not mildness. Vicious hatred and anger because of love frustrated. James Dean had them both. It was the most apt piece of casting I've ever done in my life. But it was accidental. I didn't search around a lot."

Prior to the completion of *Eden*, gossip columnist Hedda Hopper saw Dean and Dick Davalos acting rambunctious at the Warner Brothers commissary. She was so appalled by Jimmy's behavior, she lambasted him in a column, threatening to snub *Eden's* premiere. She claimed nobody could drag her to an *Eden* preview. Veteran actor Clifton Webb came to Jimmy's rescue and vouched for the young star. Based on Webb's praise of Dean, Hopper asked for a private screening of *Eden*. Overwhelmed by what she had just witnessed, Hopper wrote in her column that Dean's performance in *Eden* had "such power, so many facets of expression, and so much sheer invention." She regarded Kazan's latest discovery as "the brightest new star in town."

Hopper was so moved by Jimmy's performance, she immediately called Jack Warner and requested an interview with the rising new star. Dean agreed to meet with Hopper at her home. Evidently, the two got along very well because their meeting lasted much longer than expected.

On the final day of shooting *Eden*, Julie Harris found Dean sobbing inside his trailer on the movie set. "It's over! It's over!" Jimmy cried. Harris tried to comfort him, but it was no use. He was too overwhelmed with grief. "At that moment," Harris recalled, "he seemed more than ever to me like a little lost boy."

Warner Brothers was uncertain about Jimmy's next film. The studio considered casting him in a movie about the life of Charles Lindbergh. MGM asked Warner Brothers if they could borrow him for an upcoming film about a deranged artist. The film was called *The Cobweb*. The studio refused to allow their new star to work on the project because they felt it would be a poor career move. Reportedly, Warner Brothers was not fond of the idea of their latest heartthrob playing an inmate inside a mental institution. During his downtime, Dean agreed to be interviewed. The star met with Philip K. Scheuer of the *Los Angeles Times*, telling him he was "terribly gauche and so tense, I don't see how people stay in the same room with me. I know I wouldn't tolerate myself."

Now that Dean had a lot of time on his hands, he continued to perform in several television shows. NBC's *Philco Television Playhouse* aired an episode on September 5 called "Run Like a Thief." Jimmy played a character named Ronnie Warren who suspects his mentor is a thief. The featured stars were Kurt Kasznar and Gusti Huber.

Director Jeffrey Hayden recalled that Dean didn't want to learn his lines. Kasznar, an adept veteran actor from the Viennese school, learned all of his lines prior to the rehearsals. Jimmy, on the other hand, wanted to slowly and deliberately navigate his way into his part until he felt comfortable with his character. Dean mumbled and stammered so often during rehearsals, Huber broke down and cried. She told Hayden she felt lost, that it was virtually impossible for her to go on. The director stepped in and warned Dean to straighten up. Jimmy immediately complied to everyone's satisfaction. After the episode aired, *Variety* referred to Dean's acting as "beyond reproach."

Huber recalled that Dean talked passionately about Pier throughout the entire production. She was impressed by Jimmy's intensity and his knowledge of a wide range of topics, including classical music, jazz, art, and literature.

CBS's *Danger* television series aired an episode on November 9 called "Padlocks." Jimmy played a criminal fleeing from the law. He stops to rob an elderly woman played by Mildred Dunnock. Jimmy's intensity during rehearsals was so overwhelming, Dunnock felt intimidated. The veteran actress recalled that Dean arrived on the set like "something shot out of a cannon." John Frankenheimer directed the episode. Frankenheimer would later direct such outstanding films as *The Manchurian Candidate* starring Frank Sinatra, and *Seven Days in May* starring Burt Lancaster and Kirk Douglas. Mildred Dunnock had played Willy Loman's wife in *Death of a Salesman* on Broadway and in the motion picture version opposite Fredric March. She played a murder victim in *Kiss of Death,* starring opposite Victor Mature and Richard Widmark. Confined to a wheelchair, her character is pushed down a flight of stairs by a vengeful mobster.

General Electric Theater aired an episode called, "I'm a Fool" on November 14. Ronald Reagan was the program's host. Arnold Schulman had adapted the teleplay from a Sherwood Anderson short story. In "I'm a Fool," Jimmy's character pretends to be someone else and in the process of lying, he loses the woman he loves. Eddie Albert, best known for his role as Eva Gabor's befuddled husband in the sitcom series *Green Acres* in the 1960s, played an elderly man reminiscing about a love lost. Jimmy played a nineteen-year-old version of the Eddie Albert character. Natalie Wood played the girl Jimmy befriends and who later rejects him.

Director Don Medford remembered the first day of rehearsals quite vividly. He noticed someone on a motorcycle riding erratically toward the set. The driver changed lanes recklessly and almost hit Medford's car. As the hot shot got off his bike, Medford noticed that the driver was Jimmy. Medford warned Dean to take it easy. Jimmy responded with a smile and walked away.

Natalie Wood recalled that Jimmy was late the first day of rehearsals. "Like everybody else in Hollywood, I'd heard the stories and was frankly afraid of him," she recalled in an interview for *Photoplay*. "The longer we waited the more frightened I became, and as I went through the script, I found that he was going to make love to me." As everyone sat nervously watching the door for Dean's entrance, he unexpectedly crawled in through a large window. It was typical James Dean.

The producer of "I'm a Fool," Mort Abrahams, claimed that one prestigious actor on the show had had enough of Jimmy's experimentations and called him out on it. According to Abrahams, the actor grabbed Jimmy by the shirt and yelled, "Listen, you son of a bitch, if you give me another interpretation next time, I'll wipe the floor with you!"

"I knew him pretty well," Abrahams went on, "and the stories about him being troublesome as an actor are errant nonsense. He was an enormously imaginative and spontaneous actor. And this, of course, causes disruptions, delays, but it comes from an artistic effort. He was just beginning to get discipline of choice and he still had trouble holding a character once it was set. If I had to make a list of my most temperamental actors, Jimmy would definitely not be on it."

Pier and Vic Damone were married on November 24, 1954, at St. Timothy's. Hundreds of people attended the ceremony, including Debbie Reynolds, Jack Benny, Danny Thomas and Cyd Charisse. According to Joe Hyams, Jimmy sat on his motorcycle across the street from the church and stared at the newlyweds as they kissed for the photographers. Disgusted by the spectacle, Dean angerly gunned the engine and sped off.

The couple divorced in 1958. Pier married Italian composer Armando Trovajoli in 1962. They separated in 1969. Pier's film career had been very sketchy for quite some time. Pier was seriously considered for a part in *The Godfather*, but presumably she was turned down. On September 10, 1971, Pier Angeli, lonely and depressed, died from an apparent overdose of barbiturates at her home in Beverly Hills. She was only 39. She reportedly said at one time that Dean was the only man she had ever deeply loved.

CBS's *General Electric Theater* aired an episode on December 12 called "The Dark, Dark Hours." The director, Don Medford, desperately wanted to feature Jimmy in this latest drama. Producer Mort Abrahams did not want Dean. Finally, Ronald Reagan stepped in and convinced Abrahams to hire Jimmy. Reagan thought Jimmy had a bright future ahead of him and he wanted to star opposite Dean.

Jimmy played a hood named Bud who forces a doctor and his wife to remove a bullet from his partner in crime. Ronald Reagan played the doctor and Constance Ford played his wife. Jimmy's friend Jack Simmons had a minor role. This production would mark Medford's fourth and final collaboration with Dean in a television drama.

Don Medford recalled that General Electric rejected the original script because it sympathized with juvenile delinquents. According to Medford, he and the producer allowed Jimmy to replace the offensive dialogue with his own dialogue. General Electric finally approved the script. After the program aired, the front office received telegrams praising the show. However, the next day, Medford and Abrahams were fired. Medford claimed that Reagan called a press conference and indicated he was coerced into partaking in the drama and also added that he thought all juvenile delinquents were bastards. A columnist for *The Hollywood Reporter* wrote, "We heard many good words for James Dean's performance on Sunday night's G.E. Theater, with high praise for the gangster lingo."

Many years later, Ronald Reagan commented on Jimmy's style of acting. "I think in a way he was experimenting with his part because in an all-day rehearsal he would vary the performance, by showtime he had arrived at the performance he wanted." Reagan also commented on Deans' extremely unorthodox method of acting. "I was struck by how very much James Dean off camera resembled the James Dean you saw on camera…Most of us, after a while in pictures, hold back somewhat in rehearsals and save our punch for the take…Jimmy did not do this. He seemed to go almost all out any time that he read his lines."

ABC's *United States Steel Hour* aired an episode called "The Thief" on January 4, 1955. The teleplay was directed by Vincent J. Donehue and produced by John Haggott. Veteran actor Mary Astor complained bitterly about Dean's penchant for mumbling. "We were doing a final dress-rehearsal," she recalled. "Jimmy was six feet away from me in one scene and I could barely hear what he was saying and what I could hear seemed to have very little to do with the script. I looked over at the booth, my palms up in a 'Help!' gesture." The director asked Astor what the problem was. She was told over the speaker that, in effect, she and the rest of the cast would have to get used to Jimmy's idiosyncrasies.

Many veteran actors were not fond of the current crop of Method actors and went out of their way to belittle them. Joe Hyams recalled a time when he was having lunch with Humphrey Bogart at Romanoff's. Hyams told Bogart that many of the actors Kazan chose for *Eden* hailed from New York City. "They're all from the Actors Studio," Bogart sneered. "Mumblers all. You'll need an interpreter to understand them."

Jimmy upset a lot of people at Warner Brothers with his emotional outbursts. One time he tore a poster of his likeness off the commissary wall. To his detractors, Jimmy always had an answer. "I came to Hollywood to act, not to charm society." He told a writer for the Associated Press: "I probably should have a press agent, but I don't care what people write about me."

During his hiatus, Dean started taking acting lessons out of actor Jeff Corey's home in Los Angeles. For one exercise, Jimmy was supposed to play someone trying to help a friend who was an alcoholic. After giving his character a great deal of thought, Dean decided to play the part of a drunk who warns his alcoholic friend that he would remain drunk until his friend stopped drinking.

In January 1955, *Look* magazine carried a column called "I Predict." The column featured stories about future film stars. The article claimed that Jimmy "will be the most dynamic discovery since Marlon Brando." The following month, *Vogue* featured a story about him in a column called, "The Next Successes." They described Dean as "thin, intense, with such strong projection that he is always noticed...." *Cosmopolitan* carried a column by Louella Parsons that same month entitled, "James Dean – New

Face With Future." She referred to Jimmy as belonging "to the Marlon Brando – Montgomery Clift 'school' of acting, the professionally unwashed, unmannered, unconventional actors' group that – East or West – flourishes under the brilliant direction of Elia Kazan."

Photographer Dennis Stock first met Jimmy at a party at Nicholas Ray's home. Afterward, Dean invited Stock to a preview of *Eden*. Stock was blown away by Dean's performance. "The entire audience applauded as the house lights signaled the end," Stock recalled. Shortly afterward the photographer asked Jimmy if he could create a photo story on him. Dean readily agreed.

They traveled to New York City where Stock photographed Dean playing the bongos, relaxing in Jane Deacy's office, and walking through Times Square, along with a wide range of other activities. Stock's most famous image of Dean is when he is seen walking in a downpour near Times Square. He is hunched over in his overcoat, the collar is raised, a cigarette dangling from his lips. The photograph appears to accurately reflect Dean's introverted nature. "Jimmy was an insomniac," Stock recalled, "the worst I've ever met – so at odd times and at odd places he would simply pass out for a few minutes or a few hours, then wake up and set out again. He lived like a stray animal."

Dean and Stock traveled by train to Fairmount, Indiana. Dean appeared totally relaxed as he rekindled old memories with Marcus, Ortense, and little Markie. Before departing Fairmount, Stock joined Jimmy inside the town's only funeral parlor. Dean climbed inside one of the caskets on display and struck several poses, including one in which he pretended to be deceased. Stock's photo story of

Jimmy appeared in the March 7, 1955 issue of *Life* magazine. "Moody New Star" was the photo story's headline. The project was not an easy sell for Stock because Dean was relatively unknown at the time. Always his own best advocate, Dean had wanted his picture on the cover of *Life*, but the magazine ignored his request. Stock later claimed that *Life* "never really liked the story very much so they weren't going to give it the best display."

East of Eden premiered on March 9, 1955, at the Astor Theatre on Broadway. Tickets sold for as high as $50. Celebrities like Marilyn Monroe and Margaret Truman had volunteered to serve as ushers. Not entirely surprising, Dean refused to attend the opening, saying only that he couldn't handle the scene. No amount of arm twisting by Warner Brothers executives could change Jimmy's mind.

William K. Zinsser of the *New York Herald Tribune* called Jimmy's performance in *Eden* "remarkable." He went on to write in part: "Everything about Dean suggests the lonely misunderstood nineteen-year-old...When he talks, he stammers and pauses, uncertain of what he is trying to say. When he listens, he is full of restless energy-he stretches, he rolls on the ground, he chins himself on the porch railing, like a small boy impatient of his elder's chatter...He has all the awkwardness of an adolescent who must ask a few tremendous questions and can only blurt them out crudely...You sense the badness in him, but you also like him." John Steinbeck went much further than most critics when he applauded the film, calling *Eden* "probably the best motion picture I have ever seen."

Kate Cameron of *The Daily News* wrote this in her column: "When the last scene faded from the Astor Theater screen last night a new star appeared…James Dean." As the film opened at other theaters throughout the country, more accolades poured in. Herb Lyon, a reviewer for the *Chicago Tribune*, called Dean's work "the performance of the year." Many years later, highly respected film critic Richard Schickel went on record to say that Dean's appearance in *Eden* was "far and away his best performance."

New York Daily Mirror columnist Frank Quinn wrote that Dean was "destined for a blazing career." *Time* magazine described Jimmy as "a young man from Indiana who is unquestionably the biggest news Hollywood has made in 1955." Jack Moffitt from *The Hollywood Reporter* wrote that Dean "is that rare thing, a young actor who is a great actor, and the troubled eloquence with which he puts over the problems of misunderstood youth may lead to his being accepted by young audiences as a sort of symbol of their generation."

Some film critics were not impressed with Dean's performance in *Eden*. Bosely Crowther, the highly respected critic for the *New York Times* said in part, "He (Dean) scuffs his feet, he whirls, be pouts, he sputters, he leans against walls, he rolls his eyes, he swallows his words, he ambles slack-kneed, all like Marlon Brando used to do. Never have we seen a performance so clearly follow another's style. Mr. Kazan should be spanked for permitting him to do such a sophomoric thing. Whatever there might be of reasonable torment in this youngster is buried beneath the clumsy display."

It didn't take long for *Eden* to become America's top-grossing film. It set new box-office records in many cities across the country. Now that Jimmy had finally achieved the fame and respect he deserved, he appeared unfazed by his newfound stardom. He claimed acting was not his chief interest. What truly excited him the most was his passion for sports car racing.

Curiously, Kazan would continue to make films depicting life in rural America. Prior to directing *East of Eden*, Kazan's films by and large dealt with urban America. Examples include *A Tree Grows in Brooklyn*, *Gentleman's Agreement*, and *On the Waterfront*. After *Eden*, pastoral settings were featured in *Baby Doll*, *Wild River*, and *Splendor in the Grass*. These latter films revealed the stark contrast between the best of America versus the inherent hypocrisy embedded in its society.

Howard Thompson, a reviewer for the *New York Times*, wasn't very familiar with Jimmy. He had seen him in *The Immoralist* on Broadway and was very impressed with Dean's stage presence. Based on that experience, he went to a private screening of *Eden*. The film did not move him at all. Thompson wondered what all the fuss was about in terms of Jimmy's acting abilities. But because so many film critics praised Jimmy's performance in *Eden*, he decided to interview him. The story in part ran as follows:

ANOTHER DEAN HITS THE BIG LEAGUE

James Dean is the young man who snags the acting limelight in "*East of Eden*," which arrived at the Astor last week. Its opening has started a lively controversy over his histrionic kinship with Marlon Brando – and his professional competence. At any rate, 25-year-old Dean, a product of an Indiana farm, Hollywood, television and Broadway, has made an impression and now owns a Warner Brothers contract.

Count his supporting chore in last season's play "*The Immoralist*" as having threefold significance insofar as the rapid rise is concerned. It netted him the Donaldson and Perry awards, and, indirectly, the attention of director Elia Kazan, then scouting leads for "*Eden*" and finally his flourishing reputation for unvarnished individuality...Had he caught "*Eden*" yet?

"Sure, I saw it," came the soft, abstract reply. His verdict? "Not Bad."

"No, I didn't read the novel. The way I work, I'd rather justify myself with the adaption rather than the source. I felt I wouldn't have any trouble - too much, anyway - with this characterization once we started because I think I understood the part. I knew, too, that if I had any problems over the boy's background, I could straighten it out with Kazan."

"To me, acting is the most logical way for people's neuroses to manifest themselves, in the great need we all have to express ourselves. To my way of thinking, an actor's course is set even before he's out of the cradle."

Would he compare the stage and screen media? "As of now, I don't consider myself as specifically belonging to either. The cinema is a very truthful medium because the camera doesn't let you get away with anything. On stage, you can even loaf a little, if you're so inclined. Technique, on the other hand, is more important. My real aim, my real goal, is to achieve what I call camera-functioning on the stage."

"Don't get me wrong. I'm not one of the wise ones who try to put Hollywood down. It just happens that I fit to cadence and pace better here as far as living goes. New York is vital, above all, fertile. They're a little harder to find, maybe, but out there in Hollywood, behind all that brick and mortar, there are human beings, just as sensitive to fertility. The problem for this cat-myself-is not to get lost."

Dean was so sensational in *East of Eden*, reporters overlooked both his real and perceived past transgressions. The increased coverage of Jimmy's new-found fame did little to alleviate his mistrust toward the press. He told a Hollywood reporter from the Associated Press, "I don't care what people write about me. I'll talk to the ones I like; the others can print whatever they please." James Dean was the hottest property in Hollywood and everyone took notice. And his career was about to enter a new dimension, one that would catapult him into the stratosphere – and beyond.

Dean was an avid participant in sports during his high school years. He excelled at basketball, baseball and track.

While attending UCLA, Dean played Malcolm, the rightful heir to the throne of Scotland, in William Shakespeare's *Macbeth*.

Dean and costar Georgann Johnson in a scene from *Campbell Summer Soundstage's* "Life Sentence."

Dean enjoyed taking photographs in the early 1950s during his brief stay in New York City.

Jo Van Fleet as Kate Trask, Cal's estranged mother, and Dean as Cal Trask in a scene from *East of Eden*. Cal asks to borrow money from Kate so he can help his financially troubled father.

Julie Harris and Dean pose for a publicity photo for *East of Eden*.

In a pivotal scene from *East of Eden*, Cal Trask pleads with his father to accept his gift of $5,000 – all the money Adam lost in a failed business venture.

James Dean and Pier Angeli met on the set of *The Silver Chalice* while Dean was busy filming *East of Eden*. Their romance lasted only a few short months.

A scene from *Rebel Without a Cause* starring James Dean as the proverbial outsider. A gang tries to provoke Dean's character Jim Stark into a knife fight.

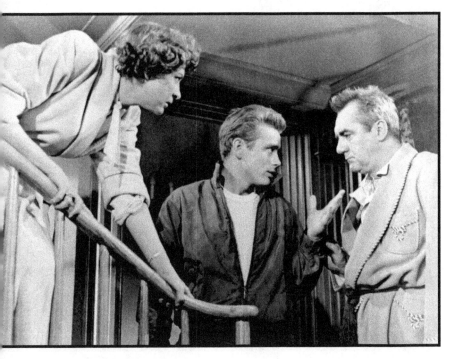

A key scene from *Rebel Without a Cause*. Jim Stark wants to turn himself in to the police after a chickie-run ends tragically. His parents, played by Ann Doren and Jim Backus, try to talk him out of it.

Dean as Jim Stark and Natalie Wood as Judy share a romantic moment in *Rebel Without a Cause.*

A publicity photo for *Giant* with Rock Hudson as cattle baron Bick
Benedict and Dean as the defiant ranch hand Jett Rink.

A scene from *Giant* starring Elizabeth Taylor as Leslie Lynnton and Dean as Jett Rink. Leslie admires Jett's attempt to improve his station in life.

James Dean's Porsche Spyder is a mass of twisted metal moments after Dean's car collides with the much heavier and bulkier Ford Tudor.

Rolf Weutherich injured in the accident

James Dean inside his wrecked car

Highway 41

STOP

Turnupseed's car approaching intersection

Highway 466

A

Turnupseed's car collided with Dean's at A and skidded to position B

B

James Dean approaching intersection

Above is a depiction of what reportedly occurred before, during, and after the deadly two-car collision involving screen legend James Dean and Donald Turnupseed.

CHAPTER 4

REBEL WITHOUT A CAUSE

Iconic image of James Dean in perhaps his most enduring film,
Rebel Without a Cause.

merica's economy was growing in leaps and bounds during the 1950s. Many of its citizens prospered under the leadership of President Dwight D. Eisenhower. Eisenhower had helped bring an end to the Korean War, a conflict which began under President Harry S. Truman. Fears of a communist takeover at the State Department were fomented by Joseph McCarthy, the controversial senator from Wisconsin. By the year 1955, America was not directly at war with any country. Although Russia and China remained a real threat, no serious signs of an impending war existed with either nation.

American households were able to enjoy vacations, weekend barbeques, and overseas travel like never before. Americans who could afford it moved out of the cities and bought new homes in the suburbs. People stayed home and watched television instead of hitting the movie theaters as the previous generation had done. Families enjoyed watching Ed Sullivan, *The Honeymooners*, dramatic and comedic teleplays, and sports. And best of all the entertainment was free.

The movie industry suffered tremendously since the advent of television. Instead of going out and spending money on food, snacks, and theater tickets, a family could stay home and watch a wide array of programs. The movie industry desperately fought back by providing movie goers with innovative film features such as 3-D, CinemaScope, and Technicolor.

Young people were beginning to enjoy a new kind of music, the kind of music many grownups found vulgar and disgusting. That strange music came to be known as rock and roll. At the forefront of rock and roll was a young man from Tupelo, Mississippi. That young man's name was Elvis Presley and he would go on to sell more records than any other musical solo act.

However, all was not well with young adults in America. In 1954 *U.S. News and World Report* carried an article about the dramatic rise in juvenile delinquency in the United States. According to one study, juvenile delinquency increased more than 40 percent between 1948 and 1953. What shocked many Americans was the fact that teenagers from affluent families were getting involved in criminal activity.

The movie industry had tackled social issues before with such films as *Gentleman's Agreement* and *Home of the Brave.* However, these movies and others like them dealt with antisemitism and racism, but not juvenile delinquency. And it appeared no one in Hollywood had made a film about juvenile delinquency among suburban middle and upper class adolescents.

The head of MCA at the time was Lewis Wasserman. He became aware of an intriguing property at Warner Brothers called *Rebel Without a Cause.* The book's subtitle was *The Hypnoanalysis of a Criminal Psychopath.* It was written by prison psychologist, Robert M. Lindner. His primary expertise was the study and treatment of juvenile delinquency. The book was based on an actual case study of a traumatized youth known as "Harold." The patient was kept under observation at the Penitentiary at Lewisburg,

Pennsylvania. Warner Brothers producer Jerry Wald found the story provocative and proceeded to shop it around to several studio executives, directors, and screenwriters. In the meantime, Lindner was paid $5,000 with the stipulation that he would receive an extra $4,000 if the story was made into a movie.

For years Wald attempted to find a studio willing to take on the project, but no one was interested. Story treatments were written by studio writers such as Theodor Seuss Geisel, a man who would later become known to the world as Dr. Seuss. Apparently, nobody seemed interested in stories about troubled teenagers. For the next several years, *Rebel Without a Cause* remained on the back burner and was nearly forgotten.

Although the story remained unsellable, the peculiar sounding title still had legs. Juvenile delinquency continued to make headlines in America and film studios were now more than willing to exploit that phenomenon. Marlon Brando's *The Wild One*, for example, proved there currently existed a huge audience for such pictures. *Blackboard Jungle* would further reinforce the theory that juvenile delinquency in our school systems was now a bankable commodity in Hollywood.

Marlon Brando had actually completed a screen test for a major role based on the newly published book, *Rebel Without a Cause*. The year was 1947, the same year he performed in Tennessee Williams' highly controversial play, *A Streetcar Named Desire*. In the end, Brando walked away from the project. Skip Homeier, an actor who specialized in playing troubled youths, also refused to sign on.

Nicholas Ray had developed an excellent reputation

in Hollywood. He had directed several well received pictures, including *They Live by Night, In a Lonely Place,* and *Johnny Guitar.* He had an inherent knack for portraying social outcasts on the big screen. At age forty-three, Ray wanted to branch out and direct a film about young people and the unique problems they face. But he wanted to focus more on problems facing middle class teenagers.

Unlike many directors, Ray accepted feedback from actors and screenwriters alike. He rarely raised his voice and was considerate and cordial to everyone on the set. Movie moguls grew apprehensive toward Ray's directorial style, but they allowed him some slack as long as he made pictures that sold well.

Ray complained to studio executives that he had grown tired of directing films strictly for monetary gain. He wanted to make pictures about young people instead of film noir type characters geared toward grownups. For once in his life he wanted to make a film he could legitimately love, something that could truly motivate him. More specifically, he wanted to make a film about middle class juvenile delinquents facing real issues of their own. The studio decided to grant Ray his wish.

Warner Brothers allowed Ray to choose his own producer. He chose David Weisbart, primarily because he was one of the youngest staff producers working for Warner Brothers. Ray thought he would probably be able to relate to the younger generation better than someone older. Weisbart had also helped edit Elia Kazan's film, *A Streetcar Named Desire.*

Ray thought that the subject matter in the book *Rebel Without a Cause* was too abnormal for the film he had in mind. Lindner, who was a psychoanalyst, pleaded with Ray to allow him to be a consultant for the film. Unfortunately for Lindner, the only thing Ray legitimately liked about the book was its title. Ray took it upon himself to write a 17-page treatment called "Blind Run." It concerned juvenile delinquency and he hoped it could be turned into a movie script. The basic premise in the treatment involved two cars driven at night by delinquents who tragically crash into each other.

Ray wanted the lead character in the film to be charismatic. He wanted an actor who could successfully convey the "conflict of violent eagerness and mistrust created in the very young." He was certain the current crop of young heartthrobs couldn't portray the lead character he had envisioned. According to Ray, Tab Hunter, Robert Wagner, and particularly John Kerr, were totally out of the question.

Elia Kazan was busy with postproduction for *East of Eden* around this time. Ray's studio offices were close to Kazan's and occasionally the two directors shared stories about their experiences in Hollywood. Kazan had even directed Ray's wife Gloria Graham in *Man on a Tightrope*. Kazan and Budd Schulberg introduced a former middleweight contender named Roger Donoghue to Ray. The fighter had trained Brando on how to box in preparation for his role as ex-boxer Terry Malloy in *On the Waterfront*. Ray considered utilizing Donoghue as an advisor for his upcoming film.

Ray asked an old friend of his, playwright Clifford Odets, to write the screenplay for *Rebel*. Odets had written many fine plays, including *Waiting for Lefty* and *Golden Boy*. His career had taken a turn for the worse when he began drinking heavily. Unfortunately, Ray couldn't utilize Odets' talent as a writer because Warner Brothers thought he was too controversial. He had named names during the House Un-American Activities Committee hearings and many in the entertainment industry refused to forgive him. However, Odets did offer some suggestions to Ray in terms of character development. According to Ray, Odets contributed the line, "I got the bullets!" It's a line Jim Stark screams at the police after they shoot and kill his friend, Plato.

Warner Brothers hired Leon Uris to write the screenplay for *Rebel*. Uris had recently written the screenplay for the hit World War II drama *Battle Cry*. The writer later gained fame for his epic novel *Exodus*. Uris and Ray spent much of their time researching data pertaining to juvenile delinquency. They witnessed what transpires during juvenile hearings and worked as social workers at Juvenile Hall. Ray was happy with Uris' enthusiasm and dedication toward the project. Unfortunately for Uris, his ideas eventually displeased the director. Ray didn't like the writer's depiction of suburban adults and their so-called petty lives. According to Ray, Uris failed to develop an understanding of what motivates and alienates teenagers. He did contribute a couple of ideas Ray found interesting, namely a sympathetic Jim Stark placing his jacket over a sleeping Plato, and Judy's attempt to replace her mother as her father's only true love.

Stewart Stern was hired to write the screenplay for *Rebel*. He delivered forty plus pages of his script in late January of 1955. The story opens on Christmas Eve, but that time period was subsequently changed to Easter because of the warmer weather during the filming of the picture. Buzz Gunderson and his gang of misfits approach a middle-aged male shopper at night and beat him senseless. A drunken Jim Stark is dragged into Juvenile Hall as Plato nervously waits to be interrogated for a senseless and brutal crime. In many ways, Plato appears to be the most disturbed teenager in the entire story. Nearby is Judy, who is blonde and sixteen. Also in the waiting room are three small children. It is not readily apparent why they are in Juvenile Hall. An officer named Ray Framek questions Judy about why she had been wandering around the streets late at night. We find out that Plato had shot and killed his next-door neighbor's puppies.

The automobile became a status symbol for young adults in the post-World War II era. The post-war economy was booming and so were the number of young people owning their very own automobile. The car gave them the freedom to go where they pleased. Cars provided the means by which the average young adult could do what they wanted without their parent's knowledge. Cars would play a crucial and ominous role in the film adaption of *Rebel Without a Cause*.

Stern made a major script change regarding the chickie-run. After Buzz's death at the bottom of the bluff, Judy screams and cries hysterically. Stern decided to tone it down and now Judy looks down at Buzz as Jim Stark moves closer to Judy and reaches out his hand to comfort her. Judy hesitantly accepts Jim's hand and they both walk away from the edge of the bluff. Plato follows the couple to Jim's car, they get in, and Jim drives away from the fiery wreckage.

Apparently, Ray's imagination did not always go over well with Stewart Stern. The director wanted to incorporate the split screen effect in order to juxtapose fantasy with reality. He wanted to reveal what goes on inside the mind of a troubled teenager as opposed to what is actually happening. Stern thought the idea of a split screen was absolutely ridiculous. He argued that the mindset of the characters should be reflected through dialogue and behavior and not via special effects.

Ray and Stern disagreed on another key element in the film. Stern wanted the entire story to be told over a 24-hour period. Ray argued vehemently against this idea because nobody would believe everything that goes on in the film could occur in just one day. Stern argued that the life of a typical teenager goes by very quickly. Because so many significant changes occur in such a relatively short period of time for a teenager, he firmly believed that the viewing audience would accept the 24-hour concept.

Nicholas Ray had been hearing stories about Jimmy's so-called antics from several sources. He had heard that Dean refused to heed the orders of television producers and directors. Dean scoffed at the idea of hitting your 'mark' during a performance. Such conventions were a hindrance and a complete waste of time to Jimmy's way of thinking. He was primarily interested in character development, experimentation, and realism. He rarely recited his lines the same way twice, sometimes even going so far as to improvise new lines. This practice often confused and exasperated his peers. Directors scolded Dean and often threatened to fire him. Jimmy was not in the least concerned about budgets and time constraints. He was in a league almost entirely by himself in terms of not getting along with fellow actors, producers and directors. He didn't seem to care about the repercussions of his actions and so he never altered his style of acting. Perhaps he thought it was a badge of honor to fight the system.

Elia Kazan invited Ray to view a rough cut of *East of Eden* in the music room at the Warner Brothers studio. Leonard Rosenman, the film's composer, was present at the screening as well. He sat at a piano and improvised some scoring during the screening of the film. Jimmy stood in a corner by himself, unshaven and hunched over. Ray must have wondered how such a young man could possibly be the next great discovery since Marlon Brando. He appeared so unassuming and nervous. Jimmy hardly spoke at all after the screening. He may have felt uneasy opening up to someone who represented old Hollywood.

Several days later, Jimmy wandered into Ray's office. Dean spoke very little at first. Ray was curious as to why Jimmy dropped by, particularly since the two of them hardly spoke to one another at their first meeting. Ray recalled later that Dean reminded him of a Siamese cat in that the animal cautiously sizes up company until it either accepts you or it doesn't. Jimmy decided he liked what he saw and heard and so he visited Ray frequently over the next several weeks. Ray sensed that Jimmy was extremely sensitive to criticism in terms of his acting ability. He thought Jimmy was prone to mood swings and erratic behavior, particularly if a director or a staff member disagreed with him.

Dean questioned Ray about the story line and the characters in *Rebel*. He seemed very intrigued about the overall theme, namely juvenile delinquency. He had played so many juvenile delinquents on television that he didn't seem to mind being typecast. After several more meetings with Dean, Ray was convinced that Jimmy was perfect for the role of Jim Stark and he told him so. Jimmy told Ray he knew someone who could teach the director about teenage violence. His name was Perry Lopez. According to Jimmy, Lopez was from a rough neighborhood in New York City and was familiar with gang violence. Lopez would appear in several movies over the years, including the 1974 film, *Chinatown*.

After the immense success of *Eden*, Jimmy appeared to grow cautious toward accepting the role of Jim Stark in *Rebel*. Ray understood Jimmy's predicament. "Agents and well-wishers were eager to advise him. It would be foolish, they told him, to appear in any film not based on a best-seller, not adapted by a $3,000 – a week writer, not directed by Elia Kazan, George Stevens, John Huston, or William Wyler. He was not a person to take this kind of advice very seriously; but intensely self-aware as he was, he could not fail to be troubled by 'success.' If these were aspects of it he enjoyed, it also added to his doubts." Two days after the premiere of *East of Eden*, the news media reported that Jimmy might very well turn down the male lead in *Rebel Without a Cause*.

Ray flew to New York City to meet with Dean so he could convince him that the Jim Stark role would be the perfect vehicle for him. Ray also spent time at the Actors Studio interviewing students for *Rebel*. Some of the actors Ray dismissed went on to become popular entertainers. Arte Johnson, who would later appear on the hit television series *Laugh-In*, was turned down for the role of Plato. At 25, John Cassavetes was considered too old and Lee Remick was dismissed because Ray thought she was not very photogenic. Cassavetes would later star in two big blockbuster films, *The Dirty Dozen* and *Rosemary's Baby*. Lee Remick would later star in such major hits as *Anatomy of a Murder* and *The Days of Wine and Roses*.

After screen testing several candidates for the role of Plato, Ray chose 16-year-old Sal Mineo for the part. Mineo had appeared on Broadway in *The Rose Tattoo* and *The King and I*. In his only film to date, *Six Bridges to Cross,* he played a New York City gang member.

Actor Tom Brannum was given serious consideration for the role of Buzz because he looked the part. The only real downside was his height. Because he was 6' 2" tall, Ray didn't like the idea of Brannum towering over Jimmy, so he was dismissed. Carroll Baker, a rising star who had just finished starring in *A Hatful of Rain,* was considered for the role of Judy. Ray even handed her a copy of the script to look over.

Jack Warner pored over the latest script and scrawled some suggestions in the margins. Mindful of the censors strict policy regarding offensive language, he crossed out several lines from the script. Chief among them were some of Jim Stark's lines, such as "Tell him to go to hell," and "Get your damn hands off me."

Surprisingly, Warner was not totally committed to hiring Jimmy for the lead in *Rebel*. He seriously thought Tab Hunter would do a wonderful job as Jim Stark. After all, Tab Hunter was already an established movie star in Warner's eyes. Hunter had even beat out Dean for the lead in *Battle Cry.* Warner also had ideas about who might make a fine Judy. He thought highly of Lois Smith's acting skills, particularly after seeing her performance in *East of Eden.*

Ray was under a lot of pressure to come up with a final script. He grew increasingly concerned that he might lose Dean if the project continued to stall. Warner Brothers wanted to give Jimmy enough time to prepare himself for his starring role in the George Stevens epic film *Giant*. Months had gone by and Ray still couldn't give the studio a script along with the names of prospective cast members. Moreover, David Weisbart and the head of production Steve Trilling were beginning to lose interest in the project. To make matters worse, several studio executives took exception to the storyline involving Plato. They didn't like the idea that Plato's mother and father neglect him. They didn't want a story that basically portrayed parents as negligent.

While Dean was in New York City, he called Stewart Stern to inform him that he harbored serious doubts about Nicholas Ray. He didn't think Ray could effectively direct him in a major motion picture. Stern warned Jimmy that he could very well face suspension if he walked away from the commitment he made with Warner Brothers. Dean finally agreed to do the picture.

Warner Brothers finally made it official. James Dean would star in an upcoming film called *Rebel Without a Cause*. A reporter asked Jimmy if he had script approval for *Rebel*. The star's answer was revealing: "Contractually no – emotionally yes. They can always suspend me. Money isn't one of my worries, not that I have any." Dean may have been alluding to the possibility that he might decide not to star in *Rebel* regardless of the repercussions.

Amazingly, Jimmy may not have starred in *Rebel* had it not been for the fact that the production of *Giant* had been pushed back a couple months. The epic saga could very well have been Jimmy's second film if not for Elizabeth Taylor's pregnancy. In any event, Warner Brothers made the announcement in mid-March 1955, that Jimmy would be starring as Jett Rink in George Stevens' epic film about Texas.

In an effort to keep Jimmy interested in making *Rebel*, Ray kept him updated in terms of new script drafts and casting considerations. In fact, Ray was so certain Dean would indeed play the lead character Jim Stark in *Rebel*, he reportedly came up with the surname "Stark," which is an anagram of "Trask," the surname of Dean's character in *East of Eden*.

The studio announced that Jayne Mansfield was scheduled to do a screen test for *Rebel*. She was 21 years old and she had won several beauty pageants. Ray flat out refused to seriously consider Mansfield for *any* part. He later claimed he never tested her with a loaded camera. The new script also implied that Judy had been arrested for prostitution. In late February, Jayne Mansfield tested once again as Judy. Somebody with influence and tenacity was obviously pulling for Mansfield to get the part. Natalie Wood and Kathryn Grant also tested for Judy. John Saxon tested for the role of Buzz while Dennis Hopper and John Carlyle tested one more time for the part of Jim Stark. Warner Brothers needed a backup plan in case Dean refused to star in *Rebel*.

Warner Brothers announced that they had signed Dennis Hopper to a term contract. He was only 18 years old and he had been featured in just one episode of a television series called *Medic*. Hopper hailed from the state of Kansas. He had worked on his grandparent's farm in

Kansas City. According to a press release, the young actor had entered the Golden Gloves boxing competition. He even came out on top in the middleweight division. Actress Dorothy McGuire encouraged him to become an actor. After his appearance in *Medic*, Hopper was reportedly offered movie contracts from three major studios.

Ray considered many other actors for the role of Judy. Contenders for the part included Margaret O'Brien, Pat Crowley, and Debbie Reynolds. Although Carroll Baker seriously considered the role of Judy, she turned it down. For weeks, Natalie Wood expressed a keen interest in playing the female lead. Initially, Ray couldn't picture Natalie as Judy. Instead, he considered her for the part of Helen, one of Judy's friends. Through sheer tenacity and assertiveness, Natalie eventually changed Ray's mind about her ability to play the gang leader's girlfriend.

Frank Mazzola was hired as a gang consultant in early February. He belonged to a 'club' at Hollywood High School called the Athenians. His gang developed a reputation for provoking fights with strangers along Hollywood Boulevard. He provided valuable information helpful to Ray in terms of gang culture. This included language, rituals, dress and gang behavior. After a couple of hours discussing teenage delinquency, Ray seriously considered Mazzola for a role in the film. Ray liked his looks and the way he carried himself. Shortly thereafter, Ray hired Mazzola to play Crunch, one of the chief members of Buzz's gang.

Mazzola was no stranger to film making. As a child actor he had bit parts in such films as *The Hunchback of Notre Dame*, *Casablanca*, and more recently, *The Boy with Green Hair*. Frank had done some stunt work and performed as an extra in several films. He also had a small role in *East of Eden*, but his brief film appearance never made the final cut. Frank came from a family deeply entrenched in the film industry. For years, his father worked as a stunt man with Western star Tom Mix and the Keystone Kops. Other family members were employed as producers and movie grips.

The two main fathers in *Rebel* were played by Jim Backus and William Hopper. Interestingly, Backus had played Natalie Wood's father in her first television performance and William Hopper had played Jimmy's father in another television drama. Surprisingly, Jimmy had very little influence when it came to steering friends toward certain roles in *Rebel*. Dean lobbied hard to deliver the role of Plato to his buddy Jack Simmons. Simmons tested for the role, but Ray was not impressed with his performance. Moreover, Jimmy campaigned especially hard for Christine White for the role of Judy, but she was ultimately turned down.

Reportedly, Ray had spotted actor Corey Allen in a local stage play called *The Pick-Up Girl*. Evidently, Ray enjoyed Allen's performance. Coincidently, Beverly Long, a future participant in *Rebel*, also appeared in the same play. Corey Allen also had small film roles in *The Mad Magician* and *Night of the Hunter*. Allen's real name was Alan Cohen. Ray contacted Cohen's agent to discuss his interest in Allen. Without the actor's approval, Cohen's agent and the studio decided to change his name to Corey Allen, presumably because it sounded more commercial. Corey Allen explained that the "big thing was to erase the circumcision."

Corey Allen's father Carl Cohen was a successful gambler and casino manager. Cohen became notorious due to a very unfortunate incident. An altercation occurred between Carl Cohen and Frank Sinatra at Howard Hughes' Sands Casino. Reportedly, Sinatra had been denied credit at a particular baccarat table. Furious, Sinatra insisted on seeing the manager about this apparent slight. An argument broke out between Cohen and Sinatra and the singer flipped over a table, causing a pot of hot coffee to land in the hapless manager's lap. Outraged, Cohen smashed Sinatra in the face. The blow split Sinatra's lip and loosened several caps.

Stern continued to make changes to the script. He had written a rather disturbing scene where Buzz's car burns near the base of a high bluff. A father and daughter watch in horror as Buzz's body burns inside the wreckage. Ray Framek, a law enforcement officer, is on the police radio providing grizzly details of Buzz's death to a police dispatcher. The part in the script where two onlookers gawk at Buzz's burning corpse was eventually removed. It was deemed too graphic and brutal by several top studio executives.

In the original script Jim Stark arrives home after the chickie-run and notices his father and grandmother playing scrabble. The two ignore Jim as he walks past them. Jim decides to confront his parents over Buzz's death and his own involvement in the gang leader's tragic demise. He wants to turn himself in to the police, but his parents try to talk him out of it. A police siren can be heard in the distance. Disgusted with his parent's reaction, Jim runs out of the house. In the film version, the grandmother is nowhere to be found during Jim's heated argument with his parents.

Ray began conducting reading sessions with the main cast members in *Rebel*. The group typically sat in a large circle in the director's living room. One night, Marsha Hunt, the actress originally hired to play Jim Stark's mother, arrived late and exchanged pleasantries with the cast members. She was the most prominent and recognizable actor in the room. She had appeared in several popular films, including *Pride and Prejudice* and *The Human Comedy*. She surprised everyone in the room with her comment, "Hello everybody. I'm what's left of Marsha Hunt." Hunt was subsequently dropped from the project, supposedly due to a scheduling conflict. Hunt suspected that perhaps her prior run-in with the House Un-American Activities Committee may have had something to do with her sudden dismissal from *Rebel*.

On March 25, Stern submitted a 'final' script to Warner Brothers. It just so happened that another movie about teenage angst opened to packed theaters, namely MGM's *Blackboard Jungle*. Bill Haley and the Comets' "Rock Around the Clock" blasted over the opening credits. The song had done rather poorly prior to the film's release, but after the movie opened the song became a smash hit. Teenagers danced in the aisles as the song blared out of the theaters sound systems.

Educational and religious leaders blasted the film as being immoral. They claimed it glorified hoodlums and chastised teachers. Coincidently or not, a New York City teacher was stabbed and thrown off the top of a roof the same day *Blackboard Jungle* opened. Warner Brothers kept a close eye on the film's box-office receipts over the next several weeks. Warner Brothers was prepared to shut down production of *Rebel* if *Blackboard* bombed.

During an interview with Philip K. Scheuer from the *Los Angeles Times*, Ray made some rather disparaging remarks about inner-city youths. This is what he had to say in part about his new film: "This is no slum study like *Blackboard Jungle*. We have put what happens in the home, the middle class home, ahead of that, ahead of the slum condition. These things are taking place on all social, economic, and cultural levels, wherever young people feel they are 'out of attention,' It is there and then that they are vulnerable to participating in and creating delinquent acts which will bring them back into attention, only this time it's negative."

Meanwhile, *Blackboard* was scoring big at the box office. *Variety* reported sensational box-office earnings in Philadelphia, Boston, New York City, and San Francisco. Juvenile delinquency films had finally proven to be very lucrative and so *Rebel* was given the green light to proceed with its production. *Variety* also reported that a movie theater in Winthrop, Massachusetts stopped showing *Blackboard* after receiving complaints from the city's Board of Selectmen.

The first day of production began on Wednesday, March 30, 1955. The cast and crew drove to Griffith Park to begin shooting some important scenes. This location was crucial to the storyline because much of the action takes place in and around the observatory. Griffith Park was built twenty years earlier by a mining tycoon named Colonel Griffith J. Griffith. He later donated the land. In the fall of 1903, the eccentric tycoon shot his wife in the face because he believed she had been conspiring with the Pope to murder him. Griffith's wife was left disfigured and she lost her right eye. Griffith served less than two years in prison for the insane attempt on his wife's life.

Sal Mineo was utterly enthralled by Jimmy's talent and overall demeanor. "We all tended to idolize him," Mineo recalled in reference to his hero. "If he didn't say good morning to me, I'd be a wreck the whole day. If he put his arm around me, that was fabulous because I knew he meant it. I always felt he was just testing people, testing to see how far he could go." According to Mineo, Natalie Wood was obsessed with Jimmy. "Every night for weeks in a row, she went to see *East of Eden*. She must have seen it over fifty times. She even taught me to play the theme song from the picture on the piano."

Because Natalie Wood and Sal Mineo were considered minors under the law, they were required to spend several hours each day with a tutor in school. A former policeman named Thomas Hennessy was assigned as their guardian. His job was to protect them from any bad influences, such as on-set profanity. Many of the cast and crew members were amused at the idea of a watchdog because both minors smoked regularly throughout the filming of *Rebel*.

Shooting began around 7:30 a.m. and ended at 5:15 p.m. Two and a half minutes of useable footage was shot over a ten-hour period. The next day, Ray directed the switchblade fight sequence. About five hundred school children arrived to watch a show at the planetarium. Just before stepping into the facility, the children hung around the set and watched Jimmy and Corey Allen face off in the famous knife fight sequence.

Beverly Long recalled that Jimmy perspired so much during the knife sequence, he had to change his shirt several times. At one point during a break Jimmy offered Allen a cup of water. Allen was taken aback by Jimmy's thoughtfulness. Allen asked him how he knew he was so thirsty. Jimmy simply replied, "I'm a lot older than you." By the end of the second day, Ray had four more minutes of useable film footage.

The movie opens with a low-angle closeup of Jimmy approaching a toy monkey holding what appears to be a pair of cymbals. The scene was shot at night at the corner of Franklin and Sierra Bonita in Hollywood. Dean slowly lowers himself onto the pavement and lays in a prone position as he gazes quizzically at the toy. He lays the toy monkey on its side and thoughtfully covers it with wrapping paper as if to protect it from the elements. He then maneuvers himself into a fetal position and lays the toy monkey near his head. This scene typifies Dean at his best. He improvised the entire sequence without any direction from the director. From that moment on Ray began to appreciate Dean's unique improvisational skills.

Steffi Sidney, the actress who played Mil, one of the gang members in *Rebel*, revealed that Jimmy did his opening scene many times. "He didn't go into the fetal position to begin with. He just looked at the monkey. He evolved. Ray and he would go off to the right. We all watched and were absolutely fascinated with the fact that it was all improvised." Beverly Long remembered being only a few feet away from Jimmy. "And I was stunned at his ability to create this whole aura for himself. It was worth everything we went through that day. We all sat there with tears in our eyes. It was so beautiful."

The movie never explains the reason for the appearance of the toy monkey nor does it really need to. In fact, the explanation is quite simple. The original opening scene was never used in the final cut. A gang of street thugs led by Buzz Gunderson assault an elderly man who is holding a bag filled with gifts. While the victim is being assaulted, he drops the package and the gifts spill out onto the street. The mechanical monkey lands on the pavement and begins banging away on the cymbals until it eventually stops. After the gang flees from the mugging, an inebriated Jim Stark appears at the scene and notices the toy monkey laying on the pavement.

It was around this time when Jimmy began receiving favorable reviews for his performance in *East of Eden*. One film critic in particular was impressed by the young star's talents. She described him as a "disturbed animal, so full of love he's defenseless. Maybe his father doesn't love him but the camera does, and we're supposed to; we're thrust into upsetting angles, caught in infatuated close-ups, and prodded, 'Look at all that beautiful desperation.' The film is overpowering."

Dean took as much time as he believed was necessary in order to work himself into whatever mood he thought was relevant. Fortunately, Jimmy was lucky to be working with a director like Nicholas Ray. Throughout the entire production, Ray insisted that Jimmy's mood swings never negatively affected the filming of *Rebel*. The director encouraged the film crew never to disturb Jimmy's concentration before each scene. According to Corey Allen, all Jimmy had to do was nod his head when he was ready and Ray would yell, "Roll em!" Corey Allen also recalled a conversation he had with the director. "Nick told me that he made an agreement with Jim not to rush Jim. And so sometimes we would wait thirty or forty minutes for Jim to come out of the trailer."

In Jim Backus' autobiography, *Rocks on the Roof,* he recalled Jimmy's intense involvement with the filming of *Rebel.* "James Dean worked very closely with Nick. May I say that this is the first time in the history of motion pictures that a twenty-four-year-old boy, with only one movie to his credit, was practically the co-director. Jimmy insisted on utter realism. And looking back, I sometimes wonder how we finished so violent a picture without someone getting seriously injured."

Jimmy prepared for his scenes inside Juvenile Hall by drinking wine and banging on bongos while listening to Wagner's "Ride of the Valkyries." The cast and crew were kept waiting for an hour before he walked onto the set. Dean performed so brilliantly that after he was through with the scene, the crew responded with a vigorous round of applause.

"When he felt ready," Backus recalled, "he stormed out, strode onto the set, did the scene, which was practically a seven-minute monologue, in one take, so brilliantly that even the hard-boiled crew cheered and applauded. He played that scene so intensely that he broke two small bones in his hand when he beat the desk, which he practically demolished. Actually, he saved the production department money with his method of making them wait while preparing himself for his one-take perfection. As a matter of fact, on the average "A" picture, seven minutes of film is considered a pretty fine full day's work."

Immediately prior to the scene where Judy breaks down and cries inside Juvenile Hall, Natalie Wood experienced a severe panic attack. Beverly Long found her crying inside the restroom. She recalled Natalie complaining, "I can't do it, I can't do it, I can't. I just can't…I can't cry." But then Natalie started crying. Long remembered telling her, "Natalie, yes you can. Look-you're crying now. Just stay in that moment, that feeling, whatever it is."

In the original script, Jim places the toy monkey on the floor of Juvenile Hall where it begins banging on a pair of cymbals. Plato and three children respond favorably to the toy monkey. Judy, on the other hand, ignores Jim's attempt at levity. The mechanical monkey mysteriously disappears entirely from the film, never to be seen or referred to again.

Initially, the script called for Jim Stark to express his rage and frustration by ranting at a Juvenile Hall officer. The script was changed so that Jim is allowed to take his anger out on the officer's desk. At first, Jim Stark scoffs at the idea, but then he has a change of heart. He smashes the desk with his fists and badly injures both hands. Ray expected Dean to hit the desk without hurting himself. Because Jimmy's style of acting demanded realism at all costs, he pounded and kicked the desk to the point where he sustained injuries to his knuckles. Ray rushed him to Riverside Emergency Hospital where X-rays were taken of both hands. He was fortunate not to have broken more than one bone, but both hands were badly bruised. For the next several days Jimmy wore elastic bandages over both hands.

The scene where Jim and Judy meet the following morning was shot at the Baldwin Hills location in Los Angeles. Jim engages in some friendly banter with Judy and offers her a ride to school. She tells him, "I go with the kids." Just as she rejects Jim's offer, a car pulls up filled with members of Buzz's gang. For no apparent reason, somebody in the car yells "Hey, Stella!" an obvious reference to Brando's Stanley Kowalski in *A Streetcar Named Desire*. Perhaps out of jealousy, Buzz asks Judy about Jim. "What's that?" Buzz inquires. "Oh, that's a new disease," Judy replies. Not satisfied with her answer, Buzz presses the issue. "A friend of yours?" Judy responds by quickly changing the subject. She says to Buzz, "I'm glad they let you out." Judy is possibly referring to the proposed opening scene where Buzz and his gang assault an innocent victim. The assault scene never made the final cut. Judy's line also suggests Buzz may have been arrested after the mugging. For some inexplicable reason the line is left in the film.

The unpardonable act of Jim Stark mistakenly stepping onto the 'sacred' circular plaque near the main entrance of Dawson High School serves to remind the audience that Jim is the 'new kid,' the proverbial outsider. While Stark is being reprimanded by a school monitor, the gang stares disapprovingly at him for his apparent transgression. Already the film is setting up the strong possibility of a confrontation between the outsider and a gang of misfits looking for someone to bully.

In the initial script, Plato recognizes Jim Stark in the hallway at Dawson High School. His locker door is open and taped to the door is a photograph of Burt Lancaster. A Warner Brothers executive ordered that the picture of Lancaster be replaced with a photograph of Alan Ladd. The executive reasoned that Lancaster never made a picture for Warner Brothers and so why give him free publicity, compliments of Jack Warner. Ladd deserved a favorable nod from the studio because of his stellar performance in the hugely successful George Stevens film, *Shane*. During that same sequence, Judy was supposed to have smoked a cigarette inside the school corridor, but the censors refused to allow her character to smoke on school property.

For the first time the knife fight sequence reveals the seriousness of Jim's predicament. Stark is forced to react to the gang's taunts when Buzz pierces one of Jim's whitewall tires with a switch blade. As the air rushes out of Jim's tire, he exhales, as if air has been let out of him as well. Stark tries to diffuse the situation by cracking jokes while he's in the process of replacing his damaged tire with a spare. The original script called for Stark to say to Buzz, "You watch too much television," after Buzz slashes Jim's tire. This comment was later deemed too lame. Instead, Jim says, "You know something? You read too many comic books." Failing to draw Jim into an altercation, Buzz continues to badger him. When the gang starts to mimic a chicken, a clear sign that they mean business, Jim turns on them. "Is that meaning me? Is that meaning me?" Buzz tells him that it does.

According to the original script, Buzz slaps Jim across the face after Stark asks Judy, "Why do you hang around with such rank company?" It was decided Buzz should shove Jim instead. Initially, Ray had assembled a huge throng of teenagers to witness the knife fight. Beverly Long remembered that Ray was schooled on how real gangs rumbled. They kept their 'events' very low-keyed so as not to alert the authorities. Ray drastically reduced the size of Buzz's gang to just a few gang members

The knife fight incident stands in stark contrast to the beautiful California landscape seen in the distance. Ray noted that "Jimmy knew how to move. He was in tune with his body and understood how to use it as a carefully tuned instrument. He learned more studying dance with Katherine Dunham (choreographer) than he did from the Actors Studio. He knew what I wanted - the precision of a dancer."

Jack Warner was deeply troubled in terms of how the censors would react to *Rebel*'s script. He was well aware that the Motion Picture Production Code had been around since 1934. The Code did not allow films to show or make reference to, among other things, nudity, rape, incest, homosexuality, lewdness, obscenity, offensive language, and drug addiction. The Legion of Decency went even further and forbade Roman Catholics from watching films depicting taboo subject matter under pain of Mortal Sin.

The Hays Office regulated the moral content of every film produced in America. Geoffrey Shurlock, an agent working for the Hays Office, reviewed early drafts of the *Rebel* script. He was adamant about cutting the knife scene from the movie altogether. Ray stepped in and convinced Shurlock that he would tone down the scene's violence significantly. After all, it was such a pivotal moment in *Rebel*. Shurlock responded by writing a memo to Jack Warner. He wrote in part: "If this knife duel is to be approved it will have to be treated without too much emphasis, and not shown in too much detail."

Several changes to the script were immediately implemented. For example, the original script called for Buzz to say, "No killing," as he explains the knife fight rules to Stark. Instead, he says, "No sticking," a far less ominous threat. Also removed from the script was the idea of Jim jabbing Buzz "again and again." Dean strongly suggested that no prop knives be used in the film. He wanted as much realism as possible. "We all argued against Dean's decision to use a real knife," Nick Adams recalled. According to Adams, Jimmy gave a look that suggested real switchblades must be utilized. Ray agreed with Dean and so real blades were used. It was illegal to own switchblades in California, so Warner Brothers borrowed several of them from Juvenile Hall. The knives had been confiscated from various gangs in and around the Los Angeles area. Frank Mazzola taught Dean and Allen how to properly handle the weapons in a real fight.

In an attempt to reduce the chance of Dean and Allen getting seriously injured while rehearsing the knife fight, both actors wore metal chest protectors under their shirts. The first few takes were a disaster. Joe Hyams, a reporter covering the filming of *Rebel* wrote: "The boys circled each other gracefully and menacingly but neither one wanted to close the distance enough to make the fight look real: each was fearful of hurting the other." Dissatisfied with the lack of action, Ray called for a break.

Shooting resumed and this time the two actors were a lot more animated. Their jabbing was so intense, the cast and crew thought someone might get seriously hurt. At one point during the action, Ray suddenly yelled "Cut!" Cory Allen had inadvertently nicked a part of Jimmy's ear and blood trickled down Dean's neck. Furious, Jimmy yelled at Ray for stopping the action. "Don't you ever cut a scene while I'm having a real moment! That's what I'm here for!" Immediately after his wound was treated, Dean quickly changed into another clean white shirt and resumed shooting the scene. After the final footage was shot, the crew broke out into a thunderous ovation.

After filming the knife fight scene, Corey Allen went to the Hamburger Hamlet for an inexpensive meal. Ray entered the establishment and approached Allen. Ray told the actor that the knife fight had to be done over again. In fact, every scene had to be redone. Warner executives decided the film had to be shot in color instead of black and white. According to an article in *Time*, CinemaScope pictures had to be shot in color. Apparently, nobody in the front office was aware of this essential tidbit of information. There are those who believe the real reason for the change had more to do with Jack Warner himself. After having watched Dean's magnificent performance in *East of Eden*, Warner became convinced that he had an up-and-coming young star on his hands. The extra cost of filming in color would be more than offset by massive ticket sales.

Mushy Callahan, a former world junior welterweight boxing champion, had coached Jimmy on the set of *East of Eden*. He was instrumental in helping choreograph the knife fight between Jim and Buzz. Dean was on the verge of accepting the role of Rocky Graziano in an upcoming production of *Somebody Up There Likes Me*. Primarily for that reason, he spent quite a bit of time taking boxing lessons from Callahan and another fighter, Roger Donoghue.

Dennis Hopper had this to say about Nicholas Ray: "I got into terrible problems with him because we were both fucking Natalie Wood. Her parents were starting to figure it out, and Nick snitched on me! I was furious with him: the studio came down on me, and he came out of it as pure as snow. So, on the chicken run, I took him aside and told him we were going to get into a fight on the set.

He said, 'You know, someday you're gonna have to figure out how to do things without using your fists, you're gonna have to start using your mind.' At that point, I lost my aggressiveness."

Sometime during the filming of *Rebel*, Jimmy was permitted a day off to prepare for his role in *Giant*. A wardrobe test was scheduled for him, but he never showed up. Instead, he drove to Bakersfield, California to sign up for an auto race. The next day Jimmy raced his Speedster at Minter Field. The conditions were horrific, even for seasoned drivers. He came in third behind a couple of pros and first in his class. Jimmy finished ninth in his second race. The winner of that race, Johnny Von Neumann, drove a Porsche 550 Spyder. Jimmy's car was not in the same class as Von Neumann's 550. From that day forward, Jimmy was determined to own a 550 Spyder. Dean had been obsessed with professional racing for quite some time. Kazan had banned him from racing, but Nicholas Ray was of a different stripe. He encouraged Jimmy to race. "I felt it was good for Jimmy to do something on his own with clarity and precision," he explained.

Jimmy was permitted to voice his opinion regarding the script. He was also encouraged to suggest ideas about character development. One key scene in the original script took place in the parent's bedroom, but Jimmy felt much more comfortable near the staircase in the living room. The staircase became the focal point between Jim Stark and his parents. The mother, who is apparently the dominant member of the family, maneuvers herself to the top of the stairs during a vicious argument while Jim's father remains at the bottom, and Jim is caught in the middle. The positioning of Jim and his parents on the staircase drives home the interconnection between each family member. Ray ordered the art director to build the downstairs area on a sound-stage to replicate his living room and staircase.

Actors playing gang members soon discovered many of their lines had been discarded. Ray had decided there were far too many gang members in the film, and so he used fewer actors. He didn't want the Jim Stark character to be overshadowed by so many other characters when just a handful would suffice. After the film switched to color, actor Ken Miller was fired and Tom Bernard found his lines cut from thirty to just one. You can hear him say offscreen, "I bet he fights cows," a reference to Jim Stark during the scene inside the planetarium.

Nick Adams remained a problem throughout much of the production. He was often accused of stealing impro-visations from other actors. Steffi Sidney claimed Adams stole her bit featuring an impression of Hitler directly after the knife fight sequence. According to Sidney, she had improvised that bit of business during the black and white sequence, but Adams later lifted it and made it his own.

Sadly, many of the actors who played gang members harassed Sal Mineo throughout the entire production of *Rebel.* Subsequently, Mineo became withdrawn and stayed to himself most of the time. According to Beverly Long, Mineo acted 'weird' but that the other actors "could have been nicer."

The cast and crew returned to the Griffith Observatory on Monday and they began filming in color. The initial scenes were shot inside the facility because it was closed to the public, it being the Monday following Easter. At one point of the shoot, Sidney sneezed and Natalie Wood responded by saying, "Gesundheit!" The whole incident had not been planned, but Ray decided to include it in the final cut.

Ray began hearing rumors that Dennis Hopper was having an affair with Natalie Wood. Furious, Ray fired him in front of the entire cast outside of the observatory. Steve Trilling warned Ray he couldn't sack Hopper because he was under contract to Warner Brothers. Ray responded by not directing the actor any further and he gave all of Hopper's lines to Jack Grinnage, another actor who played a gang member. Rumor had it that Ray was also having an affair with Wood.

The planetarium scene is vital to the film because it is at this location where the main characters initially interact with each other. The lecturer tells the students that the problems of humanity are meaningless when compared to cosmic events. He further states that Man, existing alone, won't be missed. When the lecturer references the constellation Cancer, Buzz playfully slides his fingers past Judy's face and grabs another gang member's nose. Jim Stark shares in this lighthearted moment by laughing gently to himself. Immediately after the lecturer mentions the constellation Taurus the Bull, Stark lets out a loud "Moo!" The gang members do not appreciate Stark's sense of humor and they proceed to belittle him. This scene is important at another level in that it establishes a connection between Jim and Plato. The two outsiders gravitate toward one another. Plato asks Jim, "What does *he* (the lecturer) know about Man alone?" Plato's vulnerability is exposed and Jim appears to accept a fellow outcast as his friend.

Ian Wolfe, a veteran actor from the 1930s, played the planetarium lecturer. His first major role had been that of Maggs, Captain Bligh's right-hand man in *Mutiny on the Bounty* from 1935. He had also performed in a couple of Ray's earlier films, *They Live by Night*, and *On Dangerous Grounds*.

Natalie Wood was intimidated by Jimmy's genius. Jackie Perry, a friend of Wood's, recalled her state of mind during the production. "She was scared to death because she felt James Dean could act circles around her. The moment Jimmy begins giggling uncontrollably as he's being frisked by a police officer was both fascinating and alarming to her. His ability to improvise amazed and frightened her. She questioned her ability as an actor and wondered if her performance would register with movie goers."

Actress Ann Doran, who played Jim Stark's mother in *Rebel*, got the role quite by accident. She had been a veteran actress for many years. She made her screen debut in 1922 in *Robin Hood*. She was called in to replace Marsha Hunt as Jim's mother. Doran received a call at her home at six in the morning and was told to report to Warner Brothers studio. No one filled her in on the role or the name of the film she was to perform in. However, she was told that James Dean was starring in the film.

At one point during rehearsals Ray told Jimmy he wasn't satisfied with his performance. Clearly upset, Jimmy walked up to a wall and started banging his head and fists against it. Actress Marietta Canty tried to console a very distraught James Dean. According to Canty, she kindly advised him that if he kept hitting his head against the wall he could develop a concussion. "Who cares?" he replied.

Canty told Jimmy that she cared about him getting hurt. "Well, God doesn't care. Just look at the dirty trick he played on me with my mother and father."

The mansion used near the end of the film was owned by oil tycoon J. Paul Getty. Ray received permission to shoot for five days in mid-April. Getty had planned to demolish the mansion once Ray was done filming inside the facility. The Getty mansion used in *Rebel* was the exact location chosen for *Sunset Boulevard*. At one point Sal Mineo collapsed from swinging a heavy pool hose. The actor was also cautioned to be careful handling the antique Spanish candelabra because it was to be used for an upcoming Liberace film entitled *Sincerely Yours*.

Elizabeth Taylor arrived at the studio for a short visit. Jimmy met with her at the Warner Brothers commissary. They seemed to hit it off from the very beginning. Dean even gave Taylor a ride in his Porsche Super Speedster. Jane Deacy also stopped by to present her client with offers for several Broadway productions slated for the following year.

Jimmy was criticized for imitating Jim Backus' Mr. Magoo character near the end of the film. A studio official advised Dean Mr. Magoo was not a property of Warner Brothers. He suggested that Jimmy should imitate a Warner Brothers cartoon character such as Bugs Bunny. Not surprisingly, Dean totally ignored the official's warning and his flawless impression of Mr. Magoo made the final cut.

Dean's highly unusual acting style was beginning to draw a lot of attention in the press. In an April 8 article, Sidney Skolsky wrote in his "Hollywood is my Beat" column: "Jimmy, before going into a scene, will take a short run around the sound stage, or Jimmy will jump up and down in one place before going into playing a scene. Dean has to be in action before going in action."

Harold Heffernan's column in the *Valley Times* included several revealing quotes from Jimmy. "An actor should never have a best performance. Once he gets in that category, he's a dead duck. He not only limits himself as to his capabilities, but he automatically throws a psychological block at theater goers. I can honestly say I consider my present role in *Rebel* better than the Cal part I did in *East of Eden*. And in each succeeding picture, I shall think of its character as better than the one before. I must always feel that my best is yet to come. If I can't keep such a thought in mind, I'll quit the business."

Jimmy once confessed to Dennis Hopper that he did not intend to make acting his only career choice. "My talents lie in directing even more than acting. And beyond direction, my great fear is writing. I can't apply the seat of my pants right now to write – I'm too youthful and silly, but someday…"

While Jimmy was still making *Rebel*, CBS's *Schlitz Playhouse of Stars* aired an episode in early May called "The Unlighted Road." Jimmy portrayed Jeffrey Latham, a drifting Korean War veteran who unwittingly gets caught up in a racketeering scheme. Dean was paid a respectable $2,500 for just a few hours work. He would never again perform in another episode for television.

Rebel closed down production on May 27, 1955 and post-production activity immediately commenced. Jimmy, Sal, and Natalie were instructed to dub certain parts of their dialogue. Mineo had to redo many of his lines due to his thick Bronx accent. After all, he played a teenager from California. Reportedly, Jimmy also presented problems because he had mumbled many of his lines.

Dean's popularity among movie fans was now soaring. In April's edition of *Motion Picture Magazine*, Jimmy didn't even make the list of most popular movie stars. However, in May's edition he was ranked fourth, just behind Marlon Brando, Tony Curtis, and Rock Hudson. An article in *Parade* magazine had this to say about Dean: "Jimmy dresses like an unmade bed; lives in a one room $30 a month garage apartment; roars to work on a high-powered motorcycle." A publicity man claimed that "one can sit with Dean all afternoon and he won't open his mouth. He's worse than Brando who at least is articulate."

Natalie Wood admitted that her favorite scene in *Rebel* never made it in the final cut. It was a scene with just her and Jimmy. "I was in the car. I was waiting for him and he comes up and we talk to each other. There was a section of the scene where I imply that I've sort of been around, that I'm not really pure. I say to him, 'Do you think that's bad?' And he says, 'No, I just think it's lonely. It's the loneliest time.' I thought it was a wonderful line-right on the cutting floor."

Many of the cast members thought Jimmy and not Ray was the real director. Ann Doran claimed that all Ray did throughout the production was yell, "Turn them over, Action, and Cut." "Jimmy just took over the picture," Doran recalled. Dean and Doran were at odds with each other from the very beginning. "Jimmy and I kind of squared off. He was not too sure of me. The first scene we did together was at the police station, where he was rattled - rattled as a person, rattled as a character. So he was fighting back at anybody…that's just the way he worked. And I tried to play it to him, to give it to him, to be a little too sweet… it gave him something to bump off of. And as I watched him work, and worked with him, it was wonderful, because there was this wonderful giving to you, and giving it back."

Dean had grown fond of Ann Doran during the filming of *Rebel* and often referred to her as "Mom." He opened up to Doran about personal issues and how he still grieved over his mother's passing. Doran listened to Dean with a great deal of empathy and understanding. They continued to see each other right up until Dean left for Texas to begin work on *Giant*.

In Jim Backus' autobiography, *Rocks on the Roof*, he recalled the scene where Jim and his parents argue after the chickie-run. "The crucial scene in *Rebel* was where Jimmy and I had a terrible argument at the top of a staircase, at the climax of which he threw me down the flight of stairs, across the living room, into a chair which went over backward, and tried to choke me to death. There is only one way to do such a scene. I had to remain completely passive and put my trust in Jimmy. If I, for any reason, got tense, we both could have been severely injured or even possibly killed."

"Due to the tremendous intensity with which Jimmy Dean approached his work, people got the impression that he was rude, ill-tempered and surly," Backus recounted. "At first, I must admit, I felt the same way. After I got to know him, I realized that he was very shy, although a very warm person. I was one of the few people who knew what his real ambition was. He secretly wanted to be a baggy pants comedian and was quietly working on a night-club act. Believe me, he would have 'killed' the people."

In terms of Jimmy's genius as an actor, Backus had this to say: "He had the greatest power of concentration I have ever encountered. He prepared himself so well in advance for any scene he was playing, that the lines were not simply something he had memorized – they were actually a very real part of him. Before the take of any scene, he would go off by himself for five or ten minutes, and think about what he had to do, to the exclusion of everything else. He returned when he felt he was enough in character to shoot the scene"

"Jimmy trusted Nick a great deal," recalled Natalie. "And I think Nick was very fatherly towards Jimmy. He really was to Sal and myself as well. But I think Nick just absolutely understood Jimmy, they were completely in tune, their personalities. I guess maybe Jimmy reminded Nick of himself a great deal. So there was never any friction, as there was between Jimmy and other directors that he worked with. It was just a wonderful blend. Nick brought up this feeling of trust in Jimmy."

Stern detested many of the lines used in the final version of the film. He hated the idea of Jimmy's mother staring into the camera and mouthing, "I don't understand. You pray for your children. You read about things like this happening to other families, but you never dream it could happen to yours." According to Stern and many other critics, the line came off as too preachy. The line was actually attributed to the mother of a 19-year-old Los Angeles boy who had recently been stabbed to death by another boy. The mother's quote appeared in the newspaper the day after the incident. Apparently, someone from Warner Brothers must have read the article about the stabbing and suggested that the line be added to the script.

A rather sensitive moment in the film occurs at the crime scene near the end of the film. Jim Stark's father tries to console his distraught son over the killing of Plato. The father tells Jim, "Stand up and I'll stand up with you. I'll try and be as strong as you want me to be." The scene focuses on the father's attempt to make up for the moments when he appeared weak and subservient.

Originally, Ray envisioned a totally different climatic ending to *Rebel*. He wanted Plato to climb to the top of the planetarium and from there he would be shot and killed by police gunfire. An expensive replica of the dome was deemed too costly according to producer David Weisbart and so that plan was scrapped. Stewart Stern suggested that Plato should wave a gun in the air immediately outside the entrance to the planetarium. It would be at this point when alarmed police officers would shoot the seemingly dangerous teenager.

There is real significance in terms of when Plato is killed in the film. He appears to have died sometime around dawn. Stern wanted to show a connection regarding the "doomsday dialogue" between Jim and Plato inside the planetarium and at the base of the dome near the end of the film. Earlier in the picture, Plato asks Jim if he thinks the world will end at night. Jim replies with apparent certainty, "Uh-uh – at dawn."

Stewart Stern and Nicholas Ray were at loggerheads over the director's insistence that the film's ending have a Hitchcock moment. Ray wanted to be seen walking toward the planetarium as police cars leave the crime scene. Stern thought the idea was a bad one, but eventually he gave in to Ray. Dean thought the idea was horrible as well. The director can be seen wearing what appears to be a light-colored trench coat while carrying a business briefcase. Stern claimed that Ray was determined to put his stamp at the end of what would become his most popular and consequential film.

Many of the actors associated with *Rebel Without a Cause* continued to appear on television and in films for several more years. The producer, David Weisbart, moved to 20th Century Fox by 1956. He produced two Elvis Presley films, *Love Me Tender* and *Flaming Star*. In 1967, after completing work on *Valley of the Dolls*, he suffered a fatal stroke while playing golf. He was only 52.

William Hopper, who played Judy's father, appeared as private detective Paul Drake in the popular *Perry Mason* television series. He died in 1970 at the age of 55.

Ann Doran, the actress who played Jim Stark's shrewish mother, continued to work in feature films and on television. She appeared in *The Explosive Generation* (1962), *Kitten with a Whip* (1964), and *Topaz* (1969). She appeared opposite heartthrob Christopher Jones in the television series, *The Legend of Jesse James* in the mid-1960s. Coinsidently, Jones bore a striking and uncanny resemblance to James Dean. She was present along with several cast members of *Rebel Without a Cause* during the unveiling of James Dean's bronze bust at Griffith Park on November 1, 1988. She died in 2000 at the age of 89.

Jim Backus' career flourished on television in the 1960s. He played the shipwrecked millionaire Thurston Howell III on the enormously popular sitcom series

Gilligan's Island. Backus died in 1989.

Nick Adams' appearance in *Rebel* helped him garner a role in the hit television Western series *The Rebel.* He received an Academy Award nomination for a supporting role in *Twilight of Honor* (1963). His career steadily declined and on February 5, 1968, his body was found inside his home by his attorney. He had apparently overdosed on medication he had been taking for a nervous disorder. He was 35.

Dennis Hopper appeared in several feature films including *Gunfight at the O.K. Corral* (1957), *From Hell to Texas* (1958), *Cool Hand Luke* (1967) and *True Grit* (1969). But it was his role in *Easy Rider* that revived his floundering career. He continued to appear in several hit films including *Apocalypse Now* (1979), *Blue Velvet* (1986), *Hoosiers* (1986) and *Speed* (1994). He died from prostate cancer in 2010. He was 74.

Corey Allen's career never really took off after *Rebel.* He had very minor roles in such films as Nicholas Ray's *Party Girl* (1958), *Sweet Bird of Youth* (1962) and *The Chapman Report* (1962). He turned to directing and in the 1980s won an Emmy for directing one episode for *Hill Street Blues.* He died in 2010 at the age of 75.

Sal Mineo appeared as the famous drummer in *The Gene Krupa Story* (1959) and as a Jewish rebel fighting for freedom in *Exodus* (1960). He was nominated for an Academy Award for a supporting role (his second), but lost to Peter Ustinov for *Spartacus.* He turned to directing with various degrees of success. He was stabbed to death outside his Hollywood home in 1976. He was only 37.

Natalie Wood's career had its share of ups and downs

after *Rebel.* She starred in *West Side Story* (1961), *Splendor in the Grass* (1961) and *Love with the Proper Stranger* (1963). In the midst of staging a comeback, Natalie drowned while filming *Brainstorm* (1981). She was only 43.

Rebel Without a Cause would remain Nicholas Ray's greatest achievement. After *Rebel,* Ray searched for another James Dean. Impressed with Elvis Presley's performance in *Love Me Tender,* he wanted the rock and roller to play the outlaw Jesse James in *The True Story of Jesse James.* The role eventually went to Robert Wagner. Ray went on to direct *Party Girl* (1958), *King of Kings* (1961), and 55 *Days at Peking* (1963). He was never able to duplicate his earlier successes and his career subsequently floundered. Ray died from lung cancer on June 16, 1979. He was 67 years old.

Rebel Without a Cause. is beyond question a James Dean film. Jimmy dominates practically every scene he is in. There are some fine moments in the film when Natalie Wood, Sal Mineo, and Corey Allen shine as well. But it is James Dean who fascinates us with his unique brand of acting and magnificent screen presence. There is probably no other actor before or since who could have created a sense of both vulnerability and unhinged anger as well as James Dean in this film. As exceptional an actor as Marlon Brando was, it is doubtful his performance as a bullied teenager would have been as convincing as Dean's sensitive portrayal. Brando simply looked too confident in his own skin. Montgomery Clift, on the other hand, may have been able to tackle the role of a young Jim Stark convincingly had he been a few years younger. But it is James Dean who ultimately fascinates us with his brilliant portrayal of teen-age angst and disillusionment.

CHAPTER 5

GIANT

**Dean as the unruly ranch hand Jett Rink
in George Stevens' classic film *Giant*.**

By 1955 George Stevens' reputation as a great director was unquestioned. Stevens had already earned an Oscar in the Best Director category for *A Place in the Sun*. Like so many others, Jimmy was in complete awe of Stevens' contributions as a film maker. In one interview he went so far as to refer to Stevens as "the greatest of them all – even Kazan." Unfortunately for Dean, he would eventually arrive at a far different conclusion regarding his idol.

Stevens had been directing movies since the early days of silent films. He had directed over thirty Laurel and Hardy shorts. In 1935 he filmed his first smash hit, *Alice Adams*. Four years later he directed *Gunga Din*, and in 1942 he directed *Woman of the Year* starring the incomparable Katharine Hepburn. He served as president of the Screen Directors Guild for several years. In 1951 he directed what would become his greatest and most successful achievement up to that point, *A Place in the Sun*, starring Elizabeth Taylor and Montgomery Clift. He was nominated for best director for *Shane*, but lost out to Fred Zinnemann for *High Noon*. He also received the prestigious Irving G. Thalberg Memorial Award.

Nearly twenty of Edna Ferber's novels had been made into films, a truly exceptional achievement. Edna Ferber's latest novel *Giant* sold very well, but it was frowned upon in Texas. Many of the Lone Star State's proud residents thought the novel made them out to look like racists. To make matters worse, the initial excitement of the book did not last very long, but not for George Stevens. The novel proved to be a hard sell in Hollywood, but Stevens was not discouraged. Instead, the controversy surrounding *Giant* aroused his curiosity. Stevens was certain that all of the terrible reviews criticizing *Giant* was actually beneficial. Evidently, he was a proponent of the oft-quoted tenet that there is no such thing as bad publicity. Stevens explained his point of view. "All of this bombast meant controversy, a healthy and provocative thing. And as such it served to add to my enthusiasm for putting the subject onto the screen in the best and most forceful possible form."

Giant tells the story of Bick Benedict, a young Texas cattle baron who takes a wife while visiting a family in Virginia. Back in Texas he clashes with a defiant, sullen ranch hand named Jett Rink. Rink hits oil on a small piece of land he inherits from Bick Benedict's recently deceased sister. The two strong-willed Texans remain bitter enemies to the very end. Throughout this sprawling saga, Bick's wife Leslie battles against racial prejudice and sexism.

The hatred among many Texans toward the epic novel was alarming. A Beaumont citizen informed a Hollywood columnist, "If you make and show that damn picture, we'll shoot the screen full of holes." Luckily for him the man's rhetoric and empty threats proved greater than his bite. One other Texan's threats went even further. Houston columnist Carl Victor Little had called for a public hanging of Edna Ferber.

Producer Henry Ginsberg found *Giant* to be very provocative. He collaborated with Stevens to produce a film based on Ferber's novel. In 1952 they made an offer for the screen rights to the book. Ginsberg, Stevens, and Ferber agreed to form a production company so they could control the production and distribution of films based on Ferber's future novels. They also agreed not to receive any fixed compensation for their efforts. Instead, they would receive a percentage of the profits from each project.

Giant Productions, which was formed in May of 1953, had a difficult time selling the idea of Ferber's epic story to the movie studios. However, persistence ultimately paid off and *Giant* went into pre-production in 1953. Stevens hired Fred Guiol and Ivan Moffat to write the massive screenplay for *Giant*. At the time, George Stevens' *Shane* had not yet been released to the general public and there were rumors the film was languishing due to undisclosed difficulties. To Stevens' relief, *Shane* finally hit the movie theaters and it became an overnight sensation.

George Stevens knew how to sell his movies. He explained to readers in *The Hollywood Reporter*: "I've always been sold on the idea of the picture-maker standing squarely behind his product. I've taken advantage of every opportunity afforded to go out on the road and help sell the picture I have made - to the press, public, exhibitor and anyone else who might be interested." He told the press that he had traveled "some 30,000 miles of '*Shane*' touring and that he would double that mileage both before and after completing *Giant*."

George Stevens wanted to work with Alan Ladd again, primarily because of *Shane*'s phenomenal success at the box office. Ladd deservedly won high praise for his performance as the mysterious and nomadic gunslinger. Ladd was convinced that Stevens was the greatest director in the history of Hollywood. He wanted Stevens to work with him again on any future project, and that project turned out to be *Giant*. Many top executives in the film industry believed *Giant* was the film to beat at Oscar time.

Not surprisingly, Stevens offered one of the major roles to Ladd. The actor had read and enjoyed the novel and he imagined himself playing the part of the cattle baron Bick Benedict. Stevens, however, had an entirely different idea in mind. He wanted Ladd to play Jett Rink, the surly ranch hand who despises authority. Amazingly, Ladd immediately rejected Stevens' offer. The director tried to convince Ladd that the Jett Rink part was juicier and more substantial than the Bick Benedict character. Ladd mulled the offer over for several weeks, but he eventually decided to reject the opportunity of working with Stevens. He vehemently believed he deserved to play the prosperous rancher instead of the indignant ranch hand. For the rest of his life Ladd would regret turning down what perhaps could have been the greatest role of his long and impressive film career.

Interestingly, Elizabeth Taylor was not George Stevens' first choice for the role of Leslie Lynnton, the young woman from Virginia who marries the successful Texas cattleman. He discussed the role with Audrey Hepburn, his first choice, but she turned the role down. As it turned out, Hepburn would appear in only one Western during her entire career, John Huston's *The Unforgiven* in 1961. It was not an easy film to make. At one point Hepburn fell off a horse and broke two vertebrae in her back. She also suffered a miscarriage due to the fall.

Stevens became inundated with requests from agents on behalf of their well-established clients. Irene Dunn,

Anne Baxter, Grace Kelly, Jean Simmons, and Olivia De Havilland represented just some of the leading ladies requesting serious consideration. His second choice for the role of Leslie was Grace Kelly, whom he referred to as the "most important female star" at that time.

Elizabeth Taylor began her film career at the age of ten and had appeared in a couple dozen films by 1955. She could never remember a time when she wasn't famous. Although she had appeared in Stevens' *A Place in the Sun*, that was certainly no guarantee the master director would place her above the other thirty candidates vying for the female lead in *Giant*. But in the end Stevens eventually chose Taylor for the role of strong-willed, independent minded Leslie Lynnton.

Most of the well-established actors interested in the role of Bick Benedict were much too old as far as Stevens was concerned. Heading the initial list of top contenders for the male lead was the very popular Western film star John Wayne. Other serious candidates included Gary Cooper, Charlton Heston, William Holden, Clark Gable, Robert Mitchum, Earl Flynn, Sterling Hayden, and Robert Taylor. Surprisingly, Burt Lancaster was not given serious consideration. He had starred in many Westerns and was considered an excellent actor by any measure. For a while Sterling Hayden appeared to be the frontrunner, but in the end Stevens rejected Hayden because of his age. Hayden's agent desperately tried in vain to convince Stevens that his client with the help of a little makeup could play a young man in his late twenties, but this suggestion fell on deaf ears.

Welshman Richard Burton was seriously considered for the role of Benedict by Stevens. Burton gave it some thought, but put himself out of the running. While in Spain he sent a letter to Stevens saying that, "I have worked at the 'Texas' material, but to no avail. I just don't seem to drawl in the right places and my 'You-alls' don't quite come off. There are quite a few Texans staying at this hotel – Castellana Hilton – and my efforts totally fail to impress them."

Rock Hudson wasn't even considered a viable candidate for the Bick Benedict role until much later in the process. But in the end, Stevens decided to go with the relative newcomer. Hudson was a former certified mail carrier in his hometown of Winnetka, Illinois. He had been in the navy and was discharged in 1946. He moved in with his father in Los Angeles that same year. After trying to make a living selling vacuum cleaners and driving delivery trucks, he hooked up with a talent agent at David O. Selznick Productions. He starred in several feature films, including *Taza, Son of Cochise*, and more recently, *Magnificent Obsession*.

"Of all the roles," Stevens once related, "that of Jett Rink has been the subject of much speculation, reproof, and discussion." Many established actors were considered for the role of Jett Rink. Veteran stars such as Alan Ladd, Robert Mitchum, Marlon Brando, Anthony Quinn, Charlton Heston and Monty Clift were seriously considered. "More actors have bucked for this part than for any of the others," Stevens remembered. Even Frank Sinatra's name came up for the role of Jett Rink, but that suggestion died a quick death. Stevens just couldn't visualize 'Ole Blue Eyes' as a Texan.

Dean had always wanted to make a film with George

Stevens because the director represented old school film making. Jimmy enjoyed watching and studying films directed by the old masters. Stevens was considered a prime example of old Hollywood, a relic from a bygone era, and he had directed some of the all-time greats Hollywood had to offer. Names like Alan Ladd, James Stewart, Spencer Tracy, Katharine Hepburn, and Montgomery Clift came to Jimmy's mind.

Stevens recalled how he first met Dean. "When Jimmy was working with Gadge (Kazan), he would walk back and forth past our office every day, and soon he started to drop in to talk to Freddy Guiol. When he first came into the office, my secretary was a little concerned about him being there; She didn't know him from Adam. Jimmy and Fred talked about cars and fishing and stuff – not a very fast - moving conversation, mind you - every five minutes somebody said a word."

George Stevens really became aware of Jimmy's talent when he went to see *East of Eden*. "When East of Eden was finished," he recalled, "we went to see it, and the boy was just incredible. I'm not just talking about him as an actor, but it was his acting that made his personality so sensitive. So when we cast the role of Jett Rink – which really called for a tough kind of beefy guy – I said to Fred, 'Hold on to your belt, Fred. What do you think of Jimmy Dean for the part?'"

George Stevens Jr. related a story about the time he and his father saw Jimmy on the screen for the first time. "At dinner he (George Stevens) told of his secretary complaining about a scruffy twenty-four-year-old actor in dirty jeans who loitered around their bungalow. He and Fred

Guiol found the young man to be intuitive and smart. I will never forget the feeling that night at the Egyptian when James Dean appeared on the screen. He was arresting and mysterious with hooded eyes, moving across the CinemaScope frame with catlike grace."

Stevens had watched a copy of "The Capture of Jesse James" in the fall of 1954 and liked what he saw. And what he saw was a young, unknown actor named James Dean. The episode was part of a CBS program called *You Are There*. Impressed with Dean's appearance, he made a mental note of Jimmy's performance and seriously mulled over the possibility of offering the role of Jett Rink to Jimmy.

In the November 1956 issue of *Screen Stories*, Stevens explained how Jimmy landed the part of the surly ranch hand. "Physically and temperamentally, Jimmy Dean was wrong for the part. Jett was a tall, powerful, extroverted character. There were a dozen actors who seemed more likely choices." He went on to comment that "we felt that the part needed an extremely good actor, and so we gave the script to Jimmy to read."

"So the next day I said, 'Here, Jim. I want you to take a look at this script and see how you feel about it. See if it's too far out for you.' He said, 'Okay.' There was about a half hour of conversation between us. He read it, came back to my office, put the book on the table and stood there and shook his head. Now Jimmy Dean had a way of shaking his head so that it could be both positive and negative. He'd shake it up and down, but you'd catch an angle of the negative in it. I could never imitate it. Anyway, Jimmy stood there, shook his head and said, 'That'd be a good thing.' We talked some more and he decided to do it."

Jimmy told Stevens he could play Rink because he would convince himself that he can become Jett Rink. Producer Henry Ginsberg confirmed later that he was convinced Dean was the best choice to play the bad-tempered outsider. "There were many things about this boy," Ginsberg recounted, "that many people wouldn't have overlooked. I overlooked them because he had talent." On March 16, 1955, Warner Brothers announced that Jimmy had been chosen to play the surly, ill-tempered Jett Rink.

George Stevens had heard that Jimmy was an auto racing enthusiast and that made him feel extremely apprehensive. Stevens called Jimmy at home and told him in no uncertain terms not to race while filming *Giant*. Reportedly, Dean promised the director that he would refrain from racing throughout the entire production of *Giant*. Although Jimmy had given his word, Stevens still felt a sense of foreboding.

In May 1955, Stevens and Ginsberg sent a telegram to members of the press. They were summarily invited to attend a luncheon to celebrate the launching of *Giant*. Journalists from several major magazines, including *Newsweek*, *Time*, and *Life* eagerly awaited the festivities. Several days later, the so-called "Chuck Wagon" opened at Warner Brothers studio. Every table inside the fabled Green Room proudly displayed a Texas flag in honor of the Lone Star State. Attendees were treated to large portions of Texas steaks as well as a huge cake in the shape of Texas.

Jack Warner entertained the attendees with some jokes, after which he distributed copies of Edna Ferber's novel. Warner felt somewhat uneasy about the very real possibility that the movie could blow a hole through the film's initial budget due to George Stevens' penchant for shooting practically every scene repeatedly. Warner also knew that Stevens was a stickler for detail. Reportedly, Stevens had examined 1,500 horses before choosing Alan Ladd's horse for *Shane*. The movie mogul even cracked a joke about everyone meeting again, hopefully in the near future. Stevens may have understood Warner's concern about overshooting, but based on the director's subsequent actions, he took the veiled threat none too seriously.

After the preliminary speeches were completed, Stevens introduced the cast beginning with Rock Hudson and Elizabeth Taylor, two of the three major stars in *Giant*. Then Chill Wills, Mercedes McCambridge, Carroll Baker, Dennis Hopper, Jane Withers, Paul Fix and Judith Evelyn were introduced. One actor was noticeably missing from the celebration and Stevens began to grow irritated. Jimmy finally wandered into the room wearing an old flannel shirt, blue jeans, boots, and a cowboy hat. He found himself a corner somewhere, plopped down in a chair, and sat there like nobody else mattered. A cigarette dangled from his lips as he sat motionless. If a photographer came anywhere near his vicinity, he'd throw a pair of dark sunglasses over his eyes. A photographer asked Jimmy to remove his shades, but the star refused. When asked why, Jimmy explained that he had bags under his eyes because he hadn't slept well.

A reporter who was present at the luncheon wrote that when Dean's name was called, "he squirmed a bit in his seat, fiddled with his big horn-rimmed glasses and stared at the floor." Visibly irritated by Dean's lack of cooperation to the slightest request, the reporter responded by saying, "It wouldn't kill you to stand up." Dean ignored her crack and she blasted him with "Who do you think you are – Clark Gable?" None of this goading seemed to bother Jimmy and so he continued to act disinterested in the whole affair.

Dean joined friends Lew Bracker and Joe Hyams after the luncheon had ended. Jimmy removed his sunglasses and revealed a pair of dark bags under his eyes. He looked absolutely drained. When asked what was wrong, he complained that he had hardly slept. He explained that he had been experiencing horrible bouts of depression over the loss of his mom. Jimmy simply could not shake the thought of living in a world without his mother.

Around this time, Jimmy was quoted as having said, "Maybe publicity is important, but I just can't get with it… the newspapers give you a big build-up. Something happens, they tear you down. Who needs it? What counts to the artist is performance, not publicity. Guys who don't know me, they've already typed me as an oddball."

It was exceedingly clear Jimmy did not feel comfortable with the studio establishment. He typically ate alone in the commissary, leaving the impression that he couldn't care less about anyone's opinion regarding his bare feet, shoddy outfits and mussed up hair. Many of Dean's peers and associates were shocked to learn that he was only in his early twenties. He appeared much older in his ragged clothes and unshaven face. One can argue that Dean was ostensibly a beatnik before there were beatniks.

There were those in Hollywood who thought Dean was an unruly ingrate who cared only for himself. Presumably, he once told fellow co-star Carroll Baker that you've got to treat studio heads "like shit." George Stevens Jr. was of the opinion that Jimmy could be gracious and fun to be with, but he could also be disruptive and abrasive toward anyone who crossed his path.

George Stevens was a huge believer in shooting on location. He thought that whatever hardships an actor endures on location will be reflected in the actor's performance. In the late 1930s Stevens had shot *Gunga Din* in the rugged hills of northern California. To the director the Sierra Nevada range looked very similar to the Khyber Pass territory in India. There was simply no legitimate substitute for authentic landscape. As far as Stevens was concerned, fake back lot scenery was a poor substitute for long stretches of mountains and valleys and prairies.

Giant finally went into production in early 1955. The production crew and several cast members traveled to Virginia to film the early scenes where Bick Benedict first meets Leslie Lynnton. Their initial encounter does not go well at all. Bick is incensed by Leslie's insinuation that Texas was actually stolen from the Mexican government. Although Bick is taken aback by Leslie's accusations, he is smitten by her beauty and charm and he falls in love with her. They marry shortly thereafter and subsequently travel by train to Bick's massive ranch in southwest Texas.

After Stevens completed filming the early scenes in Virginia, production moved to Marfa, Texas. The small desert town is located about fifty-nine miles from the northern Mexican border. It is here where Jimmy would spend six weeks playing the part of an obnoxious, defiant ranch hand. The Jett Rink character was based on a real-life upstart Texas oilman by the name of Glenn McCarthy. He was a highly successful wildcatter who later became one of the richest men in the entire state of Texas. McCarthy was also a land speculator who happened to own the future site of the Houston Astrodome.

On June 3 Jimmy traveled to Marfa, Texas to join the production crew and several cast members. The weather in and around Marfa was excruciatingly hot, particularly during the day light hours. To make matters worse, Marfa and the surrounding area was in the grips of a terrible drought. The actual locations used for the film were split between the Worth Evan ranch (Reata) and the Ben Avant ranch (Little Reata). Several hundred curiosity seekers and movie fans typically showed up to watch the filming of *Giant*.

Many of the cast members in *Giant* were absolutely appalled by the isolation of Marfa. There were no lively nightclubs or movie houses. Mercedes McCambridge called the location, with perhaps some exaggeration, "the ugliest landscape on the face of the earth." Marfa's schools and cemeteries, like many towns and cities throughout America at that time, were segregated. Caucasian children enjoyed much better facilities than Mexican American children. Sadly, segregation would continue to be the norm for quite some time.

Marfa was rather small and quaint, particularly in comparison to any large city like Los Angeles. It had a grocery store, a couple of bars, a few small hotels and motels, and an old movie theater which had gone belly up. While most of the cast members stayed in one of the hotels, the three male leads were lucky enough to reside fairly comfortably in a private home. In their free time, Rock Hudson, Chill Wills, and Jimmy drank Lone Star beer and played poker well into the night.

George Stevens was a master at marketing his films and *Giant* was no exception. He encouraged amateur camera clubs to come visit Marfa and take pictures of the cast and crew as well as the Ryan ranch. Stevens believed that an open set policy accounted for a great deal of free publicity. Not just ordinary folks visited the set, but reporters and journalists came in droves from all over the world to report on one of the most publicized epic films in years.

Unlike several actors who absolutely hated Marfa, Dean thrived on the location. Having been well acquainted with small towns, Jimmy had no problem adapting himself to Marfa and its citizens. He felt entirely at ease with regular people who weren't part of the establishment. As a serious actor he also realized the importance of learning the local lingo and habits of Marfa's inhabitants.

Jimmy appeared to crave womanly attention and affection. He became very close to Elizabeth Taylor and Mercedes McCambridge. "I can't tell you how he wanted to be patted," McCambridge recalled. "He was the runt in a litter of thoroughbreds, and you could feel the loneliness beating out of him." Many years later McCambridge's gravelly voice would be heard spewing out Satan's obscenities in *The Exorcist*.

Dean was very fortunate to have worked with Elia Kazan and Nicholas Ray. They were open to any suggestions he may have had in terms of character and plot development. Stevens was of a different stripe altogether. The master planned out each scene just the way he wanted it. He rarely listened to what any cast member had to say about different interpretations. One could argue that Stevens was on the same page as Alfred Hitchcock, a man who once famously said, "All actors are cattle." Stevens rarely discussed how a scene should play out other than the way he wanted it. To him, an actor was simply a necessary tool required to help tell a story.

Screenwriter Ivan Moffat wrote a profile of Jett Rink. Many people familiar with the young star may have thought this profile mirrored their perception of Dean's personality. "Of all the people in our story, the only one who did not grow up or mature, or become reconciled to this earth, was the most successful of them all: Jett Rink himself."

June marked the first month Dean actually performed in front of the cameras. As many as 2,500 residents from nearby Marfa and surrounding towns stood and watched as Jimmy and Elizabeth Taylor shared a scene together. George Stevens was not thrilled with Dean's performance and halted filming. Clearly upset, Jimmy suddenly walked toward the crowd and stared at them for a moment. Then he unzipped his fly and proceeded to urinate in front of all the adoring fans. After he was done, he zipped his fly back up and returned to the set and advised Stevens he was ready to proceed with the scene.

Dennis Hopper recalled having a conversation with Jimmy about this incident. When asked why he pulled such a stunt, Jimmy simply replied, "I was nervous. If you're nervous your senses can't reach your subconscious and that's that – you just can't work. So, I figured if I could piss in front of all those people and be cool about it, I could go in front of the camera and do just about anything at all."

Hopper constantly shadowed Dean around the set, pleading for advice on how to act natural during a performance. Backed into a corner, Jimmy told Hopper to simply do things rather than to show what you're attempting to do. In other words, if you're going to smoke a cigarette, then smoke it, don't make a big production out of it. Stop the gestures. He warned him that the simpler the action, the more difficult it will be to act naturally. It finally dawned on Hopper that the proper methodology was to work internally rather than to work externally. This was Method acting in a nutshell.

The scene between Leslie and Jett reveals a vulnerable and sensitive side of the sullen ranch hand. Rink invites Leslie into his dilapidated shack for some tea. She obliges him and sits down while he prepares her tea. She notices a book, *How to Speak and Write Masterly English*, laying on a table. Hanging on a wall is a newspaper clipping depicting a photograph of Leslie on her wedding day. She seems moved by Jett's unexpected hospitality, graciousness and eagerness to improve himself.

Curiously, the scene is not reflected anywhere in Ferber's novel. The author vehemently complained to Stevens and Ginsberg about the absurd notion that Leslie could be so kind and considerate toward someone as lowly and unseemly as Jett Rink. Against Ferber's protest, Stevens kept the scene in the final cut because it depicted Jett Rink as somewhat of a sympathetic character instead of a complete louse. More importantly, Stevens realized that any scene James Dean appeared in was pure gold.

June 8 represented the first day of shooting at the ranch. According to one source, the scene where Bick and his wife Leslie first arrive at the ranch was shot a mind-blowing seventeen times. Evidently, Stevens' attention to detail and authenticity was being put on full display from the outset.

Jett Rink is seen lurking in the background as the newlyweds climb out of their automobile. You are deliberately drawn to this lone figure peering at the young couple as they hug each other in front of their Victorian gothic style mansion. The significance of this character is unclear up to this point. The very fact that the camera repeatedly keys in on this mysterious figure suggests a certain importance to the character. He's ostensibly working on a car, but you're not really sure. Finally, there is a close-up shot of the stranger smoking a cigarette, still focusing solely and quietly on the Benedicts, but you never clearly see his eyes or his expression. Many years later, Stevens revealed his take on Dean's first appearance in the film. "In Giant there is a big house, there is the couple. There is an insignificant character in the background very remotely....the eyes of the audience go with the vanishing point to that little figure. Nothing has told them [the audience] that the insignificant figure is an important man, but they have discovered that this fellow is of interest."

A few moments later it's revealed that the man is none other than Bick's surly ranch hand and future nemesis, Jett Rink. Bick confronts Jett, telling him "The next time I tell you to git – you git!" Jett politely asks him to cool off and explains that Bick's sister Luz had asked him to stay on the ranch because she needed his help while Bick was away. Jett does a double take as he glances over at Leslie. He offers to shake Leslie's hand but she refuses. Rink then awkwardly climbs into Bick's Duesenberg and mutters to himself, "Nobody's king around here – No matter what they think." It is at this moment when Bick's antagonist is clearly revealed.

The three-story mansion's facade seen in *Giant* had been constructed at another location and subsequently shipped to Marfa in dozens of sections for reassembly. The entire three-sided structure had a hollow interior and was partially supported by huge utility poles. The cost to build the entire façade totaled a staggering $200,000, an enormous amount of money in those days.

The big, sprawling barbecue sequence was shot from June 9 through 11. Once again, Jett Rink is seen prowling around in the background, the consummate outsider, apparently uninvited to partake in the festivities. A moment later he's seen sprawled out in the back of Bick's humongous Duesenberg, his legs stretched out, his boots resting comfortably on top of the seat in front of him. It appears he might be fantasizing about actually owning the monstrous vehicle. In the background, well beyond where Jett is relaxing is the Big House in all of its gaudy, Texas splendor. Amazingly, at no time in the film does the audience see Jett Rink riding a horse. He is either driving a vehicle or working on an oil derrick. In a sense, he represents the modern Texan who's never satisfied with traditional values.

After a few days of filming, Jimmy realized that Stevens' directorial style was not conducive to his own notion of filmmaking. Stevens had developed the reputation of controlling practically the entire production from start to finish. He was by no means an "actor's director," meaning he did not allow for character development during the filming of his pictures. Much like Alfred Hitchcock, Stevens believed actors were simply a means by which a story could be told and nothing else. Jimmy felt as if his contributions were not being fully appreciated by the director.

Dean didn't like the way Stevens utilized an actor's time. Jimmy would show up early in the morning for a scheduled scene, only to find out he wouldn't be needed until much later that day or sometimes not at all. At one point, Dean became so frustrated, he didn't show up to work at all. Stevens did not take Jimmy's apparent protest lightly. Dennis Hopper recalled one particular blowup between Stevens and Dean.

"Stevens was furious with Jimmy, took him up to Jack Warner's office and threatened to kick him out of Hollywood. After they chewed his ass off for about an hour, Jimmy said, 'Are you finished? Well let me tell you something. I am not a machine. I may be working in a factory, but I'm not a machine. I stayed up all night Friday to do that scene. I prepared *all night* for that scene. I came in ready to work and you kept me sitting all day. Do you realize I'm doing emotional memories? That I'm working with my senses – my sight, hearing, smell, touch? Can I tell you that for every day you make me sit, there'll be two days next time? Then three, then four? You'll pay for it. And you're not going to stop me from working. Now let's get back to the set.'"

Entertainment gossip columnist Hedda Hopper spoke with Jimmy about the friction between Dean and the director. In her book *The Whole Truth and Nothing But*, Hopper wrote about her conversation with Jimmy.

"I've been reading some bad things about you. I understand you haven't been showing up for work. 'Right, I haven't. Stevens has been horrible. I sat there for three days, made up and ready to work at nine o'clock every morning. By six o'clock I hadn't had a scene or rehearsal. I sat there like a bump on a log watching that big, lumpy Rock Hudson making love to Liz Taylor. I know what Stevens is trying to do to me. I'm not going to take it anymore.'

"I hold no brief for Stevens," I said, "but what you don't know is that there's a man on that set who put the whole deal together. Henry Ginsberg, Stevens, and Edna Ferber are partners. It took Henry two years to do it. This is the first time in Ferber's life she took no money, only an equal share of the profits as they come in. If this picture goes wrong, Stevens can walk out, and those two years of Ginsberg's life go down the drain."

"I didn't know," Jimmy said.

Carroll Baker revealed her experience with George Stevens in her autobiography *Baby Doll.* The title of the book is in reference to a highly controversial Elia Kazan film she appeared in. According to Baker, the master director expected the entire cast to be ready in full make-up and costume on the days they were scheduled to perform. The horrific summer heat in Texas made it that much more unbearable. Jimmy finally rebelled after sitting around for three days waiting to be filmed. On the fourth day he simply refused to show up.

Baker further claimed that Elizabeth Taylor, Rock Hudson, and Dennis Hopper "carried on like absolute fools – laughing and crying and partying and drinking, and hardly ever sleeping. Jimmy refused to participate in these social gatherings. Slowly but surely, Jimmy befriended Taylor, sensing that she empathized with lost souls. He stole Elizabeth away from us. She went off mysteriously each evening with Jimmy, and none of us could figure out where they went."

Dean continued to protest against Stevens' methodology when filming a scene. Stevens shot each take from multiple angles and then selected the most impressive reels of film to create a masterpiece. It was an extremely expensive way of filming a picture, and each scene took several hours to process. Many actors found a way to adapt to Stevens' very unusual technique, but Jimmy was definitely not one of them. "I hate pictures," Jimmy told a friend, "and Stevens is no better than the others. Only he can't go wrong. Do you know he gets more footage, more film, than anybody else at Warner Brothers?"

Jimmy detested the way Stevens ran the production. And he certainly didn't appreciate Stevens' lack of patience for actors who wanted to experiment with their character. Countless takes occurred and this process unnerved Jimmy to no end. He firmly believed that two or three takes were all that was necessary, whereas Stevens might shoot anywhere between six to sixteen takes before he was satisfied with a scene.

Dean and Stevens frequently clashed because the director typically had a preconceived notion how a scene should play out. He rarely if ever asked any of the cast members for their input. Jimmy took a totally opposite approach. He worked best when allowed to experiment with the characters he portrayed. He was fluid, whereas Stevens was less flexible in terms of character development. "When an actor plays a scene exactly the way a director orders," Jimmy once noted, "it isn't acting. It's following instructions."

The fifty-one-year-old director shot each scene from a wide variety of angles. That allowed him to choose the best angle in the editing room. Stevens controlled his actions by indicating where he wanted his actors to stand. When Jimmy tried to explain to the director that this technique was foreign to his style of acting, Stevens stood his ground. Stevens told an interviewer that he "wanted to nail him quick." He went on to explain that "there's always a testing period in the beginning of a picture when an actor wants to find out who's boss. Jimmy was predisposed to do a scene as he saw it, and I had my way of doing it. Very seldom does an actor entirely favor the director's way. Some actors, and Jimmy was one of them, are too ready to debate the director's point of view, and I found myself imposing it."

George Stevens gave this account about Jimmy's penchant for tardiness: "He wasn't really late, but still, other people would have to sit around and wait. I told Jim I knew what he was going through, but he had a job to do and he'd better figure out a way to do it, and if he couldn't handle it, he'd better go to the front office and see about taking some time off to relax. The lateness stopped and we never talked about it again." Tom Pryor, a correspondent for the *New York Times*, watched some early rushes of the film. At one point, Jimmy appeared on the screen and Stevens turned to Pryor and said, "Just once, I'd like to fire that bastard." Much like Elia Kazan, Stevens never truly warmed up to Jimmy. Both directors admired his inventiveness as an actor, but despised his rebelliousness. In the end, Kazan and Stevens proudly patted themselves on the back for recognizing Dean's unique talent and permitting him to perform in their films.

Beginning on June 22, Stevens filmed the scene where Jett Rink measures off a section of his newly inherited parcel of scrubby, desolate land. Stevens didn't like the way

Jimmy walked along the property line, so he lined up some stones along one side of Rink's property and instructed Jimmy to follow the row of stones. Visibly upset, Dean tossed the stones aside. He cautioned Stevens never to over instruct his acting. Jimmy ran through the scene again, but this time he took long strides as he walked along Rink's property line. Stevens cautioned his camera man to "Stay on him." The director instinctively knew that Dean's performance in this pivotal sequence was going to be exceptional. Then Dean did something that was clearly not in the script. He instinctively climbed a windmill which bordered Rink's scrubby parcel of land. Stevens ordered the camera men to keep the camera focused on Jimmy as he climbed to the top of the structure. Dean then stood for a moment as he gazed over Jett's property. Then he slowly sat down on the edge of the platform, carefully crossed his arms, leaned forward, and stared out over the spread like a Texas land baron.

Though he might not have realized it at the time, Stevens had just experienced the genius of Jimmy's interpretation of Jett Rink's mindset. Stevens eventually understood Jimmy's self-imposed motivation for climbing the windmill. "Here's the most bereft piece of ground in the world," Stevens later commented. Stevens assumed the viewing audience would realize "the feeling within a man's heart for possessing things. It's like he owned Manhattan Island."

Film critic James Powers had this to say about Dean's masterful performance in this powerful sequence. "Stevens had directed him beautifully, taking full advantage of Dean's unusual ability to act with his whole body as much as his voice or face. A single scene, where Dean paces out the first land he has ever owned, is unforgettable. Shot from below, with only Dean's expressive silhouette seen against the sky, it has rhythm and beauty and says more than a thousand words could."

In early 1956 Stevens gave an account of what it was like to work with Jimmy during the filming of *Giant*. He recalled that Dean would sit alongside Stevens and watch the dailies, challenging the director not to like any portion of his acting. Dean wasn't just performing for the camera on the *Giant* set, he was also closely observing Stevens' technique of filming sequences and taking meticulous notes on how each camera was set up for each shot. He drew rough sketches of camera angles and kept them in a booklet. He informed a couple of friends that he wanted to own his own production company so that he could make independent films. "I want to direct because I can be a better director than actor."

Hobnobbing with the other leads in the film was never a serious option with Jimmy. He spent much of his spare time socializing with Bob Hinkle, his dialogue coach. Hinkle recalled that he showed Jimmy several rope tricks he had learned over the years. "I taught him how to build a loop with the rope. There's a lot more to it than just making a big loop. You have to work it so that you can throw if off your hand just right. Before we came back to Hollywood, Jimmy was an expert." Jimmy and Hinkle frequently hunted jack rabbits at night. Over a six-week period they shot over two hundred rabbits and a couple of coyotes. "People told me he was moody and hard to get along with," Hinkle recalled, "that he clammed up and wouldn't talk. That was a lot of nonsense. He could talk your arm off."

Not everyone got along with Dean. Chill Wills, who shared living quarters with Jimmy, eventually moved out. Reportedly, the two men got into a heated argument over Jimmy's guitar playing. Clearly upset, Wills finally smashed the guitar and stormed out of the house.

Elizabeth Taylor got to know Jimmy very well during the filming of *Giant*. They frequently stayed up until early morning talking about life in general. "He would tell me about his past life," she remembered. "Some of the grief and unhappiness he had experienced, and some of his loves and tragedies. Then, the next day on the set, I would say, 'Hi, Jimmy,' and he would give me a cursory nod of his head. It was almost as if he didn't want to recognize me, as if he was ashamed of having revealed so much of himself the night before. It would take maybe a day or two for him to become my friend again."

On July 12, after the second camera crew had completed their filming of Dean involving several exterior shots, Jimmy traveled back to Los Angeles. Bad blood still existed between the star and the director. On July 23, Jimmy had decided not to show up on the set. Stevens' associates informed the director that the actor had apparently been looking for a place to live somewhere in the San Fernando Valley. Stevens was so furious, he told several associates that he would never work with Jimmy again. He sent a memorandum to Warner Brothers explaining how horrible Dean's work ethic was. The memo detailed every instance in which Jimmy acted irresponsibly by needlessly holding up production.

Gossip columnist Dorothy Manners attacked Dean for allegedly acting so juvenile and ungrateful to Stevens and the production crew. Manners claimed that Jimmy told her he was "just dog tired." "Everybody hates me and thinks I'm a heel," he was quoted as saying to Manners.

Jane Deacy immediately jumped into action on behalf of her client. Deacy went to Warner Brothers to negotiate a new contract for Dean. Her first demand was very clear. She wanted Jimmy to be compensated as much as one-hundred thousand dollars a film instead of receiving the current rate of fifteen hundred dollars a week. Demand number two stipulated that she wanted Warner Brothers to allow her client to do nine pictures over the next six years. She wanted Jimmy to be allowed to form his own production company under the studio for the purpose of developing movie and television projects. Finally, he would be permitted to appear on television in different capacities and appear in the theater.

If Warner Brothers agreed to Deacy's demands, then her client would begin performing in the next nine films for the studio after he completed his work on MGM's upcoming project, *Somebody Up There Likes Me*, a film about middleweight Rocky Graziano's turbulent life and brutal boxing career.

Jimmy sat down with Hedda Hopper and unloaded a lot of what was on his mind. "I don't like that bullshit from anyone. I realize I'm only a small cog in a big organization like Warner's, but I'm an individual. I think I have talent, and with just a little bit of kindness, I would do anything in the world for him. I'm insecure? I feel that George Stevens is insecure – and even that I could stand, but I'll be damned if I'll be his servant. Nobody's going to be allowed to step on me."

Stevens' cinematographer recalled just how sensational Dean's performance was. "While we were making *Giant*, I think we all knew that young Jimmy Dean was giving a performance that not even the extreme adjectives of Hollywood could adequately sum up. It's not often a unit gets a feeling like that."

John Rosenfeld wrote an essay for *Southwest Revue* about a year after he visited the set of *Giant*. He found Jimmy to be the most interesting of all the actors on the set. He remembered that the young star needed very little direction from Stevens. The writer was amazed at Jimmy's sense of dedication during his free time. At one point he watched Dean gallop past a car as he tossed his hat into the open vehicle. Then he returned to the car and collected his hat as he galloped past it. He performed this very unusual and complex stunt repeatedly until he perfected it. He further noted Stevens was "eloquently appreciative of his actor."

Dean made good use of physical objects throughout the film. For instance, Jett Rink's hat became an essential fixture to his character. Lee Strasberg commented on Jimmy's use of his hat in *Giant*. "You see every actor doing it now...pulling his hat down...it's become a style. But there was nothing loose about it...when Jim did it. Inside he was saying, 'Gee, that blankety-blank,' but he couldn't quite say it. So, he pulled down that hat."

Marfa was just another small, unpretentious town to Jimmy. He felt thoroughly comfortable living and working there. He enjoyed spending time with the citizens of Marfa.

One could argue that Marfa may have reminded him of Fairmount where he grew up. He made a point of talking with cowboys and ranchers from the area. Coincidently, the movie theater in Marfa and Fairmount shared the same name, The Palace. Reportedly there was even a street named 'Dean.'

Dean was very cordial and friendly with the local citizenry of Marfa. School-age girls were mesmerized by his good looks and pleasant demeaner. One fan recalled that Jimmy enjoyed signing autographs and chit chatting with some of his admirers, whereas Rock Hudson and Elizabeth Taylor rarely intermingled with fans. One fan in particular was pleasantly surprised to find Jimmy very warm and congenial, just the opposite of how the newspapers described him.

Rock Hudson, on the other hand, found Marfa to be a "desolate place," hot, dusty, and with absolutely nothing to do. He bitterly complained that "the weather just put its thumb on us and kept us right down into the ground." What Hudson found even more upsetting and offensive was Jimmy's ability to 'steal' scenes from actors such as himself.

Hudson confessed to *The Hollywood Reporter* that he didn't like Jimmy. "He hated George Stevens," Hudson complained, "didn't think he was a good director. And he was always angry and full of contempt." He claimed Dean never smiled and was always sullen and ill-mannered. "While doing a scene in the give and take," Hudson continued, "he was just a taker. He would suck everything out and never give back."

Hudson imagined he would be the big star in *Giant*.

At the time it made sense because Jimmy was almost a complete unknown in the movie industry. Hudson reasonably believed the film critics would praise his performance not so much because of his acting, but because of his strong presence. To Hudson's constant annoyance Jimmy had an uncanny ability to attract attention to himself in a scene even if he had very few lines. Being the inventive genius that he was, Dean occasionally performed tricks with a small length of rope or he would reset his hat slightly to emphasize his everchanging moods. In scenes where Hudson literally towers over Jimmy his screen presence wasn't enough to trump Dean's exceptional acting.

Dean was clearly not a traditional actor who showed up on time, mouthed his lines, and congenially got along with the director and the rest of the cast. A reviewer for *The Nation* wrote, "Rock Hudson, Elizabeth Taylor, Mercedes McCambridge…are people who will neither astonish nor disappoint. They do what they are told and make up in experience for what they lack in imagination. For excitement, Stevens added James Dean and, as always, Dean supplied it."

Hudson vehemently detested Dean's unusual preparations before appearing in a scene. He thought it was not only unnecessary, but disruptive and extremely annoying. He hated the way Jimmy jumped high in the air with his knees tucked under his chin or how he ran around the set as fast as he could while shrieking "like a bird of prey."

One scene in particular upset Hudson. On July 19, Stevens filmed the sequence in which Bick Benedict informs Jett that his sister Luz had bequeathed Rink a parcel of land known as Buffalo Waller. Benedict tries to buy

Jett out by offering him $1,200 in hard, cold cash right then and there. Jimmy played Jett Rink as an uncouth, fidgety character nervously playing with a length of rope. Bick helplessly looks on as Jett mumbles his appreciation, but cagily decides to keep the land instead. In effect, Jimmy took an ordinary scene in which he had very few lines and made it his own. Hudson may have found Dean's 'scene stealing' disgraceful, but Stevens certainly did not. This was exactly the kind of acting the master director wanted out of Jimmy, and he got exactly what he wanted – a first class, take no prisoners performance. Stevens later commented about Jimmy's uncanny ability to draw everyone's attention to his performance. "Whoever is in the screen, it's Dean you watch – even if he has nothing to say!"

George Stevens spent a great deal of time with Rock Hudson because the star required many retakes due to apparent bouts of shyness. He stumbled over his lines and had difficulty nailing a scene down. Elizabeth Taylor received quite a bit of personal attention from Stevens as well. She had difficulty understanding her character at times, but eventually she found a way to elicit a convincing performance.

Stevens once made this observation about James Dean: "As an actor, Jimmy had the ability to reach people with movement. Using himself as a kind of clay, he could mold psychological impediments into his speech and into his movements. Instinctively, he seemed to understand all the impediments people have when they try to communicate with each other."

In time, Hudson would occasionally say a few kind words about Jimmy. He stated in an interview years later that he had "never worked with an actor that had so much concentration. I mean, he could think about this piece of glass and that's it, nothing else would interfere; which, I felt, was brilliant." With that said, he also thought Montgomery Clift would have done a much better job as Jett Rink.

By the end of July most of the cast and crew returned by train to Los Angeles. Each train car proudly bore the word Giant on it. Hudson continued to complain to his wife that *Giant* had turned out to be Jimmy's picture and not his. Dean remained in Texas to perform in some additional scenes related to Jett Rink discovering oil on his property. In an interview Jimmy stated the following: "It took me a while to accustom myself to the Texas way of life, but I regard the weeks as particularly well spent. In my desire to learn more about the character of Jett Rink, I learned much about Texas and Texans. I've gotten to like the state and the people so much. I'm apt to talk like a proud Texan even after Giant is completed."

Although Stevens respected Dean's phenomenal talent as an actor, he hated the amount of time Jimmy took to prepare for his scenes. "Dean was not my choice for the role. He had the ability to take a scene and break it down… into so many bits and pieces that I couldn't see the scene from the trees, so to speak. From a director's point of view that isn't the most delightful sort of fellow. All in all, it was a hell of a headache working with him."

One of the key scenes in *Giant* occurs after Jett Rink discovers oil for the first time. He drives up to the Big House, climbs out of his delipidated truck and slowly approaches Bick and company. Completely covered in oil from head to foot he proudly announces, "My well came in, Bick," and then laughs hysterically. Bick and Leslie tactfully tell him they're happy for him. Jett quickly ignores their condescending attitude and begins stepping onto their porch. He approaches Bick and boasts, "I'm rich Bick. I'm a richie. I'm a rich boy. Me – I'm gonna have more money than you ever thought you could have. You and all the rest of you stinking sons of Benedicts." Bick tells Leslie to go on inside the house but she refuses. Jett turns to Leslie and tells her, "Oh my, you sure do look pretty, Miss Leslie. You always did look pretty. Just pretty now good enough to eat." Furious, Bick slugs Jett in the face and knocks him down. Bick's friends pull him away from the fallen Jett and hold him back. As Bick is being held, Jett gets back on his feet and mockingly tells Bick he's acting about as "testy as an old cook." While Bick's guard is down, Jett punches him in the face, then the stomach, and finally smashes him in the groin. As Bick crumbles to the floor in sheer agony, Jett quickly leaps off the porch, jumps into his truck and drives off. Uncle Bawley stares at Jett Rink as he speeds off into the distance. He then offers these words of wisdom to the injured and embarrassed Benedict. "Bick, you shoulda shot that fellow a long time ago. Now he's too rich to kill." Thus ends the first half of *Giant*. Ironically, the location where *Giant* was primarily filmed produced no oil. The studio arranged for oil derricks to be erected in and around the property where Jett Rink discovers oil.

The beginning of the second half of *Giant* takes place twenty-five years later. It is shot almost entirely indoors. By the end of the first half of the film the audience has probably had its fill of the vast Texas landscape. The beginning of the last half of the film depicts a significantly older Jett

Rink looking approvingly over his oil holdings in the form of derricks scattered throughout his vast empire. The rest of the film deals with issues that are still relevant today, such as racism, feminism, and generational divisions.

The make-up staff gave Dean a receding hair line, gray hair, and a pencil-lined mustache. Sal Mineo, barely able to recognize his idol, said he saw him "outside the commissary, a little old man with a mustache." Some people on the set thought Jimmy closely resembled Howard Hughes, the reclusive tycoon. Ever the perfectionist, Dean was deeply concerned about his ability to pass convincingly as a much older Jett Rink.

Jack Warner wasn't at all happy with Stevens' directorial methods. In his opinion, Stevens wasted time and money shooting and reshooting scene after scene. The director respectfully took Warner's concerns under advisement, but he continued to do things his way. Warner realized he had to strike a balance between repeatedly warning Stevens about cost overruns and deadlines and allowing him to make the picture his way. Stevens understood Warner's point of view, but he felt he had a job to do as well. After all, Stevens had a reputation to uphold in terms of churning out high quality films, no matter the cost. There was one scene, for example, where Bick Benedict and Old Polo watch in disgust as Jett Rink's oil trucks roll past them. The scene is very brief, but unfortunately it required up to forty men and many hours of shooting to film the short sequence.

On August 2, Stevens shot the scene between Jett and Luz Benedict II inside the Bottle Room of the Emperador, Jett Rink's new hotel. A drunken Jett Rink attempts to flatter Luz into marrying him. Carroll Baker, a Method actor who played Luz, remembered Stevens took several takes. She also knew that Dean was notorious for changing his lines repeatedly. The actors never played the scene the same way on each take. "There was always something new he would throw in," Baker remembered. "It was never exactly the same twice over, and I'd have to be listening and watching him just like the girl in the story – a bit tense and apprehensive."

At one point during this scene, Jimmy leaned over and rested on his left side as he positioned himself directly behind Baker. It appears Jimmy may have been attempting to convey a sense of awkwardness in Jett's pursuit of Luz. His skewed and twisted frame represents yet another example of Dean's uncanny ability to utilize his entire body in order to convey certain emotions.

In Carroll Baker's autobiography, she refers to Jimmy as someone "fully committed to the scene, entirely responsive to the other actor or actors, and yet a fierce competitor for first place. He was so driven to be better than anyone else that when it looked like a tie, he wasn't above fighting dirty to regain an edge." According to Baker, George Stevens made the two actors perform their big scene over and over again so that he'd have plenty of outtakes on hand. He took the outtakes home and played them for his friends. Reportedly, Stevens had said that the nightclub scene with Jimmy and Carroll reminded him of "a great boxing match between actors."

Baker explained some of the improvisation that went on between them. "It went something like this: Jimmy sat back in the booth...I stretched forward, I sat back...Jimmy slumped to one side, I sipped my drink...Jimmy rolled his cigarette, Jimmy tossed his head…I took the rose out of the vase and twirled it…and on, and on, and on, take after take, during twenty-one hours of filming!"

Beginning on September 2, Stevens shot the banquet sequences in which Jett Rink is honored by important Texas dignitaries for his mercurial rise to power and influence. Too drunk to get up and speak, Rink slumps forward in his chair and collapses. His face hits the table and he passes out. Jimmy was very upset with his performance and asked Stevens if they could work together on the sequence. Stevens agreed. "We did this darned thing for two nights," Stevens recalled, "and then he came back to shoot it, and I think he did an excellent job with it – certainly as much as I felt the scene could do."

In their final scene together, Jett and Bick square off inside Jett Rink's liquor storeroom. Moments earlier, Rink had hurt Bick's son during an altercation. Rink is totally inebriated and Bick Benedict, so thoroughly disgusted with his nemesis, refuses to throw a punch at him, saying instead, "You ain't even worth hitting. Jett – you wanna know something true? You're all through."

Nick Adams was asked to dub some of Jimmy's lines in the scene where Rink finally attempts to give his big speech. According to Stevens, Dean's voice was so inaudible, it was difficult to make out what he was uttering. Dean wasn't around for post-production and so Stevens asked Adams for help. Unfortunately, Adams did a poor job imitating Jimmy's voice. It's curious that Stevens, a true stickler for detail, allowed such a horrible Jett Rink impression to remain in the film.

One of the last scenes in *Giant* is nowhere to be found

in the novel. Bick Benedict stands up to Sarge, the blatantly racist owner of a roadside diner. Sarge tries to eject a Mexican family from his establishment, but Bick Benedict stands up to the bigot. A fist fight breaks out between the two men, but Bick is no match against the burly, much younger opponent and he is beaten unmercifully. Bick lays on the floor nearly unconscious as Leslie tries to comfort him. In spite of her husband's terrible thrashing, Leslie proudly considers Bick to be a real hero fighting against racial discrimination.

When Jimmy arrived back in Los Angeles he reconnected with a nineteen-year-old Swiss-born actress named Ursula Andress. They had met prior to Dean leaving for Texas to do *Giant*. One evening in mid-September Jimmy and Ursula attended a sneak preview of *Rebel* at the Village Theater in Westwood. Dean appeared pleased with his performance. Andress recalled that the pair "would fight, then make up, then fight again." According to the actress, Jimmy drove like a person possessed, taking terrible chances with his life as well as hers. Unable to cope with Dean's erratic behavior, Andress stopped seeing him and started dating actor John Derek.

In 1962 Andress would play Honey Ryder, the first James Bond heroine in *Dr. No*, also starring Sean Connery. The next year she starred opposite Elvis Presley in *Fun in Acapulco*. She was beginning to gain traction in Hollywood. Her later films included *4 For Texas*, *Casino Royale*, and *What's New Pussycat?*

On September 17, William Orr, a Warner Brothers executive and Jack Warner's son-in-law, approached Jimmy about doing a commercial sponsored by the National

Safety Council. It was a public service announcement cautioning drivers about the perils of speeding on the open road. According to Orr, Jimmy refused to sit through a five-minute interview with Gig Young, an established film star. After much prodding, Jimmy reluctantly agreed to do the commercial. Dean wore his Jett Rink outfit and stayed in character throughout the entire staged 'interview.' He fiddled with a length of rope that had a weight attached to it. At the end of the commercial Jimmy spoke directly into the camera and cautioned, "Take it easy driving. The life you might save – might be mine."

In late September Alec Guinness and Jimmy met at the Villa Capri around dinner time. Guinness had just arrived in Hollywood to do a picture with Grace Kelly called *The Swan*. Guinness had just finished filming *The Ladykillers,* a crime caper set in London. Three years later he would win an Academy Award for Best Actor for *The Bridge on the River Kwai*. Four years after that he would portray Prince Faisal in arguably his finest film, *Lawrence of Arabia*.

The two men chatted for a while and then Dean asked Guinness if he wouldn't mind taking a look at his brand-new Porsche Spyder. Guinness stared at the race car for a moment and then asked Jimmy how fast could he drive it. Dean told him it could go as fast as 150 miles per hour. Suddenly, a sickening, ominous feeling of impending doom came over Guinness. The English actor turned to Dean and said, "Please do not get into that car, because if you do, you'll be dead in a week."

Chapter 6

TRAGEDY STRIKES

**Dean and auto mechanic Rolf Weutherich on their way
to an auto race in Salinas, California.**

On Friday, September 30, 1955, at approximately 7:30 a.m., Jimmy heard his name being called by his landlord, Nicolas Romanos. Romanos was also the maître d' at the Villa Capri, Dean's favorite restaurant. He had been renting his $250 a month log house for the past several weeks. Curiously, the place had no bedroom, just a loft with a cot. Dean had to climb a ladder and crawl through a trap door to get to it. The house had a seven-foot stone fireplace in the living room and an old wheel lamp that hung from a beamed ceiling. A large white bearskin rug covered the living room floor. The house was conveniently located at 14611 Sutton Street in Sherman Oaks, California. Unfortunately, it was destroyed in a fire several years later.

Dean had installed a pair of large speakers which were attached to a beamed ceiling. He listened to a lot of music on his new hi-fi system. Jimmy enjoyed listening to a wide variety of music, including Bartok, Bach, Brubeck, Jimmie Rodgers, and Frank Sinatra. Bullfighting posters and a pair of mounted horns hung from the walls. Cameras, tape recorders, bongos, and records could be found scattered throughout the house. A reporter noticed a hangman's noose strung ominously from the ceiling, further evidence of Dean's morbid sense of humor.

Dean had recently dropped off his precious Siamese kitten Marcus at Jeanette Doty's apartment. Elizabeth

Taylor had given Jimmy the kitten as a gift. He had asked Jeanette if she would take care of Marcus while he was away and she agreed. He had left her specific instructions on exactly what to feed his kitten. He explained to Jeanette that he was leaving town to race at the Salinas Municipal Airport over the weekend. After the races he had planned to visit San Francisco before heading home.

Jimmy had purchased a brand-new silver Porsche 550 Spyder two weeks earlier for $7,000, the most money he had ever spent on a single item. He had traded in his Porsche Speedster to help pay for it. The Spyder's body was made of thin aluminum and it could go as fast as 150 miles per hour. "It'll be hard to catch," Jimmy liked to boast. Dean and Bill Hickman, a fellow racing enthusiast, had driven the race car up and down the highway several times between Sherman Oaks and Los Angeles in order to break it in before Jimmy's big race. Bill Hickman sat in the passenger seat while Dean practiced shifting, cornering, and accelerating in his super-charged Porsche Spyder.

Jimmy slid into a pair of faded jeans and his signature white T-shirt and stepped outside of his apartment at around 7:45 a.m. Waiting for him was his beloved Spyder which he had hooked up to the back of his Ford station wagon. Earlier in the week, Jimmy had driven his car to George Barris' customizing shop in Compton. He had the number '130' painted in black on both doors and across the front and back of the race car. He also had the words, 'Little Bastard' painted in bright red across the back bumper. Evidently, the name had been given to him by his racing buddy, Bill Hickman. In turn, Dean referred to thirty-four-year-old Hickman as the 'Big Bastard,' presumably because of his friend's massive size. Apparently, it was an inside joke between the two friends. Hickman would later portray a hitman in two films, *Bullitt* (1968) and *The Seven-Ups* (1973). He also went on to play a New York City detective in the 1971 film, *The French Connection*.

Jimmy arrived at Competition Motors at around 8 a.m. Rolf Weutherich, Dean's mechanic, immediately started checking the Spyder over. Twenty-eight-year-old Weutherich was a former Luftwaffe pilot during the final stages of World War II. He had worked as a service mechanic at Competition Motors for several years. He had met Jimmy at a California track and the two race car enthusiasts became close friends. Rolf spoke with a thick German accent. Weutherich helped roll the Porsche off the trailer and into the garage where the German would make some final adjustments.

At approximately 10:00 a.m. Bill Hickman and Sanford Roth entered the facility. Roth's purpose was to photograph Jimmy at the race track and also during his vacation in San Francisco. Dean had first met Roth on the set of *Giant*. At that time Roth was finishing up his photo essay on Dean for *Collier's*. Hickman and Roth were instructed to follow Jimmy in his Ford station wagon to the races in Salinas. Jimmy had originally planned to have his Spyder towed to Salinas, but at the last minute he decided to drive the car himself. He reasoned that the Spyder needed breaking in and also it could use some more mileage. Apparently, nobody tried to convince him that this might be a terrible idea. The car was really meant for racing, not driving on the open highway. But this was Jimmy's show and he called all the shots. Supremely confident in his ability to drive the

Porsche Spyder, getting into an accident on a bright, sunny day was probably the last thing on his mind.

Sometime around noon Winton Dean and Charles Nolan Dean, Winton's younger brother, arrived at the garage to see Jimmy off. Dean seemed genuinely excited to see both of them. Jimmy proudly drove his uncle around the block several times in his Spyder. Afterward, Rolf completed all the necessary adjustments to the race car's engine, even repairing the safety belt on the driver's side. While Rolf cleaned up, Jimmy and some friends, including his father and uncle, walked a short distance to the Hollywood Ranch Market for some donuts and coffee. Shortly afterward they returned to Competition Motors. Charles Dean warned his nephew to be careful driving the Spyder. Jimmy just laughed and replied, "That's my baby!" At around 1:30 p.m., Roth took a picture of Jimmy and Rolf sitting in the Porsche with their arms raised in a triumphant gesture. Jimmy slipped a pair of clip-on sunglasses over his prescription eye glasses. Dean's safety belt was left unfastened as he drove off.

The two vehicles stopped off at a filling station off Ventura Highway. Jimmy refueled the tank and then they drove toward Highway 99 heading north through the mountains. Dean and Hickman took turns passing each other on the open road. Roth took several pictures of Jimmy driving his Spyder. Dean continued wearing his sunglasses, but Rolf had forgotten to bring a pair Jimmy had given him. Dean smoked his Chesterfield cigarettes almost as fast as Rolf could light them.

Around three o'clock the caravan stopped off at Tips, a roadside diner. Jimmy enjoyed a glass of milk and Rolf consumed an ice cream soda. Hickman and Roth finally arrived at the diner and ordered sandwiches. Jimmy talked about the upcoming races scheduled for Saturday and Sunday. He had never formally signed up for any of the events, but he was hopeful the sponsors would still allow him to race. Dean was advised not to drive too fast during the race, that experience was more important than winning at this stage in Jimmy's racing career.

The caravan continued heading north on Highway 99. As they entered Kern County the topography turned from hilly terrain to gently rolling hills. At around 3:30 p.m. a highway patrolman was cruising Highway 99 when he spotted the small, silver Porsche Spyder traveling north as he drove south. According to the patrolman, the vehicle appeared to be speeding. Patrolman Otie V. Hunter immediately made a quick U-turn and started pursuing the Spyder. He clocked both cars at seventy miles per hour, well over the fifty-five miles per hour speed limit. Hunter pulled up in between the Porsche and the Ford station wagon and hit his horn in an effort to get their attention. Jimmy quickly pulled over.

Hunter climbed out of his patrol car and approached the Spyder. He warned Jimmy of his excessive speed and asked to see his driver's license. Jimmy explained to Hunter that he was on his way to Salinas to race and that the Porsche needed more mileage on it so that it would be ready for the event. He informed the patrolman that his car wouldn't run right under eighty. Hunter wrote out a ticket for speeding anyway. He gave Hickman a ticket as well because he was going 20 miles per hour faster than the allowed speed limit for a vehicle pulling a trailer.

The caravan arrived at Bakersfield and stopped off at Stan's Coffee Shop. They stayed for a while before heading north. As they drove out of town, they noticed Disney's *20,000 Leagues Under the Sea* starring Kirk Douglas was playing at a drive-in. *East of Eden* was scheduled to begin its run the following week. Moments later they drove by Minter Field which had previously served as an air base during World War II. Jimmy had raced there five months earlier. He finished first in his class and third overall. During that same meet Arizona race car driver Jack Drummond died when his car flipped over.

Dean and his caravan turned west onto Highway 466 at Famosa. The stretch of road has since been renamed Highway 46. Barbed wire lined the shoulders of the route on both sides, possibly to help keep tumbleweed from rolling onto the highway. There were quite a few cars on the road around this time. Eastbound traffic included families on their way to a high school football game between the Drillers and the Bearcats. Westbound motorists included drivers towing their race cars to different racing events.

Around five o'clock Jimmy and Rolf arrived at Blackwell's Corner, a combination filling station and grocery store located at the intersection of Highway 33 and 466. Dean bumped into Lance Reventlow, a fellow race car acquaintance. Twenty-one-year-old Reventlow was the son of the Woolworth heiress Barbara Hutton. He had also been ticketed for speeding. Reventlow showed off his 300 SL Mercedes Gullwing and Dean did likewise with his Porsche Spyder. Reportedly, Hickman approached Jimmy and warned him about cars turning in front of him. He cautioned Dean that it was beginning to get dark and his silver Porsche might be hard to see. Jimmy laughed and told the 'Big Bastard' not to worry. Dean and his entourage left Blackwell's Corner and continued heading north where they planned to have dinner in Paso Robles at around 6:00 p.m. As Jimmy sped off, his safety belt remained unfastened.

Twenty-three-year-old Donald Gene Turnupseed was born in Portersville, California, a rural community nestled in the eastern Central Valley. When Turnupseed turned twenty in 1952, he enlisted in the navy. He served aboard a hospital ship somewhere off the coast of Korea. Turnupseed was discharged after he had completed his tour in April, 1955. He wanted to acquire an electrical contractor's license, so he enrolled at the California Polytechnic Institute, or Cal Poly, in San Luis Obispo. The G.I. Bill helped pay for his tuition. The student drove a black and white 1950 Ford Tudor back and forth between Cal Poly and Tulare, where he lived. He put up with a lot of rough teasing because the Tudor resembled a police car.

Around 4:30 p.m., Donald Turnupseed climbed into his 1950 Ford Tudor and headed home for Tulare for the weekend. He drove north on Highway 101 to Paso Robles. He crossed over the Salinas River and drove east on Highway 466. He passed through the rural town of Shandon shortly after 5:30 p.m. He saw a sign that indicated Cholame was up ahead.

Tom Frederick, a twenty-eight-year-old beekeeper and his brother-in-law Don Dooley were fast approaching Cholame. Frederick's brother Paul was following them in a separate car. They were on their way to a high school football game in Bakersfield. The Paso Robles Bearcats were playing the Bakersfield Drillers. They had just passed Moreno's

Cholame Garage on their left. It was a combination filling station and grocery store. Turnupseed passed Frederick's car at about 60 miles per hour. Both cars were not far from where Highway 466 and 41 intersect. Highway 466 and 41 joined to form the prongs of a Y fork.

Turnupseed approached a highway sign that indicated Bakersfield was straight ahead and another sign which indicated Hanford was on the left. The only STOP sign in the entire area was located where Highway 41 merged with 466. Unfortunately, there was no left turn lane for motorists wanting to enter Highway 41 off of 466. The student veered left heading toward Highway 41. He suddenly slammed on his brakes and the Ford Tudor skidded thirty feet. Turnupseed pulled the steering wheel as hard as he could to the right, but it was too late. At this very moment, the Porsche Spyder and the Ford Tudor collided. The driver's side of the Spyder's front end smashed into the Ford's left front end. Upon impact, Rolf's head smashed up against the Spyder's dash board. The left front fender on both vehicles was ripped away as the race car flew up into the air. According to one witness, the Spyder flipped over several times before landing near the edge of the highway facing west. Rolf had been thrown from the Porsche and landed several feet from the Spyder. He laid in a prone position, bloodied and dazed.

Tom Frederick pulled his car over and immediately ran over to the Spyder. He saw another man still in the car. According to Frederick, he saw a lot of blood and two arms that were twisted and lifeless and bent every which way. Tom flagged down a motorist and had him race up the highway to Moreno's garage for help. Dazed and disoriented, Turnupseed slowly climbed out of his car and was seen rubbing his left shoulder. His nose had a deep gash and he was bleeding, but other than that he appeared fine. Paul Frederick rushed over to the Spyder and knelt close to the driver's head. Paul held his sunglasses under Jimmy's nose to see if it might fog up, but it did not. He was fairly certain the driver was dead.

A registered nurse jumped out of her car and ran over to the wreckage. After carefully observing Dean's body, she was convinced he had sustained a broken neck based on the position of his head and neck. She checked Jimmy's wrist and quickly determined there was a faint pulse. According to Tom Frederick, the driver of the Ford Tudor repeatedly told him he didn't see the Porsche Spyder. "I couldn't see him," the driver claimed.

The impact of the crash had caused Jimmy's body to be thrown backwards. He lay on his back with his arms outstretched. His head rested eerily over the passenger door, hanging lifeless at a sickening 90-degree angle, another indication that his neck had probably been broken.

Just before 6 p.m., California patrolman Ernest Tripke received a call regarding an accident where 466 and 41 meet. He was just coming on duty when he was alerted. He sped east on Highway 466 toward the location of the accident. Patrolman Ronald Nelson, a friend of Tripke, also received a call. He switched on his police siren and raced toward the scene of the collision.

Moments later an ambulance driven by Paul Moreno arrived at the scene. Rather than parking the ambulance on the same side of the highway close to the wreckage, Moreno, for some inexplicable reason, parked on the opposite side of the highway from where the Spyder rested. Forty-one-year-old Paul Moreno, a giant of a man, and Collier "Buster" Davidson, his much smaller assistant, ran over to the wreckage.

Meanwhile, Bill Hickman and Sanford Roth were fast approaching the site of the crash. At first it looked to them like a road block, but when they drove closer to the wreckage, they noticed an ambulance and several police cars and the 1950 black and white Ford Tudor. They saw what was left of the Porsche Spyder, a crumpled mess of metal lying next to a utility pole. Hickman pulled over and ran toward the Spyder, his heart pounding faster and faster. Hickman bent down where Dean lay and held his friend in his arms, crying for Jimmy to open his eyes, or at least show some sign that he was still alive.

Roth started snapping pictures of Jimmy's lifeless body. One foot was entangled near the clutch as he lay pinned down in the wreckage. Hickman yelled at Roth to stop taking photos. "You son of a bitch!" he screamed. "Help me, come here, help me!" Roth immediately stopped snapping pictures of Dean. It's unclear what became of those particularly grizzly photos. Hickman felt Jimmy's body move slightly and then he heard air escaping from his friend's lungs. It may have been Jimmy's last breath leaving his torn and twisted body. No one knows for sure. Hickman felt fairly certain that Dean had succumbed to his injuries and died inside the wreckage.

Moreno pulled Jimmy's foot loose from under the steering wheel, and then he and Davidson gently lifted Dean onto a gurney. They strapped Jimmy securely and covered him with a blanket. Roth snapped pictures of

Moreno and Davidson carrying Jimmy toward the ambulance which was parked directly across the highway. After they placed Jimmy inside the ambulance, the two men returned to the wreckage.

Roth snapped more pictures of Moreno and Davidson standing next to the seriously injured Rolf. Towering over the wreckage stood Turnupseed, his hands partially hooked into his pants pockets. The two men strapped Rolf onto the gurney and carried him across the narrow highway. They carefully slid Rolf and his stretcher next to Jimmy's. Davidson maneuvered his way inside the back of the ambulance and sat down. With the back door now securely closed shut, Moreno slid behind the wheel and drove off with the siren blasting its signature sound. Moreno headed west toward the nearest hospital, War Memorial. It was located about thirty miles away in Paso Robles. Hickman and Roth jumped back into the station wagon and followed Moreno to the hospital.

In the meantime Officer Donald Nelson began taking statements from witnesses. Nelson looked at Turnupseed and asked him what had transpired. The officer did not detect any evidence of alcohol on the student's breath.

"I was going to turn," the student explained. "When I got to the intersection, I started to slow down. Just before I made my turn, I looked straight down 466 but didn't see the car. I was already in my turn when I heard the tires and saw him. I tried to miss him, but I couldn't." Nelson asked Turnupseed how fast he was going at the time of impact. The driver claimed he was traveling at 55 miles an hour. Turnupseed showed the officer his driver's license and provided him with his home address.

Moreno continued driving west on 466 when a car suddenly swerved in front of him. The car slammed into the side of the ambulance, causing Davidson to be thrown against some ambulance tanks at the head of the two gurneys. The collision's impact woke Rolf up. He looked over at Jimmy and saw that his face was covered by a respirator. He could not tell if Jimmy was dead or alive. Moreno jumped out to inspect the damage and then climbed back in and continued driving west. He noticed the left side of the ambulance had a fresh crease.

Moreno finally reached the emergency entrance to the hospital. It had taken him approximately twenty minutes to reach his destination. Hickman and Roth pulled up directly behind the ambulance. Moreno and Davidson removed Rolf from the ambulance first and delivered him over to the hospital attendants. Moreno told the attending physician Dr. Robert H. Bossert that they should check Dean's condition first. The doctor climbed into the back of the ambulance and examined Jimmy. Bossert immediately concluded that he had suffered a broken neck. A slight grating noise could be heard when he moved Jimmy's head. His face was covered with bruises and large cuts. It appeared he had lost a lot of blood judging by the whiteness of Dean's skin. He concluded both forearms were broken and a leg had been fractured. Dr. Bossert declared Jimmy dead after completing his examination of the body. Bill Hickman and Sanford Roth were in shock. This *couldn't* be happening. Moreno's next stop was the Kuehl Funeral Home in Paso Robles.

Meanwhile, news of the horrible tragedy traveled quickly. An operator at War Memorial Hospital telephoned Warner Brothers studio. A policeman working for the studio received the call and was informed that James Dean was dead. The policeman immediately called Henry Ginsberg and relayed the terrible news. Ginsberg called Dick Clayton, Jimmy's agent, and informed him of Jimmy's passing. Clayton in turn called Jane Deacy and told her the bad news. Clayton drove to Winton's residence to inform him of his son's death. Evidently, he didn't want Dean's father to find out via a news broadcast. He felt it would be more humane to hear the horrific news from someone Jimmy knew personally.

Moreno pulled up to the mortuary where Martin Kuehl worked. Kuehl took possession of the body while Bill Hickman stood nearby, smoking one cigarette after another, clearly still shaken by Jimmy's death. Just a few hours ago his friend was happy and looking forward to the races in Salinas. After the mortician cleaned up Jimmy's wounds, he allowed Hickman to see Jimmy. Hickman noticed his friend had several cuts and his forehead appeared pushed in. Because Jimmy had lost so much blood, his body appeared gaunt and blue veins were very noticeable just beneath the skin. Hickman was so traumatized by the tragedy that he couldn't sleep for several days.

Hickman stayed at the mortuary as Kuehl prepared the body for burial. The mortician handed Bill Hickman Jimmy's wallet. He examined the contents and discovered there was no money in it. Evidently, someone had removed all of Jimmy's remaining cash and pocketed it. Hickman was outraged that somebody, possibly Moreno or Davidson, had stolen money from Jimmy's wallet. Cars started slowly passing by the mortuary after fans became aware that Dean had died just a few hours earlier in a brutal car collision near Paso Robles.

Kuehl examined the body more closely and noticed the left side of Jimmy's face was badly damaged as compared to the right side. He also noticed small pieces of glass were embedded in the skin. Both upper and lower jaws were broken. He also determined that there was hardly any blood left in the body. The mortician determined that an autopsy was not required because Jimmy's death was clearly caused by a two-car collision. Patrolman Tripke stopped by the mortuary around 8 p.m. to inspect Jimmy's body for his official report. He had requested a blood sample in order to determine if there was any evidence of alcohol in Dean's body. The mortician's phone became inundated with calls from not only within the United States, but from around the world. One hysterical caller shouted into the phone, "He's not dead! I know he's alive!"

Back at the crash site, Officer Nelson took pictures of the two cars involved in the collision and the point of impact and any skid marks. Several other patrol officers arrived at the crash site and inspected evidence that might shed some light on the cause of the accident. Moreno returned to the scene of the accident with a tow truck. He towed the Ford Tudor and the Porsche Spyder to his garage. Turnupseed asked an officer what should he do next now that the authorities were done asking him questions. He was without any means of transportation because his car had been towed away. He was told to catch a ride with someone. Evidently, it was perfectly legal in 1955 to bum a ride in the state of California. Not knowing who to ask, he started walking north along Highway 41 toward Tulare which was a good fifty miles away. He was able to hitch a ride along the way. Turnupseed arrived at a Tulare hospital at around 11:00 p.m., whereupon a doctor examined and treated his injuries.

Winton Dean, accompanied by the chief of security for Warner Brothers, arrived at Kuehl's funeral home on Saturday, October 1, the day after the accident. He was greeted by a very traumatized Bill Hickman who embraced Winton. Dean's father signed for and took possession of all Jimmy's personal effects. He had brought with him a suit for his son to be buried in and he chose a simple bronze casket. Dean's bloodied clothing was subsequently destroyed. Before leaving, Winton made arrangements for Jimmy's body to be transported to Los Angeles.

The evening of the crash, George Stevens and several cast members were in the Warner Brothers projection room screening rushes. The phone rang and Stevens answered.

"No-my God!" he yelled. "When? Are you sure?" The director hung up the phone, stopped the rushes, and turned on the lights. He was clearly upset.

"I've just been given the news that Jimmy Dean has been killed."

No one said anything at first. It was too much to process. It sounded like a bad joke. Carroll Baker recalled that "death was present in that room."

"I can't believe it, George; I can't believe it," cried Elizabeth Taylor.

Stevens glanced over at her.

"I believe it," Stevens said to her. "He had it coming to him. The way he drove, he had it coming," he snarled, insensitively.

Visibly shaken, Taylor hurried to her dressing room and threw up. Overwhelmed with grief, she left for the day.

The next day George Stevens called Taylor back to the set to complete her final scene. After all, Stevens thought, the show must go on. Taylor told Stevens she had been up the entire night crying over Jimmy's death. She was obviously too distraught to work. Stevens told her he didn't care. She needed to come in and finish her scene. Pressured to return to the set, Elizabeth worked on the scene. Before she left for the day, she screamed at Stevens. "You are a callous bastard! I hope you rot in hell!"

Taylor suffered from excruciating abdominal pains the next day and was rushed to the hospital. Reportedly, she punished George Stevens by not reporting back to the set for two weeks. Production had to be shut down until she returned.

On the evening of Jimmy's accident, Natalie Wood, Nick Adams and Sal Mineo had gone to see Arthur Miller's play, *A View from the Bridge*. The play featured Richard Davalos, the actor who had played Caleb's brother in *East of Eden*. Afterward, they enjoyed dinner at a restaurant in Chinatown. "We were all together – all Jimmy's friends," Natalie remembered. "We were talking about what a great future he had, and how in a few years he'd be the greatest thing that ever hit Hollywood. Jimmy's going to outlive everyone of us at this table."

After dinner they walked back to the Warwick Hotel where they were all staying. Natalie went straight to bed because she had to get up early the following morning to perform in a musical version of *Heidi*. The next day, Wood's limo driver broke the news to her about Jimmy's death. After the live broadcast of *Heidi*, Natalie immediately returned to the hotel. Still in shock, she spoke to Sal

Mineo over the phone about Jimmy and how much they missed him. "We heard the terrible, unbelievable news of Jimmy's death in an accident," Wood recalled. "And we realized that he had been killed almost as we were talking about him the night before."

The morning after the accident a local reporter called Turnupseed to find out what had happened. "I looked, but I didn't see him coming," he explained. He also told the reporter that he had overheard a man telling a cop that Jimmy had sped past him shortly before the incident. He complained that a patrol officer did not offer to help him make his way home to Tulare. He also complained that he didn't receive treatment for his injuries until five hours after the collision.

The day after the accident Mercedes McCambridge and her husband drove up Highway 466 on their way to San Francisco. They stopped at a store to fill up on fuel. Mercedes overheard a woman telling her husband that they had Jimmy's Spyder in the garage. The actress ran over to see the car and screamed, "Oh my God!" in disbelief. The sight of the crumpled, blood smeared race car was more than she could bear. A woman working at the store told the actress that a local man had caused the accident when he turned in front of the Porsche. Not long after, Mercedes came down with a fever and was taken to Saint John's Hospital for treatment.

The day after Jimmy died his home in Sherman Oaks was burglarized. Joe D'Angelo, Dean's stand-in for *Giant*, reported that the star's home had been ransacked by "vultures." Alarmed by what had just occurred at his home in Sherman Oaks, Jimmy's friends removed for safe keeping everything they could out of his other home on West Sixty-eighth Street in New York City.

On Monday morning the deputy coroner John Stander signed a death certificate. The official document indicated that on September 30, 1955 at 5:45 p.m., James Byron Dean had primarily died from a broken neck along with several other fractures and internal injuries.

The afternoon edition of the *Paso Robles Daily Press* carried the story of Jimmy's death on the front page with pictures of the two wrecked cars and a small picture of Dean. It mentioned that the deceased was one of two 'speed-loving young men' involved in the accident. Without any sufficient, credible evidence, the newspaper had already concluded Jimmy must have been speeding immediately before the collision, thus clearly causing the accident.

John Stander loaded the casket carrying Jimmy's body into a hearse and drove it to the Los Angeles Airport. Stander stopped along the way to refuel. A group of young people stood and stared, apparently realizing Jimmy's body was inside the black hearse. Stander removed the Kuehl Funeral Home placards from the outside of the hearse so as not to draw attention to the fact that the deceased star was inside. Winton Dean met Stander at the airport and received the casket bearing his son's body.

Meanwhile in Paso Robles, Sheriff-coroner Paul E. Merrick announced that he was ordering an inquest to ascertain the true cause of Jimmy's death. The *Daily Press* named several witnesses who would be testifying in the Paso Robles City Council Chamber at 10:00 a.m. the following Tuesday. The article indicated that Jimmy had a 'reputation for fast driving' and that he had been ticketed for speeding earlier that day. Evidently, certain people in the media were determined to paint Dean as the sole culprit in the fatal collision.

Inside the War Memorial Hospital in Paso Robles, Rolf Weutherich lay suffering from excruciating pain caused by a broken jaw and smashed femur. A young blonde woman who claimed to be an acquaintance of Jimmy's asked Rolf what had happened around the time of the accident. Heavily sedated with painkillers, Rolf tried to answer her questions. He told her he was conscious inside the ambulance and he believed Jimmy was still alive, although he couldn't be certain. He also noticed the Pan Am ring Jimmy had given him was no longer on his finger.

On Wednesday, October 5, Sheriff Paul E. Merrick, Deputy District Attorney Harry Murphy, coroner's assistant Albert Call, and officer Ernest Tripke visited Rolf to see if he could shed some light on the fatal collision. Judith Rooney was on hand to record the deposition. Rolf answered questions through an interpreter. He recalled quite clearly patrolman Hunter handing Jimmy a speeding ticket near Bakersfield. Once they turned onto Highway 466, Rolf was under the distinct impression that Jimmy was traveling somewhere between 60 to 65 miles per hour. Rolf admitted that Dean did travel faster at times, but he was not traveling faster than 65 miles per hour when the two cars collided. Just before the crash, he believed the Porsche was in fourth gear. He wasn't sure if Jimmy had changed gears just before the collision.

Murphy asked Rolf if he remembered seeing any oncoming vehicles swerve away from Jimmy about five minutes prior to the accident. Rolf replied that there was in fact an oncoming car in and around that time period, but it did not swerve to get out of the way of the Spyder. Rolf also mentioned that Jimmy was wearing sunglasses.

Rolf said he couldn't recall if Jimmy had said anything immediately prior to impact and he couldn't recall if Dean yelled or screamed. He remembered Jimmy turned the wheel to the right in an effort to avoid a collision with the Ford Tudor. He said he didn't remember if Jimmy applied the brakes. Rolf admitted Jimmy wasn't wearing the safety belt at all during their entire trip to Salinas.

Murphy asked him how long prior to the impact did he notice the Ford Tudor coming toward them. Rolf replied that he couldn't remember seeing the car approach them – that everything happened so fast. Rolf explained that he could not remember anything just prior to impact, but that he did remember seeing the Ford Tudor at the time of the collision. The following morning, Rolf was transferred to the Glendale Sanitarium for further treatment and observation.

The funeral service for Jimmy was held on Saturday, October 8, at 2:00 p.m. at the Fairmount Friends Church in Fairmount, Indiana. Three thousand people showed up to pay their respects. Flags at the Warner Brothers Studio were flown at half-mast. Sadly, Hollywood was not well represented at Dean's funeral. Nicholas Ray, Elizabeth Taylor, Natalie Wood, Julie Harris, and Edna Ferber did not attend. Some sent flowers instead. Warner Brothers sent a wreath. Producer Henry Ginsberg, Nick Adams, and Jimmy's buddy Jack Simmons were thoughtful enough to pay their respects. The pallbearers were all former classmates of Jimmy. After the eulogy was read praising the actor's short but consequential life, a church organist solemnly played Dvorak's "Going Home." Shortly thereafter Dean was buried in Park Cemetery, less than a mile from where he grew up on his aunt and uncle's farm. For two weeks guards were stationed around the grave site to deter intruders from stealing pieces of the tombstone or perhaps absconding with Dean's corpse altogether.

Winton Dean inherited his son's estate, which totaled approximately $96,000 after taxes. Jimmy had signed off on a $100,000 accident insurance policy just prior to his death. Many of Dean's personal assets were sold, including his horse Cisco, his Triumph motorcycle, and his Ford station wagon. Dean also had a balance of about $3,000 in an account with the Chase National Bank of New York.

Martin Landau sent a letter to the Winslows expressing his sadness over the tragic death of his close friend. Reflected below is a portion of that letter.

I am writing this letter because I know and understand how much you meant to Jimmy. It is hard to believe that he is gone. Last Christmas night, Jimmy had dinner at home with me and my family. For three years my mother had heard me speak of Jimmy, and although they had spoken to him on the telephone, this was the first time they had ever met him. They practically fell in love with him, as did my entire family, and feel now as though they've lost a son.

The news of Jim's death was a terrible shock to me. I can't begin to imagine what his loss must mean to you who raised him and were closer to him than anyone else in the world. I want you to know how terribly sorry I am.

I wish I were better at expressing my sympathy. This boy had every reason in the world to live. None of the comforting phrases apply. All there is to be grateful for is that, young as he was, he had shown his genius, and that remains, even though a thin substitute for his continuing life.

On October 11 at approximately 10:00 a.m., an inquisition into the death of James Dean was held in Paso Robles, California. The inquest was headed by coroner Paul Merrick. Eight witnesses were called on to provide testimony and two depositions were read into the official record. Amazingly, Donald Gene Turnupseed was never called on to provide his side of the story. It cannot be overstated that refusing to include Turnupseed as an essential witness to the fatal collision in which he was directly involved is shocking to say the least. No one at the inquest even offered an explanation as to this strange and puzzling development. It will be shown that other witnesses to the fatal collision testified freely at the inquest, but for some inexplicable reason that defies logic, Turnupseed was given a free pass.

Paul Moreno was the first witness to testify at the inquest. Deputy District Attorney Harry Murphy asked Moreno to describe what he saw when he arrived at the scene of the accident. After Moreno answered some preliminary questions, District Attorney Herbert Grundell took over the questioning. He asked Moreno the following: "Anything on the road would either have to be outlined or bled into the color of those mountains, is that correct?" Grundell might have been attempting to establish a premise he hoped Morena would faithfully agree to. The premise being that the landscape impeded Turnupseed's ability to see Dean's car approach him from the east. Morena immediately took the bait and concurred with the attorney's assessment. One could reasonably argue that Grundell was clearly attempting to clear Turnupseed of any wrongdoing by conveniently blaming the scenery and not the driver of the Ford Tudor for the collision.

When Moreno was asked to describe the color of the Porsche, he answered: "Silver gray or something. It blended in with the horizon, the background, and the mountains very well." It is unclear how Morena could be absolutely certain that Dean's car was impossible to see as it approached the Ford Tudor at that particular time of day. In an effort to drive home his claim early in the proceedings, Grundell once again fixated on the scenery and Turnupseed's alleged inability to see the Porsche prior to the collision. "It shows the mountains you have described and the road becomes delineated or merged into the scenery?" Moreno dutifully answered, "That is right."

It's important to note that no one at the inquisition represented James Dean. Otherwise, they likely would have mentioned that the silver Porsche Spyder stood out in stark contrast against Highway 466's blacktop. This business of blaming horizons and mountains could arguably have been a convenient distraction designed to exonerate Turnupseed. Moreover, someone representing Dean probably would have asked if Turnupseed had even bothered to signal that he was about to make a left turn. There was no evidence presented at the inquest to suggest that he did signal.

Murphy then read the deposition of Dr. Robert H. Bossert into the record. In the document, Murphy had asked Bossert if there were any indications the deceased wore glasses at any time prior to the collision. Bossert told

Murphy the victim was not wearing glasses during his examination.

Murphy: "Was there any evidence that any glasses might have been on him?"

Bossert: "I didn't examine his eyes closely, but he had numerous cuts about the face and bruises about his face. If he had been wearing glasses they could have easily been knocked off."

Murphy: "Those cuts he had about his face, could they have come from the glasses being broken in the accident?"

Bossert: "...it is difficult to tell whether they came from glasses."

Patrolman Ernest Tripke was called on next to testify. Murphy continued to hammer away at Turnupseed's alleged inability to see Dean's car just prior to impact.

Murphy: "Now, considering the color of the car, the height of the car, the time of day and the amount of sunlight, do you have any opinion as to how hard or difficult or easy it would be to see this car coming up the highway?"

Tripke: "Well, it would blend in well with the highway color and the horizon, it being silver gray."

Officer Tripke had brought with him a rather large diagram to help explain what had occurred at the intersection of 466 and 41. He testified that the point of impact occurred in the westbound lane, the lane Jimmy was in when Turnupseed turned in front of him. In other words, according to patrolman Tripke, Jimmy had the right of way at the point of impact. Turnupseed's statement claiming not to have seen the Porsche Spyder was suspect, at least just prior to the time of the collision. The fact still remained that the point of impact occurred while Jimmy was in *his own lane*, that he clearly had the right of way the moment the two cars collided.

District Attorney Grundell asked the patrolman if he had detected any alcohol on Turnupseed's breath. He replied that he had not. The patrolman stated that he saw Jimmy's body at the mortuary around 8:00 p.m., the night of the accident. It was determined that Jimmy's driver's license had a restriction in that the driver was required to wear corrective lenses. He was asked if he saw any evidence of glasses at the accident site. Tripke replied that he found a part of a frame belonging to a pair of glasses. When asked if he knew where this piece of evidence was, he replied he was unaware of its current location.

Thomas Frederick was the next witness to be called to the stand. He had been heading east on 466 at the time of the collision, the same direction Turnupseed was traveling.

Murphy: "Did you see the collision?"

Frederick: "Yes sir, I did."

Murphy: "Where were you when the collision occurred?"

Frederick: "Well, I was approximately 50 yards behind the Ford."

Frederick's testimony is critical in terms of whether or not Turnupseed was *capable* of seeing Jimmy's Porsche as it approached the Ford Tudor. If Frederick could see Jimmy's car approaching Turnupseed from a distance of *50 yards*, which is half a football field, then why couldn't Turnupseed see Jimmy's car as well from an equal distance? Frederick faced the exact same landscape as Turnupseed did, yet the background did not impede Frederick's ability to see the Porsche 50 yards away. One can make a very strong, credible argument based on Frederick's statement that Turnupseed *did* see Jimmy's car approach him, but that Turnupseed took it upon himself to cut in front of the Porsche.

Murphy: "Had you seen the Ford previous to this?"

Frederick: "That is right. He passed us about half a mile before we got to the intersection."

Frederick estimated that the Ford Tudor was traveling around 40 to 45 miles per hour right before impact. Murphy asked the witness if he had spoken to the driver of the Ford after the accident. Frederick claimed the driver told him he couldn't see the Porsche just prior to the collision.

Murphy: "You saw the Ford begin to make its turn. What did the Ford do then?"

Frederick: "Well, he started to make his turn and he acted like he saw the Porsche, and started to cut back to the right."

If Turnupseed did not see the Porsche just prior to the collision as he claimed, then why would he suddenly turn his car to the right unless he *did* see the Porsche approaching him. The very fact that Turnupseed did not follow through with his left turn indicates that he probably misjudged his chances of avoiding a head-on collision with the Porsche. Tom Frederick's testimony flatly discredits Turnupseed's claim that he only became aware of Dean's car at the moment of impact.

The next witness called to the stand was Patrolman Otie V. Hunter. He was asked whether Dean had been wearing glasses at the time he was pulled over for speeding. Hunter claimed he was not sure if Dean was wearing glasses while he was writing his citation for a traffic violation.

Patrolman Ronald Nelson was sworn in next. Nelson testified that Turnupseed told him that he was traveling roughly 55 to 60 miles an hour just before approaching where Highway 41 converges with Highway 466. The driver of the Ford told Tripke he had slowed down as he approached the entrance to 41. He said he looked straight down 466 and claimed he did not see Dean's car approaching him until Turnupseed had made his turn.

In the end, the jury agreed that Dean did not meet his death through any criminal act and that he was probably traveling at a very high rate of speed.

The two-lane highway in Cholame where the accident took place was widened in 1959. A safety island was built at the intersection where the two drivers had collided four years earlier. The area looks significantly different than how it looked on the day of the fatal crash. Undeterred by all the changes, people still flock to see the site of the accident.

Many years later, Ron Nelson was asked to comment on what transpired on September 30, 1955. He disagreed with the idea that Dean was traveling at a high rate of speed just prior to the collision. "If he'd been going ninety miles per hour, I don't think there'd be anything left of the car or even the mechanic that was with him." Nelson theorized that Dean may have been traveling 55 miles per hour just before the impact. He based this theory primarily on the skid marks and where the Porsche ended up in relation to where the collision occurred. Had Dean's car been traveling at a high rate of speed, the Porsche would have been tossed much farther away from the spot where the two cars collided.

The Porsche Spyder Jimmy drove that fateful day was towed to several high schools in the Los Angeles area in an effort to warn students about the dangers of driving on the open road. Dr. William F. Eschrich later purchased the wreck for a thousand dollars and installed parts of the engine in his own vehicle. He loaned the transmission to a friend who had it installed in his race car. The friend, Dr. Carl McHenry, drove the car in a race and was subsequently killed.

Donald Turnupseed was forced to give a deposition in Fresno, California on March 8, 1958. An attorney for Jimmy's insurance company questioned Turnupseed about the fatal crash on September 30, 1955. The driver of the Ford testified that he had left Cal Poly between the hours of twelve and one o'clock in the afternoon. He claimed he was traveling between 45 and 50 miles an hour when he started to make his turn to go onto Highway 41. Attorney A. H. Brazil asked Turnupseed if he had been looking in the direction of Highway 466 before starting his turn. He answered in the affirmative. He suggested that there was no traffic to speak of. He was then asked to confirm that he did in fact look directly up Highway 466 before veering left to get onto Highway 41. He claimed he did not see any vehicle whatsoever coming toward him from the opposite direction.

"I was driving along and then I heard this screaming of an engine or saw it first, I am not sure which, in other words. It both happened and I had – it was right under me, or there was a collision." He stated he heard the sound of the other car's engine about three seconds prior to impact. The attorney counted out three seconds and Turnupseed immediately changed his answer. He now testified that the time frame was "closer than that." Realizing his initial answer did not help his case, he now told a completely different story, a story that would hopefully exonerate him from any guilt.

"No, it was closer than that. It all happened right about the best as I could tell, at the same time."

"A snap of the fingers you might say. Is that right?"

"Yes."

Turnupseed at this point was obviously fitting "facts" to help bolster his tenuous claim that there was no way he could have possibly avoided a collision with Jimmy's car. Turnupseed was asked how could he have possibly determined how fast Dean's car was going if he never saw the Porsche until the moment of impact. "Just from the sound of the engine would be the only way," Turnupseed replied. Evidently, Turnupseed was now a self-proclaimed expert on judging the speed of a car based on the sound of its engine. And if he did hear the sound of the Spyder's rather distinctive roar of the handcrafted power unit, why did he blatantly ignore it?

Rolf Weutherich remained an active rally driver for Porsche in the 1960s. It appears he never fully recovered from his horrific injuries dating back to that fateful day in September of 1955. Each of his four subsequent marriages ended in divorce. At one point, he allegedly attacked one of his wives with a knife. He spent some time as a patient at the Weissenhauer Psychiatric Hospital for observation and treatment. In 1968 Rolf severed his ties with Porsche.

Rolf continued to receive "fan" mail because of his business relationship with Jimmy and the accident. In 1981 he signed a contract with a publisher so that he could reveal to the world his experiences in America and his friendship with James Dean. On July 20 of that same year, he left a bar in his hometown of Kupferzell and drove home in his Honda. At around 10:50 in the evening, a witness saw the Honda speeding toward the middle of town going at approximately 65 miles per hour. As Rolf tried to make a turn, he lost control of his car and smashed into the front of a house. A doctor tried to revive him but was unsuccessful. Rolf Weutherich was only fifty-three when he succumbed to his injuries.

Shortly before Dean's death, he had agreed to appear in several major television productions. He had signed on to portray a boxer in Ernest Hemingway's "The Battler." It was scheduled to be broadcast live from New York City on October 18, 1955. His part eventually went to Paul Newman. Dean had also been chosen to play Billy the Kid in a feature film called *The Left Handed Gun.* The film was released in 1958 with Newman assuming the role of the outlaw. Dean was also looking forward to playing the lead in *Hamlet* on Broadway.

Not long after the fatal collision, a note belonging to Jimmy was discovered. He had indicated in the handwritten note upcoming appointments with an occultist, a dentist, and presumably a therapist, (he had written Dochead). He also expressed the need to sell his motorcycle and to prepare for his upcoming role in "The Battler." Finally, he wanted to begin practicing a Welsh accent for his role in the television production of *The Corn is Green.*

The horrific, senseless death of James Dean set into motion a tsunami of books, magazine articles, newspaper columns, collectibles and memorabilia the likes of which had not been seen in decades. Jimmy had been in Hollywood for a year and a half and he had already touched the hearts and minds of fans throughout the entire world. Dean's immortality was ensured by an unexpected and tragic early death. The outpouring of grief was staggering, particularly among Dean's most loyal fan base – teenagers. But no one could have predicted the events that were about to unfold. Out of death, a true American icon was about to be born.

CHAPTER 7

DEAN'S LASTING IMPACT

Perhaps James Dean's most iconic image.

For weeks on end, folks from all over the world stopped by the quiet little town of Fairmount, Indiana to pay their final respects to the young man they had grown to love and admire. It was practically unheard of for fans to make a pilgrimage to the hometown of a deceased Hollywood star. Not satisfied with just visiting Dean's gravesite, some curiosity seekers wanted to speak to the Winslow family and perhaps take home some of Jimmy's personal belongings.

Shortly after Dean's death, the *Los Angeles Times* printed a front-page story with the heading: DEATH PREMONITION BY DEAN RECALLED. In part, it said that Jimmy frequently confessed to Hollywood friends about a premonition of death, that he was always in a hurry because he didn't think he had long to live in this world.

"Dean died at just the right time," Humphrey Bogart once said. "He left behind a legend. If he had lived, he'd never have been able to live up to his publicity."

Montgomery Clift was quoted as saying, "James Dean's death had a profound effect on me. The instant I heard about it, I vomited. I don't know why."

Pop records were released in an effort to cash in on the James Dean phenomenon. Records such as "Jimmy Plays the Bongos," "The Ballad of James Dean," "His Name was Dean," and "Jimmy Dean's First Christmas in Heaven" were just some of the songs that filled the airwaves. Clips of hair claimed to have belonged to Dean, bubble-gum cards, photographs, and toy monkeys flooded the marketplace. And of course, red jackets sold by the thousands. It seemed like everybody wanted to emulate James Dean.

The reaction to Jimmy's untimely death was swift and overwhelming. One publicist admitted that he was wrong when he referred to Dean as a legend. He was in fact a religion. Warner Brothers was totally unprepared to handle the massive amounts of letters that kept pouring into the studio. The influx of mail finally reached a point where the studio had to do something out of the ordinary. They outsourced the job of receiving and processing mail addressed to Dean to some independent firms. This allowed Warner Brothers to concentrate their resources on publicity campaigns designed to promote other stars.

Warner Brothers studio executives were unsure about when to finally release *Rebel*. It was unclear how Jimmy's fans might respond if the film was released just weeks after his untimely death. The studio didn't want to be accused of cashing in on the young star's fatal accident and popularity. The decision was finally made to release the film and hope for the best. After all, *Rebel* cost Warner Brothers quite a bit of money to produce. Warner Brothers spent enormous sums of money touting Dean's presence in the film. "This kid has a chip on both shoulders!" blared the advertisements.

Rebel Without a Cause premiered on October 26, 1955, a mere twenty-six days after Jimmy was killed. It was hard for many fans, particularly young people, to accept Dean's passing. The media took full advantage of this peculiar mindset. Magazines flooded the newsstands with articles that perpetuated a kind a cult following among the hardcore James Dean fanatics. Articles had titles like, "Elvis Hears from James Dean," "How Jimmy Dean Still Works Miracles for Others," and "Jimmy Dean Fights Back from the Grave."

Rebel Without a Cause received mostly favorable reviews after its release. Some of its detractors couldn't relate to the film's primary message regarding teenage angst and a sense of disillusionment with established norms. Bosley Crowther, film critic for the *New York Times*, claimed that *Rebel* was too slick for its own good, adding that utilizing color and CinemaScope went against the realism Nicholas Ray attempted to convey. Crowther did admit that the film "is a violent, brutal and disturbing picture of modern teenagers...it is a picture to make the hair stand on end." *Variety* described the movie as "exciting, suspenseful, and provocative," and called Dean "a talent which might have touched the heights." More accolades soon followed:

"The most moving job of all is turned in by James Dean."

"The best thing about the film is James Dean, a player of unusual sensibility and charm."

"His rare talent and appealing personality even shine through this turgid melodrama."

A film critic for *Saturday Review* wrote that Dean "reveals completely the talent latent in his *East of Eden* performance."

Rebel shot to number one almost instantly. Reportedly, it outgrossed *East of Eden* in its first week. The film was released nationally on November 9 and it stayed in the top ten for several weeks. Throughout the fall of 1955, teenagers lined up for blocks to see Jimmy in *Rebel* and some of the more rabid fans watched the film dozens of times. Audiences at the Paramount Theatre in Los Angeles applauded loudly and often throughout the entire screening of *Rebel*. Fans called television stations and demanded that they rerun Dean's earlier television appearances.

The role of Jim Stark and the young, charismatic actor who portrayed him became and remained indistinguishable for many of Dean's fans. Through James Dean, Jim Stark symbolized the pain many teenagers experience in a world dominated by adults. He represented the misunderstood adolescent trying desperately to fit in with society's traditions.

A full year after *Rebel's* release, Natalie Wood and Jim Backus continued to receive huge amounts of fan mail requesting personal information about Dean. Over the next several months, Warner Brothers would receive tens of thousands of letters praising Dean's mesmerizing performance. Author Jack Kerouac, a huge fan of *Rebel*, went so far as to compare the cult-like status of Jimmy to that of Saint Teresa.

One can reasonably argue that *Rebel Without a Cause* surpasses *The Wild One* and *Blackboard Jungle* in several ways. Generally speaking, the acting in *Rebel* appears more natural and less melodramatic than the performances in the other two films. The reason for this may have been due to Dean's enormous influence on the other cast members and to Nicholas Ray's realistic approach to the film. Moreover, the Jim Stark character is much more relatable to young people than the rambunctious motorcycle leader portrayed by Marlon Brando. Dean's character says, "I don't want any trouble," whereas Brando's character is looking to raise hell. When he is asked what is he rebelling against, he answers with a flippant, "What've you got?" Furthermore, *Rebel* was also shot in color, giving it a more contemporary, modern feel.

More than any other film geared toward attracting a youthful audience, *Rebel Without a Cause*, for better or worse, helped spawn a flood of teenage exploitation films in the latter half of the 1950s. Not surprisingly, several cast members from *Rebel* would go on to play similar roles in pictures such as *Crime in the Streets*, *Rock, Pretty Baby*, and *Dino*, all featuring Sal Mineo. Corey Allen played a gang leader in *Juvenile Jungle* and Steffi Sidney played a young gang member in *The Hot Angel*. Other films followed on the heels of *Rebel*, including *High School Confidential*, *Dragstrip Riot*, *The Wild Ride*, and *The Delinquents*. Some films focused on so-called female delinquents such as *Hot Rod Girl*, *Eighteen and Anxious*, *Live Fast, Die Young*, and *Dragstrip Girl*. Not to be outdone, horror films got into the act with such gems as *Teenagers from Outer Space*, *The Blob*, and *I Was a Teenage Werewolf*, starring Michael Landon. Landon would go on to star in the enormously popular Western television series, *Bonanza*.

The popularity and influence of *Rebel Without a Cause* remains a worldwide cult phenomenon even to this day. The film's influence on pop culture will likely remain strong for generations to come. Posters of Dean in his familiar red jacket and upturned collar can be seen in diners, popular restaurants, clothing stores, movie theaters, concert halls, and malls throughout the entire world.

Unlike many films from the 1950s, *Rebel* foretold

the emergence of the anti-hero. Dean helped usher in a non-conformist attitude among adolescents in the 1960s. He portrayed a teenager unafraid to question and confront society's traditional values. Hollywood in the 1960s changed as well. Films like *The Graduate* and *Easy Rider* reflected a seismic change in the kinds of movies young people wanted to experience.

With over 800,000 feet of *Giant* footage to examine and edit, Stevens had before him a monumental task. It would take him an entire year to finally bring to fruition the masterpiece he had always dreamed of. It was not shot in CinemaScope because he wanted to emphasize height as well as width. "I want height and I want to be able to edit freely. Height because the movie is a world of upright things and tall men." Furthermore, many in the film industry claimed CinemaScope had a tendency to distort faces reflected on the screen. This flaw was later corrected by the utilization of Panavision.

Even George Stevens was not spared the wrath of Dean's more rabid fan base. Some sent him death threats, warning Stevens that if he cut a single foot of Jimmy's performance, he would face an appropriate response. Stevens found those letters extremely unsettling. He was also fully aware of the fact that he had never edited posthumously an actor's performance in any of the films he had directed. In effect, he was venturing into uncharted territory.

After several tedious months of editing, George Stevens was ready to present an early test screening of *Giant*. It was held on May 22, 1956. Although the film lasted an incredible three hours and thirty-five minutes, no one in the test audience walked out. Not only that, the ending was followed by a huge ovation. Some overly optimistic film critics speculated that *Giant's* popularity might even surpass that of *Gone With the Wind*.

Warner Brothers announced that the film would be released in the fall. The advance publicity campaign for *Giant* was unparalleled for its time. Much of the publicity centered around Dean, not its two main leads, Elizabeth Taylor and Rock Hudson. It was largely touted as James Dean's last picture. *Saturday Review* didn't hold back on the James Dean phenomenon when it said this about the upcoming release of *Giant*: "It's Dean, Dean, Dean...It is the late James Dean as Jett Rink that the audience will be watching with fascination and love. For as everyone knows, this young man who died in an auto smashup has caused a mass hysteria at least equal to that caused by Valentino."

The premiere for *Giant* occurred on October 10 at the Roxy Theatre in New York City. Reviews were generally very favorable. Bosley Crowther at the *New York Times* enjoyed it immensely. *Time* and the *Chicago Daily News* praised it. Most film critics thought Dean's performance was brilliant. A few days later, the film premiered at Grauman's Chinese Theatre in Hollywood and it was received with a great deal of adulation. Stevens became annoyed when he discovered *Giant* had been heavily edited in Mexico. Censors cut about thirty minutes from the film because it depicted blatant bigotry against Mexicans.

On October 16, *Look* put Jimmy on its cover in response to the sudden surge in Dean's popularity brought on by the release of *Giant*. Dressed as his character Jett Rink, Dean looks relaxed as he stares far into the distance. Next to his image is the headline: "James Dean – The story of the strangest legend since Valentino." Found inside the magazine were images of Dean on the set of *Giant*.

Film critics considered *Giant* to be George Stevens' masterpiece. *Time* carried an article about Jimmy's outstanding performance as the surly Texas ranch hand turned oil baron. "He has caught the Texas accent to nasal perfection and mastered the lock-hipped, high-heeled stagger of the wrangler, and the wry little jerks and smirks, tics, and twitches, grunts and giggles, that make up most of the language of a man who talks to himself a good deal more than he does to anyone else...[he] clearly shows for the first and fatefully the last time what his admirers always said he had: a streak of genius."

Bosley Crowther, columnist for the *New York Times*, raved about Dean after seeing his performance in *Giant*. "Mr. Dean plays this curious villain with a stylized spookiness -a sly sort of off-beat languor and slur of language that concentrates spite. This is a haunting capstone to the brief career of Mr. Dean." Just a year earlier, Crowther had criticized Jimmy's performance in *Rebel* as simply a horrible Brando impersonation.

A critic for the *New York Herald Tribune* praised Dean's performance. "His earlier depiction of the amoral, reckless, animal like young ranch hand will not only excite his admirers into a frenzy, it will make the most sedate onlooker understand why a James Dean cult ever came into existence."

When Lee Strasberg first heard the news of Dean's fatal car accident, he took it in stride. In fact, he almost expected it. Jimmy's death didn't really hit him hard until he saw *Giant*. Afterward, he cried because he had just witnessed a truly remarkable performance by a promising young film star. Strasberg called Jimmy's tragic death a "waste."

Even George Stevens praised Dean's performance, although it was rather underwhelming. "Dean was a good boy and he filled the bill perfectly," he told an interviewer for *Time*. "He wasn't always a joy to work with, but find me any actors who aren't difficult. You gamble along with young people and hope their performance comes off. We gambled with Dean and we won." Later, Stevens gave a kinder account of Dean. "There is no part of Jimmy I don't like, no part of him that hasn't always the attraction that goes with complete naturalness."

Henry Ginsberg had grown to respect Jimmy's inventiveness and star appeal. "In sixteen months of acting, he left a more lasting impression on the public than many stars do in thirty years," Ginsberg acknowledged. "I can understand why the impact of his personality was so great. Though he was not an easy person to know, he was an exciting and stimulating person to be with." He was not alone in his assessment. Just a few months after Dean's death, literally hundreds of James Dean fan clubs sprang up across several continents. Just a couple of years after his demise, the Hollywood Foreign Press Association named Dean the "World's Favorite Actor."

Many years after *Giant*'s release, Stevens recalled a scene where Dean wanted his character to pour himself a whiskey from *his* flask rather than drinking Bick Benedict's liquor. Dean reasoned that Jett Rink was too proud to drink his archrival's whiskey. Stevens insisted that Dean should do the scene exactly as written, that Rink would drink Bick Benedict's liquor. "His idea was too damn smart," Stevens recalled, "and he didn't explain it to me, so I didn't get it then. But he really knew that character, and that's the best tribute I can pay to his talent as an artist."

In 1956 Nicolas Ray recounted some memories of Jimmy. They were part of an essay he had written about the film star. "The last time I saw James Dean was when he arrived without warning at my Hollywood home, about three o'clock in the morning. That evening we had met for dinner. We had talked for several hours of many things, of future plans, including a story called Heroic Love that we were going to do. When he reappeared later, he had been given a Siamese cat by Elizabeth Taylor and he wanted to borrow a book of mine on cats before driving home."

In terms of Jimmy's mood swings, Ray recalled the following incident. "He swerved easily from moodiness to elation. The depression could lift completely and unexpectedly as it arrived. Once it was cured by going to see Jacques Tati in The Big Day. Unshaven, tousled, wrapped in a dyed black trench coat, glasses on the end of his nose, he was morose as he entered the theater. Within ten minutes he was laughing so wildly that nearby members of the audience complained. He ignored them - there was nothing else to do, the spell of laughter and delight grew more and more irresistible. Before the film was over, he had to leave, making his departure a series of hurdles over the ashcans in the aisle."

A year after Jimmy's death, Sal Mineo recalled conversations he had with Jimmy. "If there was one thing that bugged Jimmy it was hypocrites. I think that the most important reason we got along so well together was that we were always honest with each other and never pulled punches. He hated people who put up fronts."

"Jimmy was shy," Mineo continued. "He was so shy

that he was hard to communicate with. Often you couldn't get to him and if you were lucky enough to talk to him, most often both of you were at a loss for words. But if by chance you could get through to him, and Jimmy liked you, then he would come out of his shyness and talk freely and honestly with you."

In 1956 Natalie Wood and Sal Mineo were nominated for Oscars for their roles in *Rebel*. Amazingly, Dean was not nominated at all for his brilliant portrayal of Jim Stark, the character he's most famous for. However, Jimmy would be nominated for Best Actor for *East of Eden* that same year. Wood ultimately lost to Jo Van Fleet for *Eden*, and Mineo lost to Jack Lemmon for *Mister Roberts*. Hedda Hopper, perhaps Jimmy's biggest supporter, was so furious Dean did not win the Oscar for Best Actor, she demanded the Academy honor Jimmy with a special honorary Oscar the following year.

Natalie Wood clearly benefited from her role as Judy in *Rebel*. The media followed her everywhere, seeking interviews, asking questions about her friendship with Dean. Nick Adams and Dennis Hopper reportedly introduced her to Elvis Presley, a devoted fan of James Dean. Wood was surprised to discover that the 'King' didn't drink or smoke. Presley took her for a spin around Memphis on his motorcycle while fans and the paparazzi followed them everywhere. Presley was obsessed with Dean and he pressed Natalie for information about Hollywood's latest and biggest legend. Apparently, Wood was so overwhelmed by all the attention Elvis received, she ended her relationship with Presley and returned back to Hollywood.

It's an understatement to say that Elvis Presley was a

huge fan of Jimmy. According to Nicholas Ray, Presley got down on his knees inside an MGM cafeteria and recited entire passages of dialogue from *Rebel* to Ray. It was as if Presley was auditioning for a part in the film. The director, totally taken aback by Elvis' infatuation with Dean, had never experienced such devotion to a film actor as Presley displayed that day. Ray discovered that the singer had seen *Rebel* perhaps dozens of times and had learned all of Jimmy's lines from the film.

Frank Mazzola, the actor who played Crunch in *Rebel*, and Elvis Presley met one day via a mutual friend. According to Mazzola, Presley wanted to know everything the actor knew about Dean. Mazzola claimed that it seemed Presley knew the entire script of *Rebel*, including Crunch's lines. "I got the sense that Elvis wanted to be Jimmy in a strange kind of way."

Elvis Presley was the biggest act in show business in 1956. No one even came close. His records sold in the tens of millions and there was no end in sight. In July a twenty-one-year-old Elvis Presley was interviewed by Hy Gardner, a prominent, longtime Broadway columnist for the *New York Herald Tribune*. For years Gardner conducted celebrity interviews on television and radio. He was the host of a very popular show called "Hy Gardner Calling." The following captures a part of his July 1 interview with Presley.

Gardner: "They predict that Elvis Presley will be another James Dean. Now have you heard that?"

Presley: "I've heard something about it, but-uh-I would never compare myself in any way to James Dean because James Dean was a genius in acting. Although I'll say that-uh-I sure would like to. I mean I guess there's a lot of actors in Hollywood that would like to have the ability that James Dean had but I would never compare myself to James Dean in any way."

Elvis Presley wasn't the only rock and roll singer to be moved by Dean. Rockers like Gene Vincent and Eddie Cochran reflected some of Jimmy's cool persona. So confident of Dean's influence on early rock and roll music, trade magazine *Music Connection* labeled him "the first rock star." British rockers like Adam Faith, Billy Fury, and Cliff Richards were captivated by Dean's image. After watching *Rebel*, Faith confessed that he "wanted to be James Dean." Sadly, England saw fit to ban *Rebel* to teenagers until 1968.

On February 18, 1957, Jimmy received an Academy Award nomination for Best Actor for *Giant*. Warner Brothers had decided not to place Dean's name for consideration in the best supporting category. The best supporting category made sense to some because Jimmy was in the picture for about a fifth of the running time. The studio also made the decision to place Rock Hudson's name for consideration in the best actor category as well. The odds of Dean winning an award for best actor diminished somewhat because now he was competing against his male co-star. In any event, on March 27, 1957, Yul Brynner went on to win the Academy Award for Best Actor for his outstanding performance in *The King and* I. Anthony Quinn won the award for best supporting actor for his role in *Lust for Life*. Earlier, he had won that same award for his brilliant performance in *Viva Zapata!*

Amazingly, *Giant* received ten Oscar nominations in several major categories, but only won a single award. The Best Director award went to George Stevens. Sadly,

Stevens' next few films would pale in comparison to *Giant*. He went on to direct another blockbuster epic film, *The Greatest Story Ever Told*, which was released in 1965. Although his direction was extraordinary, the film received horrible reviews and did poorly at the box office. Stevens threw in the towel after his film, *The Only Game in Town* (1970), starring Elizabeth Taylor and Warren Beatty, failed miserably at the box office. He died a few years later.

In 1956, producer George W. George and director Robert Altman began working on a new project, a biographical film about the life of James Dean. Elvis Presley was seriously considered for the role of James Dean. A young, relatively unknown actor named Robert Conrad was also in the running, presumably because Conrad bore somewhat of a resemblance to Dean. The idea of using actors was ultimately discarded and instead the creators of *The James Dean Story* decided to make a documentary about his life. Marlon Brando was asked to narrate the documentary. Initially he considered the offer, but eventually turned it down.

The James Dean Story was billed as "a different kind of motion picture," which is another way of saying it was a documentary. It presumably utilized a novel technique in which the camera zooms in and out of still photographs. Staged reenactments were frequently used, sometimes involving the Winslows themselves. People who had known Dean were asked to offer their perspective of Jimmy. In an attempt to appeal to teenagers, a theme song, "Let Me Be Loved," was sung by Tommy Sands. The film was released in 1957 and it did horribly at the box office. It was panned as either a shameless exploitation piece generated strictly for profit or a well-meaning attempt to pay tribute to a genius who died much too young. Shortly thereafter, Warner Brothers acknowledged their horrible mistake and yanked the movie out of theaters and sold it to television.

Nick Adams appeared at the premiere of *The James Dean Story* in Marion, Indiana, wearing Dean's trademark red jacket and jeans. He gave countless interviews to various fan magazines. Some of his stories sounded far-fetched. He claimed cops circled his house continuously to deter thieves from breaking in and stealing souvenirs Jimmy had supposedly given him. He also distributed photographs of a car he claimed he and Jimmy had worked on together.

Through contacts, Adams ingratiated himself with Elvis Presley. He first met the 'King' while Presley was making *Love Me Tender* in Hollywood. Some believed that Presley's manager Colonel Tom Parker promoted and manipulated Elvis' 'friendship' with Adams. Most likely, Parker realized both men could mutually benefit from their association with each other. Naturally, Adams had a lot more to gain from their relationship than Presley, but that probably didn't matter to the Colonel. Elvis' association with someone who supposedly had been a close friend to James Dean was a big plus for the singer's image.

Esquire magazine carried an article written by John Dos Passos called "The Death of James Dean" in its October 1958 issue. "James Dean is three years dead but the sinister adolescent still holds the headlines." For a time, interest in the James Dean phenomena seemed to fade. Evidence was everywhere. In 1961, James Fuller's stage version of *Rebel Without a Cause* closed shortly after it opened. September 1965 marked the tenth anniversary of Jimmy's death and no one seemed to care except some diehard James Dean fans. The *New York Post* carried an article under the head-line, "Decade Has Dimmed James Dean Luster." It read in part that "the Dean craze has all but vanished, apparently the victim of malnutrition." All of this was about to change in the coming decades. James Dean was about to be rediscovered by a whole new generation of devoted fans.

James Dean's growing popularity had a profound effect on the pop and rock music scene and the film industry in the 1960s and 1970s. Major rock bands and pop stars began referencing Dean in their songs beginning in the 1960s.

The Beach Boys recorded a track referencing Jimmy's tragic death in the song, "A Young Man is Gone." It was off their 1963 *Little Deuce Coupe* album.

In the early to mid-1970s, rock musicians accepted Dean as one of their own. Some cultural critics began labeling Dean as "the first rock star." John Lennon reportedly proclaimed that the Beatles never would have existed without James Dean. Elvis Presley enjoyed being called the "James Dean of Rock and Roll."

"American Pie" by Don McLean became a huge hit when it was released in 1971.

"Now for ten years we've been on our own, and moss grows fat on a rolling stone, but that's not how it used to be, when the jester sang for the king and queen, in a coat he borrowed from James Dean..."

Grease, a rollicking musical featuring songs from the early days of rock and roll, opened in early 1972 at the Eden Theater in New York City. Prominently displayed among a collage of photo blowups was a huge iconic photograph of James Dean.

In 1972, Lou Reed had a giant hit single called "Walk on the Wild Side."

"Jackie is just speeding away, thought she was James Dean for a day."

In 1973, David Essex had a massive hit called "Rock On."

"And where do we go from here? Which is a way that's clear, Still looking for that blue-jean baby-queen, Prettiest girl I've ever seen, See her shake on the movie screen, Jimmy Dean Jimmy Dean..."

The Eagles released "James Dean" in 1974.

"You were the lowdown rebel if there ever was, Even if you had no cause..."

Bruce Springsteen idolized Jimmy and reportedly carried around a biography of the star for several months. According to *Time* magazine, Springsteen represented "a '50s hood in the James Dean mold." David Bowie's character Ziggy Stardust was referred to as "James Dean with a guitar."

Elroy Hamilton wrote an article in the *Chicago Sun-Times* in early 1971 in which he said in part: "This scene of The Establishment versus The Youth-the climax of *Rebel Without a Cause*, when the Los Angeles police shoot Plato as Jim Stark cries out that he has the bullets to the gun Plato is holding - somehow seems to be an early version of the deaths in Easy Rider, and, perhaps, of those at Kent State, though the intervening years seem to have added the extra ingredient of hatred."

Prominent film stars of the 1970s and beyond praised Dean for his unique and inventive approach to acting. Some thought of Jimmy as a symbol of rebellion and discontent toward society in general.

In a 1971 interview, Dustin Hoffman discussed Dean's influence. "When I initially started in acting in college, James Dean was the big hero there in films, and Marlon Brando. My secret fantasy was that I would be like James Dean and Marlon Brando. Then I came to New York and New York kicked that out of me after about three or four years. Then I decided, 'I don't want to be like Brando or Dean, I just want to be a really good working character actor. That's all I ever wanted.' I convinced myself that that's all I ever wanted, because that's all I hoped to achieve."

During an interview with Tony Perkins, talk show host Dick Cavett brought up the subject of James Dean. "Every actor of your time was supposed to have been influenced by James Dean," Cavett said to Perkins. "Were you in any way?"

"Well, I was certainly impressed by the originality of his talent," Perkins replied. "Of course, it was popular at that time of his emergence to compare him unfavorably with Brando. Fifteen or twenty years later – if you look at them-they are not that similar. That was poverty-stricken minds who were making that comparison. I think he was an original talent. I don't think there's anybody who has come along since Dean that had the originality or the passion he had."

"There's a lot of jealousy about Jimmy," Sammy Davis Jr. observed. "Why should people still have a kind of thing about him after all these years after he's passed? There are only two people in the world within my lifetime creating that thing. One was Marilyn Monroe and the other was James Dean."

"Jimmy had that genius, that mysterious certain

something," Harvey Keitel observed. "When you watched him play you wanted to learn how to play that way. He was an inspiration to me to play honestly, to play truthfully, to play deeply."

"There are moments - behavior - in 'East of Eden' that are pure magic," Johnny Depp once stated. "'Giant' is pure magic. Rebel is a bit dated and is sort of a strange vision of the 1950s, but his work in that is amazing." Depp was so moved by Dean, he stayed in the exact same room Dean lived in at the Hotel Iroquois in New York City so he could channel the dead actor's spiritual essence.

"I was a kid when Dean came out," Al Pacino recalled. "Dean was the inspiration. Even the red jacket he wore in 'Rebel Without a Cause,' you saw that red jacket popping up all over the place. He really reached people in a way. It was kind of a phenomenon when you think of it. I wonder what it would be like today, that kind of a person. He made that connection with his audience. And I remember at that time my mother loved him. He reached everybody."

Robert De Niro once commented that of the three films Dean made, East of Eden was his favorite. "When you saw James Dean do 'East of Eden' he was great, but you can't do what he could do." De Niro considers Marlon Brando, James Dean, and Montgomery Clift his favorite actors.

Dennis Hopper once commented on the ubiquity of Jimmy's image. "I mean, I can go to Europe, I'm going to Sweden. I go into a nightclub, and there's James Dean, Humphrey Bogart, Marilyn Monroe on the wall. Going to Paris, there he is…"

Nicolas Cage decided to become an actor after watching East of Eden. "I saw the scene where James Dean goes to bring the money on the birthday, and his father says to him, it's not good enough, and he has the breakdown. That was so painful to watch, and it was so real to me, that I knew acting was what I wanted to do."

"His life was not so much a struggle as it was a quest," Martin Sheen once mused. "His purpose, not so much to achieve, as it was involvement. If anyone would've stopped James Dean in his lifetime and said, 'tell me what you're all about' he might just as well have shrugged and said, 'I'm just passing through here.' A product of the 1950s generation, he had an overwhelming impact on my generation and on me personally."

James Dean is one of the few actors who transcends time itself. James Franco, a huge fan of Dean who once played his idol in a film made for television, wrote a poem explaining Jimmy's impact: "Dean's ghost never stops, launched from that moment, off the back of his image, and shot through every generation thereafter."

Andy Warhol wrote that Dean "is not our hero because he was perfect, but because he perfectly represented the damaged but beautiful soul of our time."

Many years after Dean's death, director Daniel Petrie was asked to talk a little about Jimmy. Petrie had directed Dean in several television programs. "He was a joy to work with," Petrie recalled. "He was not in any way difficult whatsoever. He came to work, he was a real pro. He was very quiet. He was constantly astounding you by virtue of – 'Whoa, where did he ever come up with that?' He had an incredible innate ability that he was born with. Jimmy Dean had a God-given gift."

Kazan continued to go on record expressing his

feelings about Jimmy, many of them surprisingly and unduly harsh. Obviously a very opinionated individual, he shared his thoughts about what he perceived to be Jimmy's personal and professional shortcomings in terms of the star's performance in *Eden*. "God, he gave everything he had in that film," Kazan recalled. "He didn't hold anything back. At the very end of the shooting, the last few days, you felt that a star was going to be born. Everybody smelled it; all the publicity people began to hang around him."

"He was never more than a limited actor," Kazan claimed, "and he was a highly neurotic man – obviously sick, and he got more so. His face was very poetic – wonderful, and very painful, full of desolation. There are moments when you say, 'Oh, God, he's so handsome – what goodness is being lost here?' Directing him was like directing the faithful Lassie. I either lectured him or terrorized him, flattered him furiously, tapped him on the shoulder, or kicked his backside. He was so instinctive and so stupid in many ways – and most of all I had the impression of someone who was a cripple inside. He was not like Brando. People compared them but there was no similarity. He was a far, far sicker kid, and Brando's not sick, he's just troubled."

It's exceedingly clear Kazan thought Jimmy wasn't in the same league as Brando. "Marlon was well trained by Stella Adler, had excellent technique. He was proficient in every aspect of acting, including characterization and makeup. He was also a great mimic. Dean had no technique to speak of. When he tried to play an older man in the last reels of *Giant*, he looked like what he was; a beginner." Rather harsh words coming from someone who chose Dean over dozens of other eligible young actors who campaigned vigorously for the Cal Trask role in *Eden*.

Kazan recalled the strange effect Jimmy had on young people. "The balcony was full of kids at a Hollywood preview who had never seen Jimmy before, and the moment he came on the screen they began to screech, they began to holler and yell and the balcony was coming down like a waterfall. Every time he made a move it was like…like Janis Joplin might have affected an audience, or Frank Sinatra when I was a young man. Every move he made…it was a landslide. I've never seen anything like it in the movies in my whole life, including Marlon Brando."

"The goddamn kid became a legend overnight and the legend grew more intense with every showing," Kazan went on. "When my friend Nick Ray cast him in *Rebel Without a Cause*, he intensified Dean's spell over the youth of the nation. It was a legend I didn't approve of. Its essence was that all parents were insensitive idiots who didn't understand or appreciate their kids and weren't able to help them. Parents were the enemy." Kazan read many letters thanking him for what he had done for Dean. Several fans asked the director to become a sponsor for a network of James Dean fan clubs. Kazan never responded to any of those requests.

A new generation of film stars continue to praise Dean's talent as an actor. Austin Butler, the Oscar nominee who brilliantly portrayed Elvis Presley in the 2022 film, *Elvis*, reminisced about his idol. "James Dean was the actor I obsessed over as a kid," Butler recalled in an interview. "I watched 'Rebel Without a Cause' so many times. 'East of Eden' too. It seems almost impossible what Dean was doing, the animalistic power that he had."

There have been some very prominent actors who

thought Dean was not only highly over-rated but down right annoying. Oscar winner and multi-nominee actress Shirley MacLaine claimed Dean was an "expert" mumbler. "So, I think he got away with obscuring clarity with English. I don't like him."

Robert Duvall claimed that Dean wasn't all that great. "He was good," Duvall admitted, "but there was Brando, and there was Steven Hill in the Actors Studio, those were the two guys. James Dean came in third."

James Dean certainly had his share of criticism while he was alive and he continues to receive negative criticism even today. Critics don't necessarily focus so much on his acting skills as they do on what he represents. For example, columnist George Will blamed *Rebel Without a Cause* for much of the youthful turmoil during the 1960s. He complained that "Dean played himself-a mumbling, arrested-development adolescent-to perfection. Feeling mightily sorry for himself as a victim, his character prefigured the whiny, alienated, nobody-understands-me pouting that the self-absorbed youth of the sixties considered a political stance." Director Peter Bogdanovich shared Will's opinion when he said that *Rebel* was "pretty irresponsible" and "gave birth to an entire generation of self-indulgent teenagers. It had tremendous impact."

In September 1980 thousands of adoring fans showed up in Fairmount to celebrate the twenty-fifth anniversary of James Dean's death. Martin Sheen spoke at a memorial service and confessed that James Dean "created one of the century's most unique inventions – himself." Sheen later spoke to a reporter and had this to say about his idol. "When I was in acting school in New York years ago, there was a saying that if Marlon Brando changed the way people acted, then James Dean changed the way people lived. He was the greatest actor who ever lived - he was simply a genius."

By the 1980s Dean had become one of the most revered American cultural figures of the 20th century. He shared this distinction with only two other artists, namely Marilyn Monroe and Elvis Presley. What separates Dean from his peers is that he had only starred in three feature films. Monroe and Presley's careers lasted far longer than Dean's.

There were signs in the 1980s that indicated Dean's influence was alive and well. Marfa, Texas, the location where *Giant* was primarily shot, continued to generate some interest during the decade. *Come Back to the 5 & Dime, Jimmy Dean, Jimmy Dean* was released in 1982. It tells the story of how the film impacted the lives of a group of women living near where *Giant* was filmed. Kevin Costner starred in *Fandango* (1985), a film about four University of Texas graduates who spend one night near where the Reata scenes were shot.

Dean's headstone was stolen in 1983 but was later discovered resting on a tree stump on a desolate country road. A week later it was stolen again and replaced. The headstone was stolen yet again in 1998 but was recovered shortly afterward. The current headstone is reportedly anchored by a hidden steel rod running deep into the ground.

In the summer of 1988, Bob Dylan played a concert in Indianapolis. After the concert, Dylan visited Fairmount to pay his respects to one of his idols, James Dean. He stopped by Jimmy's gravesite and the museum honoring Dean on Washington Street.

As a tribute to Dean's outstanding performance in *Rebel Without a Cause* and his connection to the Griffith Observatory, the city of Los Angeles erected a bronze bust of Dean in November of 1988. Sculptor Ken Kendall commemorated the bust in honor of Dean's contribution as an actor and on his impact as an American icon. The monument also serves as a reminder of Jimmy's ever-growing popularity.

Marlon Brando referenced Dean in his 1994 autobiography, *Songs My Mother Taught Me*. He indicated in the book that Jimmy became "a symbol of social change during the 1950s...a sense of alienation was rising among different generations and different layers of society...he was not only on his way to becoming a good actor, but he had a personality and presence that made audiences curious about him...he was awfully good in that last picture, and people identified with his pain and made him a cult figure."

There was a major resurgence of interest in Dean within the music industry beginning in the 1990s. Chuck D of Public Enemy referred to rapper Tupac Shakur as the "James Dean of our times. Basically, a *Rebel Without a Cause*." In preparation for his performance in *8 Mile*, Eminem studied James Dean's performance in *Rebel*.

Dean was referenced in Madonna's "Vogue" in 1990, REM's "Electrolite" (1996), Chris Isaak's "American Boy" (2002), The Killers' "Under the Gun" (2004), and Rufus Wainwright's "Peach Trees" (2004). More examples followed, including "Speechless" by Lady Gaga (2009), "Rather Die Young" by Beyonce (2011), Lana Del Rey's "Blue Jeans" (2012), Taylor Swift's "Style" (2014), Adam Lambert's "Ghost Town" (2015), "Gorgeous" by X Ambassadors (2015), and

Ariana Grande's "Moonlight" (2018), to name just a few.

What saves James Dean from extinction, many may argue, is due to the timeless image he projects. His likeness can be found on merchandise everywhere. Be it New York, Paris, Tokyo, London, or Berlin, stores selling Dean's image on jackets, watches, jeans, T-shirts, footwear, greeting cards, books, and magazines sell out faster than they come in. Even the United States Postal Service got into the act and issued James Dean commemorative stamps in 1996. They remain some of the fastest selling stamps ever offered by the postal service.

James Dean's film career was tragically cut short, yet his legend continues to attain greater heights. Not even his harshest critics can deny his staying power in a world content on destroying its heroes. He is a contradiction of attitudes and emotions. Dean has been accused of being narcissistic, overly ambitious, inconsiderate, self-centered, rude, and dangerously disruptive. He has also been described as deeply intuitive, brilliant, compassionate, inventive, and original. When Jimmy appears on screen, he demands your attention – and he gets it. Time and time again. Without fail. All eyes are drawn to his ever-changing facial expressions or the way he contorts his entire body in a maddening display of emotions. You watch him intently because you might miss something intriguing if you look away for just an instant. That's because Dean creates an aura of unpredictability in all of his characters. Whether it's Cal Trask, Jim Stark, or Jett Rink, anything is possible with Dean at the helm.

Dean symbolizes youthful unrest and disillusionment in a world dominated by an older generation. His image never suffers from the vagaries of middle age as many of his followers did. Dean was able to achieve greatness on the screen by combining a magnetic screen presence with excruciating self-doubt. He projects both a tough exterior and a sensitive nature which film fans find endearing.

Dean's image as a brooding nonconformist is so pervasive, it frequently casts a shadow over his brilliance as an actor. He is regarded as a cultural icon far more often than he is as a genius. In each of his three films, Dean portrays an outsider bent on getting his own way – with tragic results. He represents to us the quintessential rebel waging war against the establishment's norms and traditions and he will forever be regarded as the symbol of the ultimate nonconformist bent on defying authority.

No other movie star has received as much adulation for so few films as James Dean. Part of the reason may be due to the fact that Jimmy suffered from an unexpected and tragic death at such a young age. It is virtually assured that the legend of James Dean will continue to grow with each new generation. The Reverend Xen Harvey may have come closer to the truth in terms of Dean's legacy when he said these words at Jimmy's funeral service on October 8, 1955.

"The career of James Dean has not ended. It has just begun. And remember, God Himself is directing the production."

BIBLIOGRAPHY

Alexander, Paul. *Boulevard of Broken Dreams: The Life, Times, and Legend of James Dean.* New York: Penguin Books, 1997.

Backus, Jim. *Rocks on the Roof.* New York: G.P. Putnam's Sons, 1958.

Baker, Carroll. *Baby Doll: An Autobiography.* New York: Arbor House, 1983.

Bast, William. *James Dean: A Biography.* New York: Ballantine Books, 1956

Beath, Warren Newton. *The Death of James Dean.* New York: Grove Press, Inc., 1986.

Bosworth, Patricia. *Marlon Brando: A Biography.* New York: Penguin Group, 2001.

Bosworth, Patricia. *Montgomery Clift: A Biography.* New York: Harcourt Brace Jovanovich, 1978.

Bracker, Lew. *Jimmy & Me: A Personal Memoir of James Dean.* Illinois: Fulcorte Press, 2013.

Brando, Marlon with Lindsey, Robert. *Brando: Songs My Mother Taught Me.* New York: Random House, 1994.

Dalton, David. *James Dean: The Mutant King.* San Francisco: Straight Arrow Books, 1974.

Eisenschitz, Bernard. *Nicholas Ray: An American Journey.* Minneapolis: University of Minnesota Press, 1990.

Finstad, Suzanne. *Natalie Wood: The Complete Biography*. New York: Broadway Books, 2020.

Frascella, Lawrence and Weisel, Al. *Live Fast, Die Young: The Wild Ride of Making Rebel Without a Cause*. New York: Simon & Schuster, 2005.

Graham, Don. *Giant: Elizabeth Taylor, Rock Hudson, James Dean, Edna Ferber and the Making of a Legendary American Film*. New York: St. Martin's Press, 2018.

Greenberg, Keith Elliot. *Too Fast to Live, Too Young to Die: James Dean's Final Hours*. Milwaukee: Applause Theatre & Cinema Books, 2015

Holley, Val. *James Dean: The Biography*. New York: St. Martin's Griffin, 1995.

Hudson, Rock & Davidson, Sara. *Rock Hudson: His Story*. New York: William Morrow and Company, Inc., 1986.

Hyams, Joe. *James Dean: Little Boy Lost*. New York: Warner Books, Inc., 1992.

Kazan, Elia. *Elia Kazan: A Life*. New York: Alfred A. Knopf, 1988.

Kazan, Elia. *Kazan on Directing*. New York: Vintage Books, 2009.

Kelley, Kitty. *Elizabeth Taylor: The Last Star*. New York: Simon & Schuster, 1981.

Linet, Beverly. *Ladd: The Life, The Legend, The Legacy of Alan Ladd*. New York: Arbor House, 1979.

Martinetti, Ronald. *The James Dean Story: A Myth-Shattering Biography of an Icon.* New York: Carol Publishing Group, 1975.

McCambridge, Mercedes. *The Quality of Mercy: An Autobiography.* New York: Times Books, 1981.

McCann, Graham. *Rebel Males: Clift, Brando and Dean.* New Brunswick, NJ: Rutgers University Press, 1991.

McGilligan, Patrick. *Nicholas Ray: The Glorious Failure of an American Director.* New York: It Books, 2011.

Michaud, Michael Gregg. *Sal: A Biography.* New York: Three Rivers Press, 2010.

Moss, Marilyn Ann. *Giant: George Stevens, a Life on Film.* Wisconsin: Terrace Books, 2004.

Rathgeb, Douglas. *The Making of Rebel Without a Cause.* North Carolina: McFarland & Company, Inc., 2004.

Schickel, Richard. *Elia Kazan: A Biography.* New York: Harper Perennial, 2005.

Spoto, Donald. *Rebel: The Life and Legend of James Dean.* New York: HarperCollins Publishers, Inc., 1996.

Stevens, Jr. George. *My Place in the Sun: Life in the Golden Age of Hollywood and Washington.* Kentucky: University Press of Kentucky, 2022.

Walker, Alexander. *Elizabeth: The Life of Elizabeth Taylor.* New York: Grove Press, 1990.

Winkler, Peter. *The Real James Dean: Intimate Memories from Those Who Knew Him Best.* Chicago: Chicago Review Press, Inc., 2016.

Young, Jeff. *Kazan: The Master Director Discusses His Films.* New York: Newmarket Press, 1999.

Document:

Transcript of Testimony and Proceeding in The Court of San Luis Obispo County State of California In the Matter of the Inquisition upon the body of JAMES DEAN: 10/11/1955 10:00 o'clock a.m.

INDEX

A Hundred Different Lives (book),106

"A Young Man is Gone," 274

Abe Lincoln in Illinois (play), 99

Abrahams, Mort, 116-18

Actors Studio (New York), 38, 39, 55, 56, 68, 75, 85, 119, 150, 166, 281

Adam -12 (TV show), 37

Adams, Joe (role), 69

Adams, Nick, 34, 167, 170, 180, 219, 240, 244, 269, 273

Adler, Stella, 279

African Queen, The (film), 86

Albert, Eddie, 115

Aley, Albert, 66

Alias Jane Doe (radio series), 34

Alice Adams (film), 185

Allen, Corey, 155, 159, 160-61, 168, 180, 181, 263

All My Sons (play), 85

Altman, Robert, 272

American Academy of Dramatic Arts (New York), 38

"American Boy," 283

"American Pie," 274

Anatomy of a Murder (film), 151

Anderson, Sherwood, 115

Andress, Ursula, 220

Angeli, Pier, 108-10, 114, 116, 117

Antony, Marc, 90

Apocalypse Now (film), 180

Armstrong Circle Theatre (TV show)

 "The Bells of Cockaigne," 77, 78

Asphalt Jungle, The (film), 38

Associated Press, 119, 125

Astor, Mary, 118

Astor Theatre (New York), 121

At Sea with the Navy (film), 37

Axe of God, The (play), 35

Ayers, Lemuel, 60

Baby Doll (book), 204

Baby Doll (film), 123

Bach, J.S., 44, 225

Bachir (role), 80

Backus, Jim, 155, 162, 173, 176-77, 179-80, 262, 287

Baker, Carroll, 151, 154, 194-95, 204, 217-19, 239, 287

Bancroft, Anne, 49

Barris, George, 226

Bartok, Bela, 44, 225

Barton, James, 54

Bast, William, 25, 31-34, 36-39, 46, 49-50, 56, 58-59, 287

Battleground (film), 39

Battle Cry (film), 99, 146, 151

Battler, The (TV play), 254

Baxter, Anne, 189

Beach Boys, The, 274

Beatles, The, 3, 274

Beat the Clock (TV game show), 45

Beatty, Warren, 272

Begley, Ed, 79

Beiderbecke, Bix, 28

Bellah, James, 30

Ben Casey (TV show), 54

Benny, Jack, 15, 116

Bergere, Lee, 94

Bernard, Tom, 170

Bernstein, Leonard, 97

Berry, Martha, 58

Betsy, The (film), 66

Beyonce, 283

Bigelow Theatre (TV series), "T.K.O.," 36, 37

Bishop, Richard, 54

Blackboard Jungle (film), 143, 157-58, 262

Blackwell's Corner, 230-31

Blob, The (film), 263

"Blue Jeans," 283

Blue Velvet (film), 180

Bogart, Humphrey, 69, 86, 119, 259, 277

Bogdanovich, Peter, 281

Bonanza (TV show), 70, 263

Bonney, William H. (Billy the Kid), 16, 254

Bora, Kathryn von, 35

Bossert, Robert H., 236, 247-48

Bowie, David, 275

Boy with Green Hair, The (film), 154

Bracker, Lew, 195, 287

Brackett, Rogers, 34

Bradon, Hank (role), 76

Brainstorm (film), 181

Brando, Marlon, 5, 43, 46, 50, 52, 72, 77, 86, 90, 92, 101, 106, 111-12, 119-20, 122-23, 143, 145, 149, 164, 175, 181, 190, 262-63, 266, 272, 276-77, 279, 280-83, 287, 289

Brannum, Tom, 151

Brazil, A. H., 252-53

Brennan, Walter, 94

Breslin, Patricia, 55

Bridge on the River Kwai, The (film), 221

Bronco (role), 72-73

Brookshire, Adeline, 17, 19-22, 59

Brubeck, Dave, 225

Brynner, Yul, 271

Bullitt (film), 227

Burton, Richard, 189-90

Butch Cassidy and the Sundance Kid (film), 75

Butler, Austin, 280

Byron, Lord, 9

Cabaret (film), 99

Cage, Nicolas, 277-78

Cagney, James, 79

Call, Albert, 243

Callahan, Mushy, 168

Cameron, Kate, 121-22

Campbell Summer Soundstage (TV show)
"Life Sentence," 76
"Something for an Empty Briefcase," 68-69

Canty, Marietta, 172-73

Carey, Timothy, 99-100

Carlyle, John, 153

Carradine, John, 65

Carson, Robert, 54

Casablanca (film), 154

Case, Ethel, 19, 25

Casino Royale (film), 220

Cassavetes, John, 150-51

Cat on a Hot Tin Roof (film), 100

Cavett, Dick, 276

CBS Television Workshop (TV show) "Into the Valley," 51

Chapman, John, 63

Chapman Report, The (film), 180

Charisse, Cyd, 116

Chicago Daily News, 265

Chicago Sun-Times, 275

Chicago Tribune, 122

Chinatown (film), 150

Chuck D (rapper), 283

Clavell, Butch, 55

Clayton, Dick, 38, 237

Clift, Montgomery, 5, 43, 50, 86, 120, 181, 185, 190-91, 215, 259, 277, 287, 289

Coburn, Charles, 38

Cobweb, The (film), 113-14

Cochran, Eddie, 271

Cohen, Alan, 155

Cohen, Carl, 155-56

Cohen, Mickey, 109

Collier's, 227

Collyer, Bud, 45

Come Back to the 5 & Dime, Jimmy Dean, Jimmy Dean (film), 282

Command Decision (play), 39

Compulsion (film), 75

Connery, Sean, 220

Conrad, Barnaby, 56

Conrad, Robert, 272

Cool Hand Luke (film), 180

Cooper, Gary, 189

Cooper, Jim (role), 75

Copeland, Aaron, 96

Corey, Jeff, 119

Corn is Green, The (play), 254

Corrigan, William, 58

Corsaro, Frank, 67-68

Cort Theatre (New York), 62

Cosmopolitan, 119-20

Costigan, James, 65

Costner, Kevin, 282

"Crazy Man, Crazy," 74

Crawford, Cheryl, 56

Crime in the Streets (film), 263

Cromwell's Pharmacy (New York), 50, 55, 61, 75

Cronkite, Walter, 66

Cronyn, Hume, 72-73

Crowley, Pat, 154

Crowther, Bosely, 122, 261, 265-66

Crumpacker, Sanger, 27

Curtis, Tony, 175

Daily News, The, 121-22

Dallapiccola, Luigi, 96

Damone, Vic, 110, 116-17

D' Angelo, Joe, 241

Danger (TV show)

"Death Is My Neighbor," 70

"No Room," 66

"Padlocks," 114-15

"The Little Woman," 94

Danton, Ray, 65

Darrow, Clarence, 26

Davalos, Richard, 98, 111-13, 240

Davidson, Collier "Buster," 234-37

Davis, Joan, 33

Davis, Sammy, Jr., 276

Dawson High School, 164

Days of Wine and Roses, The (film), 151

Deacy, Jane, 38, 47-48, 51, 55, 59, 63-65, 80, 120, 173, 210, 237

Dean, Charles Nolan, 228

Dean, Emma, 13-14

Dean, James Byron:

acting technique, 47, 52-53, 57, 63, 67, 70, 78-79, 114, 118, 124, 148-49, 167, 173-74, 177, 199, 200, 203, 205-07, 211, 213-15, 218 athletic prowess, 15, 18-19, 23-25, 27-28

averse to criticism, 17-19, 22-23, 31-32, 40, 54, 56-57, 68, 78, 80-81, 111-12, 119, 148-49, 172-73, 195-96, 203-07

awards, 22, 25, 82, 124

birth of, 9

Broadway performances, 59, 60-63, 65, 67-68, 72, 80-82, 91, 96-97, 123-24, 254

car racing, 123, 169, 193, 226-27, 229-30

childhood, 11-17

college theater, 27-28, 30-32

critics reviews of, 5, 31-32, 62-63, 65, 69, 72, 77, 82, 111, 113-14, 118-24, 161, 213, 261, 265-66, 274, 281

death of, 3-6, 232-55, 259-61

early films in Hollywood, 37-38

filmmaking interests, 174, 208, 210

funeral, 244-45, 285

insomnia, 33, 43, 120

love interests, 33, 49-50, 58-59, 61-62, 69-70, 81-82, 100-01, 108-10, 114, 116-17, 220

motorcycles, 23, 62, 91, 94, 101, 107-08, 111-12, 115-16, 175, 245, 254

musical interests, 19, 27-28, 44, 68, 225

Santa Monica City College, 25-27, 29-30, 106

UCLA, 24-33, 35, 38

Dean, Mildred, 9-14, 16, 24, 176

Dean, Winton, 9-14, 19, 24-26, 28-30, 58-59, 95-96, 228, 237, 239, 242, 245

Death of a Salesman (film), 115

Death of a Salesman (play), 85-86, 115

De Havilland, Olivia, 189

Dekker, Albert, 99

Delinquents, The (film), 263

Del Rey, Lana, 283

De Niro, Robert, 277

Depp, Johnny, 277

Derek, John, 220

De Sica, Vittorio, 108

Desiree (film), 112

Desperate Hours, The (film), 69

Dickens, Charles, 20

Dillman, Bradford, 75-76

Dino (film), 263

Dirty Dozen, The (film), 151

Doan, Zeno, 10

Dr. No (film), 220

Dr. Quinn, Medicine Woman (TV show), 76

Donehue, Vincent J., 118

Donoghue, Roger, 145, 168

Dooley, Don, 231

Doran, Ann, 172, 175-76, 179

Dos Passos, John, 273

Doty, Jeanette, 225-26

Douglas, Kirk, 115, 230

Draesemer, Isabel, 34-36

Dragstrip Girl (film), 263

Dragstrip Riot (film), 263

Drummond, Jack, 230

DuBois, Roland, 24

Duffield, Brainerd, 19

Dunham, Katherine, 166

Dunlap, Dick, 77

Dunn, Irene, 188

Dunnock, Mildred, 114-15

Duvall, Robert, 281

Dylan, Bob, 282

Dynasty (TV show), 94

Eagles, The (band), 275

East of Eden (film), 4-6, 48, 88-90, 92-93, 95-99, 100-08, 110-13, 119-25, 145, 149-51, 153, 155, 159, 161, 168, 174, 191, 230, 240, 261, 269, 277, 279-80

East of Eden (novel), 87-88

Easy Rider (film), 180, 264, 275

8 Mile (film), 283

Eighteen and Anxious (film), 263

Eisenhower, Dwight D., 141

"Electrolite," 283

Elliott, T.S., 72

Elvis (film), 280

Eminem, 283

Erickson, Leif, 35

Eschrich, William F., 252

Eshleman, Richard, 35

Esquire, 273

Essex, David, 275

Evelyn, Judith, 194

Exodus (film), 180

Exodus (novel), 146

Exorcist, The (film), 198

Explosive Generation, The (film), 179

Fairbanks, Jerry, 34-35

Fairmount Friends Church (Indiana), 244

Fairmount News, 11, 23, 25, 27

Faith, Adam, 271

Falcon Crest (TV show), 65

Fandango (film), 282

Father Peyton's Family Theater, "Hill Number One," 35-36, 77

Faulkner, William, 72

Ferber, Edna, 185-87, 193, 200, 204, 244, 288

Ferris, Arbie (role), 66-67

55 Days at Peking (film), 181

Five Easy Pieces (film), 100

Fix, Paul, 194

Fixed Bayonets! (film), 37

Flaming Star (film), 179

Flynn, Earl, 189

Fonda, Henry, 30

Forbes, Kathryn, 46

Ford, Constance, 117

Ford, John, 30

Ford, Robert (role), 66

Forrest Hotel (New York), 47

Forsythe, John, 54

Fort Apache (film), 30

4 For Texas (film), 220

Fox, David, 21

Franco, James, 278

Frankenheimer, John, 115

Frederick, Paul, 231, 233

Frederick, Tom, 231-33,

249-50

French Connection, The (film), 227

From Hell to Texas (film), 180

Fuller, James, 273

Fun in Acapulco (film), 220

Fury, Billy, 271

Gable, Clark, 189, 195

Gabor, Eva, 115

Gardner, Hy, 270

Garfield, John, 85

Garrett, Pat, 16

Gazzara, Ben, 66-67

Geisel, Theodor Seuss, 143

Gene Krupa Story, The (film), 180

General Electric Theater (TV show)

   "I'm a Fool," 115

   "The Dark, Dark Hours," 117-18

Gentleman's Agreement (film), 85, 99, 123, 142

George, George W., 272

Getty, J. Paul, 173

"Ghost Town," 283

Giant (film), 4-6, 152, 169, 176, 187-89, 193-94, 196-199, 200-20, 227, 239-41, 264-67, 271-72, 277, 279, 282, 288

Giant (novel), 185-86, 220

Gide, Andre, 80

Gilligan's Island (TV show), 180

Ginsberg, Henry, 6, 186-87, 193, 200, 204, 237, 244, 267

Glenn, Barbara, 61-62, 81-82, 100

Godfather, The (film), 117

Golden Boy (play), 145

Gone With the Wind (film), 265

Gonzalez, Manuel, 30, 32

Good, the Bad, and the Ugly, The (film), 68

Goode, Richard, 54

Goodman, Benny, 19

Gordon, Michael, 60

"Gorgeous," 283

Graduate, The (film), 264

Graham, Gloria, 145

Grande, Ariana, 284

Grant, Kathryn, 153

Grapes of Wrath, The (film), 65

Grapes of Wrath, The (novel), 86

Grauman's Chinese Theatre (Hollywood), 265

Graziano, Rocky, 168, 210

Grease (play), 274

Greatest Story Ever Told, The (film), 272

Green Acres (TV show), 115

Gregory, Frank, 70

Griffith, Griffith J., 158

Griffith Park (Los Angeles), 34, 158, 179

Grinnage, Jack, 171

Group Theater (New York), 56

Grundell, Herbert, 246-47, 249

Guinness, Alec, 221

Guiol, Fred, 187, 191-92

Gunfight at the O.K. Corral (film), 180

Gunga Din (film), 185, 196

Gunn, Bill, 68, 81, 97

Haggott, John, 118

Haley, Bill, 74, 157

Hallmark Hall of Fame (TV show)

  "Forgotten Children," 58

Hamilton, Elroy, 275

Hamlet (play), 28-29, 254

Hamner, Earl, Jr., 65

Hampden, Walter, 70-71

Hanson, Nels (role), 46

Harlib, Matt, 69-70

Harris, Julie, 98-99, 100, 102, 106-08, 111, 113, 244

Harvey, Xen, 285

Has Anybody Seen My Gal? (film), 38

Hatful of Rain, A (play), 151

Hawaii Five-0 (TV show), 70

Hawthorne, Nathaniel, 67

Hayden, Jeffrey, 114

Hayden, Sterling, 189

Hayes, John Michael, 34

Hays Office, 166

Heffernan, Harold, 174

Heidi (play), 240

Heller, Franklin, 51-52, 71

Hemingway, Ernest, 72, 254

Hennessy, Thomas, 159

Hepburn, Audrey, 188

Hepburn, Katharine, 185, 191

Heston, Charlton, 189-90

Hickey, Bill, 63

Hickman, Bill, 37, 226-30, 234-37, 239

High Noon (film), 185

High School Confidential (film), 263

Hill, George Roy, 75

Hill, Steven, 281

Hill Street Blues (TV show), 180

Hinkle, Bob, 208-09

Hirsch, Albert, 54

Hitchcock, Alfred, 178, 198-99, 202

Hoffman, Dustin, 276

Holden, John, 31

Holden, William, 189

Holland, Maury, 75

Hollywood Foreign Press Association, 267

Hollywood Reporter, The 36, 118, 122, 187, 212

Homeier, Skip, 143

Home of the Brave (film), 142

Honeymooners, The (TV show), 141

Hoosiers (film), 180

Hope, Bob, 15

Hopper, Dennis, 110, 153-154, 168, 171, 174, 180, 194, 199, 203-04, 269, 277

Hopper, Hedda, 112-13, 203-04, 210, 269

Hopper, William, 155, 179

Hot Angel, The (film), 263

Hotel Iroquois (New York), 43-44, 50, 277

Hot Rod Girl (film), 263

Hough, Horace, 98

House Un-American Activities Committee, 146, 157

Huber, Gusti, 114

Hud (film), 68

Hudson, Rock, 38, 175, 190, 194, 197, 204, 212-15, 265, 271, 288

Hughes, Howard, 156, 217

Human, Comedy, The (film), 157

Hunchback of Notre Dame, The (film), 70, 154

Hunt, Marsha, 156-57, 172

Hunter, Otie V., 229, 243, 250

Hunter, Tab, 145, 151

Hussey, Ruth, 35

Huston, John, 39, 150, 188

Hutton, Barbara, 230

Hyams, Joe, 109, 116, 119, 167, 195, 288

I Am a Camera (film), 99

Iceman Cometh, The (play), 51

Idlewild Airport (New York), 94

Immoralist, The (play), 80-82, 91, 123-24

In a Lonely Place (film), 144

Inge, William, 72

I Remember Mama (play), 46

Isaak, Chris, 283

Ives, Burl, 99-100

I Was a Teenage Werewolf (film), 263

Jackson, Anne, 51-52, 68

Jacobs, W.W., 20

"James Dean," 275

James Dean Story, The (film), 272-73

James, Jesse, 66, 179, 181, 192

John F. Kennedy International Airport (New York), 94

John the Apostle (role), 35-36

Johnny Guitar (film), 144

Johnson, Arte, 150

Johnson, Georgann, 76

Jones, Christopher, 179

Joplin, Janis, 280

Jourdan, Louis, 80-81

Juvenile Jungle (film), 263

Kasznar, Kurt, 114

Kate Smith Hour (TV show), "The Hound of Heaven," 65

Kazan, Elia, 5, 55-57, 82, 85-107, 110-13, 120, 122-24, 144-45, 149-50, 169, 185, 191, 198, 204, 206, 278-80, 288-89

Keisker, Marion, 47

Keitel, Harvey, 276-77

Kelly, Grace, 49, 79, 189, 221

Kendall, Ken, 283

Kennedy, Arthur, 61

Kerouac, Jack, 262
Kerr, John, 66, 90, 145
Kerr, Walter, 62
Keystone Kops, 155
Kilgallen, Eleanor, 51-52
Killers, The (band), 283
Kimbrough, Emily, 20
King and I, The (film), 271
King and I, The (play), 151
King of Kings (film), 181
Kirkland, Muriel, 54
Kiss of Death (film), 115
Kitten with a Whip (film), 179
Kobe, Gail, 35
Kraft Television Theatre (TV series)
   "A Long Time Till Dawn," 76-77
   "Keep Our Honor Bright," 75
   "Prologue to Glory," 55
Kuehl Funeral Home, 236, 242
Kuehl, Martin, 237-39

Ladd, Alan, 164, 187-88, 190-91, 194, 288
Lady Gaga, 283
Ladykillers, The (film), 221
Lambert, Adam, 283
Lancaster, Burt, 115, 164, 189

Landau, Martin, 50, 61, 70, 80, 245-46
Landon, Michael, 263
Lansbury, Angela, 79
Lassie (TV show), 54, 279
Last Picture Show, The (film), 58
Latham, Jeffrey (role), 174
Laugh-In (TV show), 150
Laughton, Charles, 70-71
Laurie, Piper, 38
Lawrence of Arabia (film), 61, 221
Leachman, Cloris, 58
Leary, Helen, 19
Leary, Nolan, 19
Left Handed Gun, The (film), 254
Legend of Jesse James, The (TV show), 179
Legion of Decency, 166
Lemmon, Jack, 79, 269
Lennon, John, 274
Levy, Ralph, 46
Lewis, Jeanetta, 32
Lewis, Jerry, 37
Lewis, Robert, 56
Liberace, 173
Life, 121, 193
Lincoln, Abraham, 55, 57-58, 99
Lindbergh, Charles, 113
Lindner, Robert M., 142-43, 145
Little, Carl Victor, 186

Little Deuce Coupe (album), 274

Live Fast, Die Young (film), 263

Lockhart, Gene, 77-78

Loeb and Leopold, 75

Long, Beverly, 34, 155, 159-60, 162-63, 165, 170

Look, 119, 265-66

Lopez, Perry, 150

Los Angeles Times, 114, 157, 259

Love Me Tender (film), 69, 179, 181, 273

Love with the Proper Stranger (film), 181

Lowther, George, 77

Lucci, Jerry, 45

Lumet, Sidney, 66

Lust for Life (film), 271

Luther, Martin, 35

Lux Radio Theatre (radio series), 15

Lux Video Theatre (TV show)

    "The Foggy, Foggy Dew," 54

Lyon, Herb, 122

Lyons, Gene, 69

Macbeth (play), 30-32

MacLaine, Shirley, 281

Mad Magician, The (film), 155

Madonna, 283

Magnificent Obsession (film), 190

Mama (TV series), 46

Mama's Bank Account (novel), 46

Man on a Tightrope (film), 145

Manchurian Candidate, The (film), 115

Mann, Daniel, 81

Manners, Dorothy, 210

Mansfield, Jayne, 153

March, Fredric, 115

Marshall, E.G., 51-52

Martin, Dean, 37

Martin Kane, Private Eye (TV show), 53

Massey, Raymond, 99, 101-06, 111

Matador (novel), 56

Mature, Victor, 115

Mayflower, 9

Mazzola, Frank, 154-55, 167, 270

MCA, 51, 142

McCallum, Kyle (role), 54

McCambridge, Mercedes, 194, 197-98, 213, 241, 289

McCarthy, Glenn, 196-97

McCarthy, Joseph, 141

McCord, Ted, 90

McCullers, Carson, 72

McCullough, Andrew, 72-74, 94

McCullough, Clyde, 58

McDowell, Roddy, 35, 98

McGuire, Dorothy, 154

McHenry, Carl, 252

McLean, Don, 274

McLeod, Catherine, 54

McQueen, Steve, 68

Medford, Don, 67-69, 115, 117-18

Medic (TV show), 153-54

Meeker, Randy (role), 66

Member of the Wedding, The (film), 99

Men, The (film), 43

Merrick, Paul E., 242-43, 246

Middleton, Robert, 68-69

Midnight Cowboy (film), 76

Miller, Arthur, 240

Miller, Ken, 170

Miller Playhouse Theater Guild, 27-28

Milner, Martin, 36-37

Minelli, Liza, 99

Mineo, Sal, 151, 159, 170, 173-75, 180-81, 217, 240-41, 263, 268-69

Minority Report (film), 100

Minter Field (California), 169, 230

Miracle on 34th Street (film), 77

Misfits, The (film), 68

Mission Impossible (TV series), 50

Mr. Magoo, 173

Mister Roberts (film), 269

Mitchum, Robert, 189-90

Mix, Tom, 155

Moffat, Ivan, 187, 199

Moffitt, Jack, 122

Monkey's Paw, The (play), 20

Monroe, Marilyn, 121, 276-77, 282

Mooncalf Mugford (play), 19-20

"Moonlight," 284

Moreno, Paul, 231-38, 246-47

Morton, Jelly Roll, 28

Motion Picture Magazine, 175

Motion Picture Production Code, 166

Murphy, Harry C., 243-44, 246-50

Music Connection (magazine), 271

Mutiny on the Bounty (film), 172

Nash, N. Richard, 60-61

Nation, The, 213

Neal, Patricia, 68

Neighborhood Playhouse of the Theater (New York), 38

Nelson, Ralph, 46

Nelson, Ronald, 233, 235, 238, 251

Network (film), 66

Newman, Paul, 49, 59-60, 63, 68, 93, 98, 100, 108, 254

Newsweek, 193

New York (magazine), 53

New York Daily Mirror, 122

New York Daily News, 63

New York Herald Tribune, 62, 121, 266, 270

New York International Airport, 94

New York Post, 62-63, 274

New York Times, 122-23, 206, 261, 265-66

Nicholson, Jack, 53

Nickell, Paul, 54

Night of the Hunter (film), 155

Nixon, Agnes, 58

Nose, India, 16

Oates, Warren, 45

O'Brien, Margaret, 154

Odets, Clifford, 145-46

Oklahoma! (film), 74

Omnibus (TV show)

"Glory in the Flower," 72-74

On Dangerous Grounds (film), 172

On the Waterfront (film), 5, 67, 86, 97, 123, 145

One Flew Over the Cuckoo's Nest (film), 53

Only Game in Town, The (film), 272

Orr, William, 220-21

Ory, Edward "Kid," 28

Osborn, Paul, 88, 90-91

Our Hearts Were Young and Gay (play), 20

Owen, Gene Nielsen, 27-31, 106

Pacino, Al, 277

Page, Geraldine, 80

Palica, Joe (role), 69

Palmer, Betsy, 69-70

Papillon (film), 68

Parade, 175

Park Cemetery (Indiana), 245

Parker, Colonel Tom, 273

Parker, Louis N., 20

Parsons, Louella, 119-20

Party Girl (film), 180-81

Paso Robles Daily Press, 242

Payne, David, 10

Payne, Hazel, 10

"Peach Trees," 283

Peck, Gregory, 85

Perkins, Tony, 276

Perry, Jackie, 172

Perry Mason (TV show), 70, 179

Petrie, Daniel, 66, 278

Peyser, John, 70-71

Peyton Place (film), 61

Philco Television Playhouse (TV show)

   "Run Like a Thief," 114

Phillips, Sam, 47

Photoplay, 116

Pick-Up Girl, The (play), 155

Pickwick Papers (novel), 20

Picnic (play), 72

Pilate, Pontius, 35-36

Pinky (film), 85

Pitsor, Zina Gladys, 11

Place in the Sun, A (film), 43, 86, 185, 189

Poe, Edgar Allan, 28

Pogostin, S. Lee, 68, 76

Powers, James, 207-08

Presley, Elvis, 3, 47, 69, 142, 179, 181, 220, 261, 269-74, 280, 282

Pressman, David, 66

Pride and Prejudice (film), 157

Prizzi's Honor (film), 63

Pryor, Tom, 206

Public Enemy (Hip Hop group), 283

Quinn, Anthony, 86, 190, 271

Quinn, Frank, 122

Raisin in the Sun, A (film), 66

"Rather Die Young," 283

Ray, Nicholas, 92, 120, 143-47, 148-63, 165-81, 198, 244, 261-62, 268. 270, 287, 289

Ray Avery's Record Roundup, 28

Reagan, Ronald, 115, 117-18

Real McCoys, The (TV show), 94

Rebel, The (TV show), 180

Rebel Without a Cause (book), 142-144

Rebel Without a Cause (film), 4-6, 34, 48, 77, 145-81, 220, 260-64, 266, 269-71, 273, 275, 277, 280-81, 283, 288-89

Rebel Without a Cause (play), 273

Redfield, William, 53

Reed, Lou, 275

Reed, Lydia, 94

REM (band), 283

Remick, Lee, 150-51

Reventlow, Lance, 230

Reynolds, Debbie, 116, 154

Rice, Rosemary, 46

Richards, Cliff, 271

"Ride of the Valkyries," 162

Riley, James Whitcomb, 10

Rink, Jett (role), 153, 186, 188, 190-93, 196, 199, 200-02, 206-07, 211, 213-19, 221, 265-68, 284

Robert Montgomery Presents (TV show)

 "Harvest," 78-79

Roberts, Marvin, 98

Robin Hood (film), 172

"Rock Around the Clock," 157

"Rock On," 275

Rock, Pretty Baby (film), 263

Rocks on the Roof (book), 162, 176, 287

Rodgers, Jimmie, 225

Romance of Scarlet Gulch, The (play), 28

Romanos, Nicolas, 225

Rooney, Judith, 243

Rose, Billy, 81-82

Rosemary's Baby (film), 151

Rosenfeld, John, 211

Rosenman, Leonard, 48, 96-97, 105, 149

Rose Tattoo, The (play), 151

Roth, Sanford, 227-229, 234-236

Route 66 (TV series), 37

Roxy Theatre (New York), 265

Royale Theatre (New York), 81, 91

Sailor Beware (film), 37

Saint, Eva Marie, 49

Saint-Exupery, Antoine de, *The Little Prince* (novel), 64

Sands Casino, (Las Vegas), 156

Sands, Tommy, 272

Saturday Review, 261, 265

Saxon, John, 153

Scarecrow, The (play), 67-68

Schatt, Roy, 79-80

Scheuer, Philip K., 114, 157

Schickel, Richard, 122

Schlitz Playhouse of Stars (TV show)

 "The Unlighted Road," 174

Schonberg, Arnold, 96

Schulberg, Budd, 145

Schulman, Arnold, 115

Scott, William (role), 57-58

Screen Stories, 192

Scully, Joe (role), 94

See the Jaguar (play), 59-63, 65, 72

Seinfeld (TV show), 49

Seinfeld, Jerry, 49

Serling, Rod, 48-49, 77

Serpico (film), 66

Seven Days in May (film), 115

Seven-Ups, The (film), 227

77 Sunset Strip (TV show), 54

Shakur, Tupac, 283

Shane (film), 165, 185, 187, 194

Shannon, Richard, 106

Sheen, Martin, 278, 281-82

Sheldon, James, 46-47, 77-79

Sheridan, Elizabeth "Dizzy," 49-50, 58-59

Sherwood, Robert, 99

Shulman, Herman, 80-81

Shurlock, Geoffrey, 166

Shurr, Louis, 47-48, 53

Sidney, Steffi, 160, 170-71, 263

Silver Chalice, The (film), 60, 63, 108

Simmons, Jack, 117, 155, 244

Simmons, Jean, 189

Simpson, Garry, 76

Sinatra, Frank, 109, 115, 156, 190, 225, 280

Sincerely Yours (film), 173

Six Bridges to Cross (film), 151

Skelton, Red, 15

Skinner, Corneila Otis, 20

Skin of Our Teeth, The (play), 51

Skolsky, Sidney, 108, 173-74

Smith, Bessie, 28

Smith, Betty, 85

Smith, Lois, 100, 151

Somebody Up There Likes Me (film), 168, 210

Songs My Mother Taught Me (book), 283

Southwest Review, 211

Spartacus (film), 180

"Speechless," 283

Speed (film), 180

Splendor in the Grass (film), 123, 181

Springsteen, Bruce, 275

Stander, John, 242

Stanislavsky, Konstanton, 56

Stardust, Ziggy, 275

Star is Born, A (film), 54

Stark, Jim (role), 146-47, 150-51, 153, 156-57, 161, 163-72, 178-79, 181, 262, 269, 275, 284

Steiger, Rod, 49, 67

Steinbeck, John, 72, 86-88, 92, 121

Stern, Stewart, 146-48, 152, 156-57, 177-79

Stevens, George, 6, 43, 86, 150, 152-53, 165, 185-99, 200-19, 239-40, 264-68, 271-72, 289

Stevens, George, Jr., 191-92, 195-96, 289

Stewart, James, 191

Sting, The (film), 75

Stock, Dennis, 120-21

Strasberg, Lee, 56-57, 68, 85, 112, 211, 266-67

Streetcar Named Desire, A (film), 72, 86, 144, 164

Streetcar Named Desire, A (play), 72, 143

Studio One (TV show)

"Abraham Lincoln," 57-58

"Ten Thousand Horses Singing," 54

Studio One Summer Theatre (TV show)

"Sentence of Death," 69

"Style," 283

Sullivan, Ed, 141

Sullivan, Elliott, 58

Sun Records, 47

Sunset Beach (play), 99

Sunset Boulevard (film), 173

Swan, The (film), 221

Sweet Bird of Youth (film), 79, 180

Swift, Lela, 52

Swift, Taylor, 283

Swindell, Larry, 31

Tales of Tomorrow (TV show)

"The Evil Within," 67

Tandy, Jessica, 72

Taylor, Elizabeth, 93, 98, 100, 153, 173, 185, 188-89, 194, 198-99, 204, 209, 212-14, 225-26, 239-40, 244, 265, 268, 272, 288-89

Taylor, Robert, 189

Taza, Son of Cochise (film), 190

Teenagers from Outer Space (film), 263

Thalberg, Irving, 185

Theater de Lys (New York), 67-68

The Whole Truth and Nothing But (book), 203

They Live by Night (film), 144, 172

They Were Expendable (film), 79

Thomas, Danny, 116

Thompson, Howard, 123-25

Thurber, James, 72

Time, 122, 168, 193, 265-67, 275

Topaz (film), 179

To Them That Sleep in Darkness (play), 16

Tracy, Spencer, 191

Trask, Caleb (role), 89-90, 92-93, 98-99, 100, 103-05, 107, 110-112, 153, 174, 280, 284

Treasury Men in Action (TV show)

    "The Case of the Sawed-off Shotgun," 66-67

    "The Case of the Watchful Dog," 65-66

Tree Grows in Brooklyn, A (film), 85, 123

Trilling, Steve, 152, 171

Tripke, Ernest G., 233, 238, 243, 248-49, 251

Trovajoli, Armando, 117

True Grit (film), 180

True Story of Jesse James, The (film), 181

Truman, Harry S., 141

Truman, Margaret, 121

Trumbauer, Frank, 28

Turnupseed, Donald, 231-33, 235, 238-39, 241, 246-53

12 Angry Men (film), 66, 79

20,000 Leagues Under the Sea (film), 230

Twilight of Honor (film), 180

Twilight Zone, The (TV show), 77

Twister (film), 100

"Under the Gun," 283

Unforgiven, The (film), 188

United States Steel Hour (TV show)

    "The Thief," 118

Untouchables, The (TV show), 70

U.S. News and World Report, 142

Uris, Leon, 146

Ustinov, Peter, 180

Valentino, Rudolph, 6, 265-66

Valley of the Dolls (film), 179

Valley Times, 174

Van Druten, John, 46

Van Fleet, Jo, 99, 269

Van Patten, Dick, 46-47

Variety, 36, 72, 114, 158, 261

View from the Bridge, A (play), 240

Villa Capri (Hollywood), 109, 221, 225

Vincent, Gene, 271

Viva Zapata! (film), 86, 88, 271

Vogue, 119

"*Vogue,*" 283

Voight, Jon, 76

Von Neumann, Johnny, 169

Wagner, Richard, 162

Wagner, Robert, 145, 181

Wainwright, Rufus, 283

Waiting for Lefty (play), 145

Wald, Jerry, 143

"Walk on the Wild Side," 275

Wallach, Eli, 51, 68

Waltons, The (TV show), 65

Warhol, Andy, 278

War Memorial Hospital (Paso Robles), 235-36, 243

Warner, Jack, 6, 87, 91, 98, 113, 151, 164, 166, 168, 193-94, 203, 217, 220

Warren, Ronnie (role), 114

Wasserman, Lewis, 142

Watts, Richard, Jr., 62

Wayne, Frank, 45

Wayne, John, 30, 79, 189

Weaver, Paul, 18-19

Web, The (TV show), "Sleeping Dogs," 51

Webb, Clifton, 113

Weisbart, David, 144, 152, 178-79

Weissenhauer Psychiatric Hospital, 253

Weissmuller, Johnny, 109

West Side Story (film), 181

Weutherich, Rolf, 227-30, 232, 235-36, 243-44, 253-54

What's New Pussycat? (film), 220

White, Christine, 55-56, 155

White, Herbert (role), 20

Whitmore, James, 38-40

Widmark, Richard, 115

Wild One, The (film), 143, 262

Wild Ride, The (film), 263

Wild River (film), 123

Wilkins, Wally (role), 59, 61

Will, George, 281

Williams, Tennessee, 79, 100, 143

Wills, Beverly, 33

Wills, Chill, 194, 197, 209

Winslow, Joan, 15

Winslow, Marcus, 13-16, 18, 23-25, 28, 30, 32, 43, 59, 63-64, 82, 120, 245, 259, 272

Winslow, Marcus, Jr., 16-17, 44, 120, 272

Winslow, Ortense, 13-17, 23-25, 28, 30, 32, 43, 59, 64, 68, 82, 120, 245, 259, 272

Withers, Jane, 194

Wolfe, Ian, 172

Wolff, Frank, 31

Woman of the Year (film), 185

Women of Trachis (play), 96-97

Wood, Natalie, 78, 115-16, 153-55, 159, 162-63, 168, 171-72, 174-75, 177, 180-81, 240-41, 244, 262, 269, 287

Woodward, Joanne, 93

Wyler, William, 150

X Ambassadors (band), 283

Yale University School of
Drama, 39, 85
YMCA (New York), 44, 53
You Are There (TV show)
   "The Capture of Jesse
   James," 66, 192
Young, Gig, 221

Zapata, Emiliano, 90
Zinnemann, Fred, 74, 185
Zinsser, William K., 121